NARCOBALL

NARCOBALL

LOVE, DEATH AND FOOTBALL IN ESCOBAR'S COLOMBIA

DAVID ARROWSMITH

First published in Great Britain in 2024 by Cassell, an imprint of
Octopus Publishing Group Ltd
Carmelite House
50 Victoria Embankment
London EC4Y 0DZ
www.octopusbooks.co.uk

An Hachette UK Company
www.hachette.co.uk

Distributed in the US by Hachette Book Group
1290 Avenue of the Americas
4th and 5th Floors
New York, NY 10104

Distributed in Canada by Canadian Manda Group
664 Annette St.
Toronto, Ontario, Canada M6S 2C8

ISBN (hardback): 978-1-78840-523-2
ISBN (trade paperback): 978-1-78840-524-9

A CIP catalogue record for this book is available from the British Library.

Typeset in 10.75/16.5pt Miller Text by Jouve (UK), Milton Keynes

Printed and bound in Great Britain.

1 3 5 7 9 10 8 6 4 2

Publisher: Trevor Davies
Senior developmental editor: Pauline Bache
Creative director: Mel Four
Plate section designer: Clare Sivell
Copyeditor: Chris Stone
Deputy picture manager: Jennifer Veall
Assistant production manager: Allison Gonsalves

This FSC® label means that materials used for
the product have been responsibly sourced.

For my mother, Carolina Ospina Lleras.

For Colombia.

For football.

'Pablo Escobar would kill anyone to win a football game.'

Fernando Rodríguez Mondragón, son of Cali boss
Gilberto Rodríguez Orejuela.

Contents

Prólogo: Better a Grave in Colombia (1989)

Two men lie in the merciful shade of a ditch alongside a dusty road, their laboured breathing audible over the gentle background buzz and hum of a sultry early evening in rural Colombia. Beads of sweat soak into their collars and underarms as they lie still, pressed against the dirt of the gulley. The younger, more athletic of the two turns away from his partner, cradling a Heckler & Koch MP5 submachine gun. The other man, older, heavier set, faces the opposite direction, the glint of nickel at his waistband revealing the SIG Sauer pistol tucked into his grimy jeans. The insects drone, and the two fugitives strain their ears for the sound of any approach. These are no farmhands, and no petty criminals – this is the most wanted man on the planet, Pablo Emilio Escobar Gaviria, and his top *sicario*, the hitman known to all as 'Popeye'. The pair are on high alert, having been on the run for over two weeks straight, traversing the Magdalena Medio region of Antioquia, ever since they were attacked at El Oro, their farm hideout in the nearby town of Cocorná.

They have felt the hot breath of the authorities on their necks, not just the Colombian National Police but their elite 'Search Bloc' unit, since the raid on El Oro. At least they survived that; Mario, Pablo's brother-in-law, was not so lucky, struck by a hail of bullets as they all fled. This is not the first time they have been forced to dive into a ditch to seek cover, as they traipse between makeshift shelters and unassuming safe houses in a bid to evade the noose that has threatened to tighten around their necks ever since Pablo and his Medellín Cartel went on the offensive and started all-out war with the Colombian government. His campaign of car bombs and assassinations has rocked the country and forced those in power to take swift and deadly action. But each time could be the last.

Dirty, desperate and exhausted, Popeye summons the last of his dwindling reserves of energy for sentry duty: senses heightened, ready to rain death and destruction on anyone foolish enough to try and take him or *El Patrón*, 'The Boss', alive. El Patrón, the man he is sworn to protect with his life, the man for whom he has killed tens, by now hundreds. They both knew it could come to this, almost certainly *would* come to this. On the run, cut off from their men, just the two of them, back-to-back, surrounded. *'Better a grave in Colombia'*, as Pablo would tell anyone that would listen . . .

The fields are silent. The dirt track above empty. Still Popeye waits, tensed. There is no sign of approach. No sound of jackbooted men on the march, tyres of Jeeps spinning in the gravel, or the whir of helicopter blades cutting through the humid air. Popeye feels his pulse slow, his aching muscles begin to relax. Then the voice of his boss, *the* voice, snaps him back to attention.

'Popeye! Popeye!'

Has he somehow missed something? Have they found them? He cocks the MP5. This is it. He sneaks a glance at Pablo, and stops.

El Patrón is hunched forward, squatting on his haunches, pistol dangling casually from the fingers of his left hand – and a small, portable transistor radio pressed to his ear with his right. He turns to face his most trusted lieutenant, his deadliest assassin, his friend. A broad smile breaks out on his grimy face, his teeth a flash of white in the midst of the dark of his patchy beard.

'Colombia scored a goal!'

And just like that the tension of the moment is punctured, like a pair of lungs by a 9x19mm parabellum fired at 900mph from the barrel of a SIG Sauer. Popeye can't help but laugh. It's just so Pablo, so indicative of the mass of contradictions that make up the deadly enigma who has become Colombia and America's public enemy number one. Billionaire, criminal, narcoterrorist. Father, patriot . . . football fan. No matter how dark the day, how bloody the war, football is his joy, his escape, his cloud nine.

Four hundred miles away, in the sweltering 38-degree early evening heat of Barranquilla, on the country's stunning Caribbean coast, the game, and the goal, at the Estadio Metropolitano are huge not just for Pablo but for all of Colombia. *Los Cafeteros* – as Colombia's football team is known, named for what was the country's most famous export before the rise of Escobar and of cocaine, the drug that has made him one of the wealthiest men ever to have lived – have just taken the lead in the first leg of the vital World Cup qualifying intercontinental play-off against Oceania group winners Israel. It's a goal, like the team itself, made in Pablo's beloved Medellín. Scored by Atlético Nacional's gangly right-sided attacker Albeiro Usuriaga, the half-time substitute running on to a one-two through ball from his Medellín teammate Luis Fajardo and slotting the ball past the Israeli goalkeeper. This is a Colombia team, like Pablo himself, born of Medellín. The coach

Francisco 'Pacho' Maturana, the maverick goalkeeper René Higuita, the calm and stylish young libero Andrés Escobar in defence, Leonel Álvarez the midfield dynamo – all also cornerstones of the Atlético Nacional side that has just been crowned the best club side in South America. A side that Pablo has built, a team that he supports, that he loves . . .

On the radio the crowd of 65,000 in 'El Metro' goes wild. Pablo, dirty, desperate and hunted, hiding in a ditch, cheers along with them, as Colombia take a single, vital step closer to the dream of qualification for the World Cup. They've not been to the tournament since 1962. For all of Colombia, and for this one infamous fan in particular, the dream of seeing Los Cafeteros in World Cup Italia '90 is still alive . . .

PART ONE

OF LOVE, AND
OTHER DEMONS

(1949–1988)

Chapter One

Born of Blood and Fire (1949–1969)

———

At five minutes before midday, on 1 December 1949, Hermilda de los Dolores Gaviria Berrío gives birth to her third child, a baby boy. The child's father, Abel de Jesús Escobar Echeverri, now has three sons. Little can he or Doña Hermilda know that this tiny bundle in their arms will become the most feared man their country has ever seen: Pablo Escobar.

But the Colombia into which young Pablo is born is a land of fire and death. *La Violencia*, the brutal decade-long civil war that will claim the lives of hundreds of thousands, is raging, 20 months after the assassination of the leading Liberal Party candidate caused the country, and especially the rural poor, to take up arms against one another. On the very day that Pablo enters the world, peasant guerrillas seize the town of Puerto López, the country's geographical centre. Pablo is born into the violence and trauma of his country, a fitting omen, a portent, of his life to come.

Young Pablo grows up in a lower-middle class family, but unshielded from the grim realities of a life without privilege in 1950s

Colombia. His early years are spent on his father's cattle ranch in El Tablazo, Rionegro, in eastern Antioquia. The violence that rages across the country initially spares the family, but hard work and 800 head of cattle count for little when illness decimates the entire herd, and Abel is declared bankrupt. The Escobars are forced to move to a town on the other side of Medellín, Titiribí.

Here, Pablo's mother has secured work as a teacher. She even teaches the poorest kids in the neighbourhood for free on the weekends. But the family are far from rich themselves, they share a single bedroom in their small wooden house, with Pablo and the other children sleeping on a mattress on the floor. Life is a struggle, and there is often not enough food to go around. Pablo and his older brother Roberto must leave home at 4am if they are to be able to walk to their own school, come rain or shine, and get there on time.

One day Pablo is sent home from school for not wearing shoes. Doña Hermilda, despite herself, is compelled to steal a pair. Perhaps these were the famous first shoes of Pablo Escobar – believed to be none other than *guayos*, a pair of football boots. Wracked by guilt, Pablo's mother scrimps and saves to be able to repay the debt.

It's not the first crime in the family, nor the most significant – for Pablo's grandfather was a bootlegger, infamous for smuggling his contraband liquor in the most ingenious of ways and for bribing his way out of trouble. Little could his parents know quite how much of these entrepreneurial criminal genes Pablo would inherit . . .

Well before Pablo turns ten, in the mid-1950s, La Violencia finally comes to his town. One night a violent mob – a large group of *chusmeros*, part of an army of peasant guerrillas – descend on Titiribí. The Escobars lock their front door and cower helplessly within as the men go from house to house, dragging out the occupants who they suspect of having opposing political views and killing them in the street, hacking them to death with machetes. Pablo's parents can do nothing but try to keep their children quiet, and offer up silent prayers for their deliverance. Salvation comes in the unlikely form of their sturdy front door – which resists all attempts to batter it down. Eventually the mob gives up, sets a flaming torch to the wooden structure instead, and moves on. As the sounds of violence retreat, and the shouts and calls that signal the belated arrival of the Colombian Army instead ring out in the town, the family finally risk escaping from their burning home. Roberto carries young Pablo in his arms, through the puddles of blood that spread across dark streets littered with the smouldering bodies of the dead, where corpses hang from the few lampposts that line the way, and houses, their own included, burn to ash.

*

As soon as they are able, Abel and Hermilda send Pablo and Roberto to Medellín, to live with their grandmother. This busy, thrusting and industrial city, the capital of Antioquia, is home to around half a million people and is growing fast. Second only to the capital and seat of power (both political and economic) in Bogotá, its frantic pace and multitudinous anonymity reek of opportunity to the brothers, and it fast becomes Pablo's spiritual home. Their parents eventually join their boys but, in contrast to his enraptured sons, Abel, an Antioquenian rancher at heart, hates it so much he moves back to the countryside to work on other people's farms. He sends his paycheques back to the city, but never returns to live with his family.

It is in the unique environment of 1960s Medellín that Pablo comes of age. And it is here that he truly begins to display two key facets of his personality: his utter disdain for authority; and his joyful, exuberant, childish love of the sport that means more to the masses across the world than any other. Here, nestled high in the Aburrá Valley, in the 'City of Eternal Spring', the young Pablo Escobar takes his first steps as a Casanova, as a hoodlum, as an aspiring politico. And, here in Medellín, there is one passion of Pablo's that is a constant: Association Football, soccer . . . *el fútbol*.

Pablo's team is Atlético Nacional, a side born just two years before he was. Nicknamed *Los Verdolagas* – 'the purslanes', after the small succulent weed whose green colour adorns their shirts – they share their new 40,000 capacity, $10.5 million stadium, the Estadio Atanasio Girardot, built just a few years before Pablo's arrival in Medellín, with rivals Deportivo Independiente Medellín. Inevitably, Roberto chooses to follow DIM, as they are known, the older of the two sides, both of whom are heavyweights in the Colombian top division. From this moment onwards, the brothers take every opportunity, come what may, to go to games at the Atanasio Girardot. For Pablo, this is the beginning of a lifelong obsession with Medellín football, with Colombian football. And it is an obsession that will bring victory and joy, but also defeat, death and dishonour. Pablo will deliver up to Medellín the greatest moment in their football history, only for his spectre to tarnish this unlikely victory forever. Likewise, his influence will bring Colombia closer than they could ever imagine to the greatest footballing glory attainable, only for his legacy to turn the opportunity into ashes. But, for now, football is new, is joyous.

The young Pablo and Roberto build wooden carts and race them through the streets. They stick down their neighbours' doorbells with gum and run. But their favourite activity is street football. With the wealth required to buy a football but a distant dream, they make their own – rolling up whatever scraps of clothing they can scavenge into a ball and wrapping it tightly in a plastic bag. Whenever they can, they take to the dusty streets and kick their makeshift ball, acting out the latest Nacional and DIM rivalries, emulating their heroes from dawn 'til dusk, until the darkness descends and the limited streetlighting makes it impossible to continue.

But not everyone is so keen on these impromptu kickabouts in their streets, their neighbourhoods. Pablo and Roberto repeatedly run into the local police – who confiscate their homemade balls, ignoring their protests, and move them on in no uncertain terms. It's more than enough to enrage the young Pablo, to stoke his simmering resentment of authority, his unshakeable belief in his inalienable rights. Soon the police are his enemy number one, and he convinces Roberto, and any other young boys who will listen, to throw stones at the patrol cars whenever they see them cruising the area's streets.

Eventually young Pablo's petulant rebellion comes to its inevitable conclusion. A thrown stone, a cracked cop car windshield, and the unerring extension of the long arm of the law. While the other kids flee to safety, Pablo is scooped up. Forced to spend a day in the local jail, he is unrepentant. When asked why he is attacking police vehicles, his answer, 'we're tired of these guys taking our balls', could be a motto for his life to come.

While football is his love, Pablo harbours twin ambitions that run in tandem: money and power. He has two intertwined dreams that he not only hopes he *can* make come true, but that he fervently believes he *will* realize, and to which he devotes all the energies he is not expending on football (and the beginnings of an equally lifelong obsession with chasing pretty girls). These dreams? The fledgling ambitions of a young Pablo Escobar? To make a million dollars before he turns 22, and to become the President of Colombia. One he will achieve with aplomb, albeit not without breaking a plethora of laws, the pursuit of the other will lead to unprecedented death and destruction and bring a nation to its knees . . .

*

Then, in 1962, with Pablo on the cusp of his teenage years, Colombia take part in their first ever World Cup finals competition. They have qualified for the 16-team tournament, hosted by South American rivals Chile, thanks to a 1-0 home win over Peru in Bogotá and a 1-1 draw in the return leg, with the winner in the first game scored by Eusebio Escobar – no relation. A prolific goalscorer in the Colombian league, he would play for both Cali sides (Deportivo and América) and both Medellín teams (Atlético Nacional and Independiente Medellín) across his career, but this vital contribution will remain his only ever international goal.

Making their debut, Colombia are drawn from pot four into a group containing the Soviet Union, Yugoslavia and Uruguay. Interestingly, none of the four sides have a single overseas-based member in their squads. Of the 16 nations taking part only Spain, Switzerland, West Germany and England boast players who ply their trade outside their native country. Gerry Hitchens of Italy's Internazionale is selected alongside the likes of Bobby Moore, Bobby Robson, Bobby Charlton, Jimmy Greaves and Roger Hunt. This England side will finish second to Hungary in their group, ahead of Argentina on goal average, but will lose to eventual champions Brazil in the first knockout stage, the quarter-finals.

An early penalty in Colombia's first game is not enough as they fall to a narrow 2-1 defeat to South American rivals and 1950 champions

Uruguay. But the second game, against the Soviet Union, is one for the ages: 3-0 down inside the first 12 minutes, and still 4-1 behind well into the second half, the Colombians somehow rally. Goals on 68 and 72 minutes bring them within a single strike of their first ever point in the FIFA World Cup. And, on 86 minutes, that glorious moment finally arrives as Marino Klinger, the Millonarios forward, levels the tie. A 4-4 draw with the team who will qualify top of the group is the first great moment for the national team on the world stage. But the joy is short-lived. Los Cafeteros bow out with a 5-0 humbling at the hands of eventual semi-finalists Yugoslavia, finishing bottom of group one. At home in Medellín he may not yet know it, but when Colombia does finally return to the competition some 28 years later it will owe more than a little to Pablo Emilio Escobar Gaviria's influence.

For two teenage boys in the city, hormones raging, there is only one aim – to save enough cash to lose their virginity to one of the many local ladies of the night. The first time Pablo knows the feeling of having money in his pocket comes when, ever the entrepreneurs, he and big brother Roberto score a job delivering dentures from the factory where they are made to dentists' offices around town. Cycling has become Roberto's obsession, and he ropes Pablo in to making the deliveries by bicycle.

Roberto's passion becomes a career. He begins to win races, and is called up as a member of Colombia's national cycling team, earning himself the nickname *El Osito*, 'the little bear', the moniker given to him by a commentator unable to make out his true identity towards the end of a race as his entire face, bar the hollows of his eyes, was covered in mud. It is just as well for the family, and for Pablo, that his big brother is able to earn real money with his cycling, as in 1965 Doña Hermilda falls behind on her rent and they are threatened with eviction. It is Roberto's salary as a professional cyclist that saves the day. Already Pablo can see the dangers, the unfairness, of poverty in Colombia. It is not something he plans to suffer any longer.

While Roberto is busy with his bikes, Pablo turns to more illicit ways to make money. Together with his cousin Gustavo, Pablo embarks on somewhat of a petty crime spree, as he learns the ways of the streets, the criminal ropes, and works his way up. From knocking over fruit carts then stealing the produce in the melee and selling it on himself, to stealing gravestones and shaving off their inscriptions to enable them to be re-sold, to flogging fake lottery tickets, he'll do anything to earn a peso or two. But it's not long before the crimes get more serious, the stakes, the risk and reward, much higher.

While still a schoolboy, Pablo is already tying his criminality to his particular sense of social justice. One day he takes aside his cousin Jaime to rail against the country's inequalities, to bemoan the fact that no rich person in Colombia lifts a finger to help the poor. His solution? To steal from the rich. In 1960s Medellín one luxury item stood out most conspicuously as a marker of wealth – the motor car. And, just like that, Pablo becomes a car thief. He is calm under pressure, a young man with ice in his veins. Not only that, he is charismatic, more than capable of rallying support from the disaffected youth of his community. Initially he is not overtly violent, although he does not shy away from dishing out beatings if his grift, or those around him, are threatened, and it is only a brave or foolish man who crosses him. He is already becoming a criminal, and a leader of men, albeit on a small, and juvenile, scale.

Pablo's increasingly nefarious activities eventually bring him to the attention of contraband kingpin Alvaro Prieto, and his life of crime accelerates. Embroiled in what becomes known as the Marlboro

Wars, a violent and deadly struggle over control of Colombia's most valuable smuggled cigarette, Pablo traffics and bribes his way to the top. Desperate to prove himself to his criminal mentor, and with the conflict reaching a bloody crescendo, Pablo soon finds his unofficial job description also necessitates increasing acts of violence and intimidation for Prieto, perhaps even culminating in his notching up of kills as one day his own sicarios will on his behalf. Pablo's is a very different life from one that is just beginning in another part of Medellín . . .

In 1967 Andrés Escobar is born. His fate will ultimately become inextricably, and fatally, linked with that of his Antioquenian namesake Pablo. The two are not related, share no blood, in fact share very little of anything, at least for the next 20 years. For now, Andrés is raised in a much more affluent and genuinely middle-class family in the well-to-do Calasanz neighbourhood. As he grows up, Andrés is a good student, and a regular attendee at mass with his beloved mother. But it is her death, succumbing to *el cancer* aged only 52, that changes the young man's life and puts him unwittingly on a collision course with Pablo Escobar. In his grief he turns all his energy to the one thing he and Pablo have in common: football. And, as a result, Colombian football will never be the same again . . .

Chapter Two

Love in the Time of Cholera
(1970–1975)

———

It is 1970, and Pablo Emilio Escobar Gaviria is now 20 and well on his way to becoming El Patrón, the Pablo Escobar the world will never forget. As this tumultuous decade unfurls, he will put down deep roots that will anchor not only his criminal enterprises but his heart – in the form of both family and football.

Meanwhile, although Los Cafeteros have failed to qualify for the 1970 World Cup in Mexico, football remains Colombia's sporting obsession. The whole country is thrilled with the arrival of reigning world champions England, the top ranked side in the world who, having famously won the trophy on home soil at Wembley in 1966, arrive in South America to acclimatize and play their penultimate warm-up game before embarking on the defence of their title. For Alf Ramsey's squad of touring Englishmen, Colombia is a distant, foreign land, and indeed no England football team has ever set foot there.

It is 18 May 1970, and England, and captain Bobby Moore in particular, are about to get a rude introduction to the complex combination of money, power and politics, and crime and corruption, that defines the modern Colombia, and that Pablo himself is busy navigating in Medellín. The team are staying at the Tequendama – the height of Bogotá opulence and sophistication and the very same place where, 23 years later, Pablo's family are held under armed guard when they learn of his death. The England squad arrive at the hotel at around 4pm, straight from the airport, but their rooms are still being prepared, and so the group mill around in the lobby to chat and wait. The high-end hotel boasts a number of boutiques dotted around its perimeter, and Bobby Charlton wanders over to window-shop. Behind the glass display of the *Fuego Verde* ('green fire' – a reference to the emeralds for which Colombia, along with gold, coffee and soon cocaine, is famous) he spies a ring mounted with a glorious green stone that would make a fitting gift from his trip for his wife, and steps inside to ask the price. Bobby Moore follows his teammate, but the pair soon leave when Charlton baulks at the figure quoted by the young female shop assistant, Clara Padilla. Moments later the players are back chatting in the lobby when Padilla runs out, accusing them of theft. Soon the store owner, Danilo Rojas, appears and Moore is accused of stealing an 18-carat bracelet studded with a dozen diamonds and a dozen emeralds. The police officer stationed at the tourist office within the five-star hotel saunters over and takes the two Bobbies aside to question them. Eventually tensions simmer down, the players are all given the keys to their rooms and the episode appears closed. But appearances can be deceptive . . .

On Wednesday 20 May, kicking off at 9pm, Ramsey's England make short work of their opposition on the pitch, outclassing *La Selección* Colombia 4-0. A glancing Martin Peters header after only 90 seconds takes the sting out of the home team and the crowd of

36,000 crammed into Bogotá's Estadio El Campín, and he doubles the England lead with another close-range headed goal on 39 minutes. In the second half a pinpoint finish into the top corner from the edge of the box from Bobby Charlton, a goal which was to be his last in an England shirt, and a final nail in the coffin fourth shortly before full time – of all things a header from 5ft 5in Alan Ball – complete the rout. In truth, it is an exhibition game, with the Colombians flattering to deceive with pretty patterns to their passing but little or no penetration and no bite to their game – perhaps understandable given their lowly FIFA world ranking of 87, and the need for their opposition to remain unscathed before the start of the tournament. But this England squad will not, in fact, leave Colombia without incident.

For Rojas and Padilla have pressed charges with the Colombian police after all, and have announced as such to the British Embassy. The morning after the game, Moore is hauled in by the cops, made to give an official statement and is asked to demonstrate whether his fist is small enough to fit inside the gap in the cabinet in which the bracelet was alleged to have been on display. When his hand is deemed too big to have pilfered the item, he is let go. Case closed? Perhaps not . . .

The team fly to Quito, where they beat Ecuador 2-0. Undefeated, they are primed for their defence of the World Cup. But, back in Bogotá on a brief layover on their way to Panama, en route to Mexico, Moore is detained. Eventually the magistrate orders him to be held in a jail cell in a notorious prison in one of the most lawless parts of Bogotá. Eventually a compromise is reached, and he is placed under 'house arrest' back at the Tequendama. But with an active investigation open he is not permitted to leave with his teammates, and it is several days before he is finally able to further prove his innocence – by demonstrating that he could not have secreted the bracelet in his pocket, as the shop assistant had claimed, because his tracksuit didn't have any! Days late, Moore arrives in Mexico to join his teammates. England's defence of their title fails at the first knockout stage, and Brazil go on to win the tournament, but one story is never wrapped up – what really happened in the lobby of the Tequendama that day. Meanwhile, Pablo is a young man in love – with no inkling that it will not be too long before, just like Bobby Moore, he too will be under lock and key for the first time . . .

*

Pablo is 23 and living in Envigado, Medellín, when the most beautiful young girl, with a definite emphasis on *young*, in the La Paz neighbourhood comes to his attention. He is the young man known by the local ladies as 'the guy with the motorbike' – and he takes many of them for a ride on his red and white Vespa, bought for 3,500 pesos and paid in 300-peso monthly instalments. He hasn't yet quit full-time education, and his dreams of power still include getting a law degree as a precursor to entering politics, with the ambition of one day becoming no less than president. But he has the airs and graces of a farm boy, with his rural *paisa* accent and his white woollen *ruana* (a traditional Antioquenian poncho). He is not in the same league as the barely teenage Victoria Eugenia Henao. Her family are one of the wealthiest in the neighbourhood, so much so that even though she is one of eight kids they can afford to send her to private school and pay for her private swimming and guitar lessons. She is everything he is not. But Pablo – who is only 5ft 5in and gets angry when his friends call him 'midget' or 'shrimp' – is nothing if not determined. In pursuit of love, as in 'business' and football, he will let nothing get in his way. He woos her for nigh on a year, encouraging her to sneak off and meet him at the local ice cream parlour, enlisting family friends as go-betweens, winning over her brother Mario, and showering her with increasingly ostentatious gifts.

His perseverance pays off, and the pair officially become boyfriend and girlfriend in May 1973. But Pablo is not expending all his energies on the girl he will always call 'Tata'. He may be spending less time playing football these days, but if so it is only because his criminal career is really starting to take off. And watching football? Now that is a different matter.

In 1973 Pablo's beloved Atlético Nacional win only their second league title, as they triumph over bitter rivals Millonarios of Bogotá and Deportivo Cali. The same year marks the inauguration of the USA's Drug Enforcement Agency, the DEA, which is created by an executive order from President Richard Nixon. At this stage, the two events seem unrelated, but in fewer than 20 years' time Atlético Nacional of Medellín and America's DEA will be inextricably linked by one man: Pablo Escobar.

Meanwhile, Colombia is also bidding to host their first ever World Cup. Misael Pastrana Borrero, President of Colombia, welcomes a FIFA delegation to the country as part of the official bid for the 1986 edition of the tournament. Los Cafeteros have been in the footballing wilderness for 20 years, the one lone and unexpected high point in that time, the 1962 4-4 draw with the Soviet Union, now a distant memory. The reason stems from the weakness of the domestic league, which is due to finances, and politics. Before the outbreak of La Violencia the sport had benefitted from its hold over the populace and had been supported by those in politics, and in positions of power. After the end of the violence, and when Colombian football returned to the bosom of FIFA, the value of the sport as a political tool dwindled. So it would remain, until one man saw the potential that was being overlooked. You guessed it. Pablo Escobar. But for now, President Pastrana is busy regaling the delegates with slick and ambitious plans for the Colombia '86 bid. Whatever he says, it clearly works as, despite not having a single stadium up to the requisite standards to stage a World Cup game, come 1974 Colombia has been awarded the hosting rights. The 1986 World Cup will be hosted by Colombia. Or will it?

1974 also marks a watershed moment for Pablo the aspiring crime boss. At a football match (where else?) he is introduced to Rafael Puente, another of Colombia's major cigarette smugglers. Puente takes him under his wing, teaching him his secrets, the tools of the trade that will eventually help Pablo Escobar become the biggest trafficker the world has ever seen. He learns how to set up and utilize a network of *caletas* – secret hiding places in hollow walls and other discrete and unassuming locations where contraband, cash, weapons or anything else, even people, can be stashed. Soon the workers who find themselves under Pablo's supervision, moving the illicit goods from stash spot to stash spot, come up with a name for their driven, charismatic young boss: El Patrón. The cap fits, and the name will follow Pablo until his death.

While his love of football has brought him into contact with his new mentor, and put him on the path to realizing his ambition to earn $1 million, it also gives him a unique calling card for his political aspirations. Himself a fan of both playing and watching the game, and still not so many years removed from the boy who kicked a plastic bag of clothes around the dusty streets, Pablo has realized what few others have – that the beautiful game is the perfect way to win over the hearts and minds of the people, of the poor and disadvantaged, of those like him. While still studying to become a criminal lawyer, and as part of his dream to make it to the top of the political tree, he begins to give speeches – taking to the school's football pitches and regaling anyone who will listen with his plans to become president and to take 10 per cent of the earnings of the richest in Colombia and use that money to fund schools, roads, hospitals and football pitches.

Soon he gives up schooling to focus on his criminal ambitions, his political aspirations and Tata – the money from the former bankrolling the latter two 'projects'. When it comes to Tata, he may often be away due to the demands of his 'business', but he still manages to hire a young man to follow her around and take photos of her in a strangely controlling gesture of love, to buy her a brand new yellow Monareta bicycle and even to teach her to drive in a 1954 Ford that was one of the first cars the La Paz neighbourhood had seen – with Victoria's sister Luz Marina and her boyfriend Óscar sitting in the back as chaperones.

Pablo will also not neglect his family. He buys his mum a house, and a brand-new top of the range bicycle for his brother. Soon he is making so much money, up to $250,000 a month, and fielding so many bank accounts and fake identities, that he asks Roberto to become his accountant and to help launder his ill-gotten gains through a portfolio of extensive property investments across Medellín and Antioquia. From this partnership of brothers, the feared Medellín Cartel will eventually grow.

But what marks Pablo out from any of his rivals is his political ambition – and his belief in the power that comes with winning the love and support of the people of Medellín. No sooner is he making money than he is out using it to garner favour among the local population – taking a truck to the food market, buying up all the lettuce, meat and fish they have and driving it down to the city dump to hand it out himself to the poorest and most destitute who scavenge through the detritus to survive. He is making a name for himself and becoming a father figure to many of the most neglected of his city, and soon he will also actually become a father himself, but these two things will ultimately prove to be his downfall . . .

*

In the latter half of 1974 Pablo disappears for two months. He leaves telling Tata that he is off 'looking for work', but ends up getting arrested while driving a stolen Renault 4. He is locked up in La Ladera Prison in Enciso, on the eastern edge of Medellín. But his reputation, and his underworld connections, come to his aid, and he is eventually released when the evidence against him mysteriously 'disappears'. Young Tata has had a glimpse of what a life with this dangerous older man might bring, but it is soon forgotten as the fledgling couple are reunited.

Pablo will find himself on the wrong side of the law again in 1976, but first comes the 1975 Copa América. Held from July to October, it is the first time the tournament has gone by that name, and it features all ten CONMEBOL (the South American Football Confederation) countries. And, following on from the successful bid for the '86 World Cup, it proves an unexpected success for Colombia. Drawn into Group C, they win all four games, beating Paraguay and Ecuador home and away to finish top, having scored seven goals and conceded only one. Only Brazil can match their maximum of eight points, as they sweep Group A scoring an impressive 13 goals.

In the two-legged semi-finals, Colombia meet defending

champions Uruguay, who were given a bye past the group stages. A comprehensive 3-0 win at home in the Estadio El Campín in Bogotá in front of 55,000 has the fans dreaming. And a narrow 1-0 defeat in the return leg in Montevideo, holding out for over 70 minutes after an early Uruguay penalty, and despite the fervent home support of 70,000 at the Estadio Centenario, means a 3-1 aggregate win for Los Cafeteros. Colombia are in the final.

They will face the winner of the Brazil–Peru tie, which is thrillingly poised after a shock 3-1 away win for Peru in Belo Horizonte courtesy of two dramatic late strikes. But the drama continues in the second leg as Brazil, needing to win by two clear goals, race into the lead in Lima after only ten minutes, as Peruvian defender Meléndez puts into his own net. Just after the hour mark a second for Brazil means a goal for either side in the final half an hour will be enough for victory. But no goal comes. With the match tied at 3-3 after both legs, the finalists will be decided by the drawing of lots. When Peru are announced, fans in Colombia could be forgiven for breathing a sigh of relief at avoiding the three times world champions Brazil.

The final is another two-legged affair. The first tie is played in Bogotá, and Colombia emerge with a slender 1-0 lead to take to Lima, courtesy of a lone first-half goal. But will it be enough for the nation's maiden triumph? Six days later Peru win the return leg 2-0. But the final will not be decided by goals scored, and instead – with both teams on two points (awarded for a win) each – the tournament will be decided in a single, winner-takes-all final game play-off. Colombia have one last chance. This final match is held a further six days later, at the Estadio Olimpico in Caracas, Venezuela. Colombia are unable to reverse the momentum of the previous tie however, and slump to a 1-0 defeat. Peru have their second 'Copa', their first since 1939. Los

Cafeteros return home to Colombia wondering what might have been. They will not reach another Copa América final until the dawn of a new millennium, when La Selección Colombia of 2001 will finally bring home the cup. They will however, thanks to the rise of Pablo's beloved Nacional and his impact on both them and the national side, have some brighter, and darker, days to look forward to before then . . .

Chapter Three

A Prince Among Thieves (1976-1979)

————

1976 sees a confluence of events entirely typical of Pablo's extraordinary existence, as his love life and his life of crime are once more set on a collision course. Now 26, he has been smuggling marijuana for some time but is soon tempted into a more lucrative endeavour by his cousin Gustavo – smuggling coca paste into Colombia from Peru. The men are recruited by local gangster Mateo Moreno, also known as *Cucaracha* – the cockroach. As he explains to them, the paste is the base ingredient needed to make cocaine, the drug that is just starting to make waves in America and across the Atlantic in Western Europe.

The demand for cocaine is growing, and the processed drug can fetch a high price. For entrepreneurial criminals in Colombia like Cucaracha and Pablo, there is serious money to be made. But Colombia does not yet have the supply of raw coca to match the demand. What the criminal enterprise needs is a complex network, involving sourcing the paste from neighbouring countries where the coca crop is abundant, smuggling it into Colombia, processing it domestically and then exporting it to the US and Europe. In order to manage the logistic supply chain, and in particular the cross-border smuggling of the coca paste, Pablo needs to make contacts both nationally and internationally. He begins to travel more and more and, in March 1976, he has a meeting in Pasto, way down near Colombia's southern border with Ecuador. He convinces Tata, who is still only 15, to go with him, and to make it a secret elopement – he intends them to wed while they are down there, away from her disapproving family.

The couple fly from Medellín's Enrique Olaya Herrera airport to Cali. But before they can continue on, Tata's family intercepts them. Ever the smooth-talker, Pablo is eventually able to convince Tata's grandmother of their love and his intentions, to the extent that she obtains them an audience with the bishop of Palmira. Watched over by Tata's relatives, the pair are kept in Cali, and Pablo postpones his trip to Pasto. After a two-week wait for the requisite documentation from Medellín, on Monday 29 March 1976, Pablo Emilio Escobar Gaviria and Victoria Eugenia Henao are pronounced man and wife.

Sometime later Mr and Mrs Escobar take a belated honeymoon trip to Colombia's paradise island. San Andrés sits, surrounded by coral reefs, in the middle of the Caribbean Sea. In a candid holiday snap, the happy couple pose on the rocks, an azure sea behind them, picture-perfect fluffy white clouds dotting the blue sky overhead. Pablo, in swim shorts and slip-on soccer sandals, is the epitome of the fit, young groom, sporting a thick moustache and with his hair slicked back, his toned chest revealed by his open coral pink shirt. Tata is the demure wife, the teenage bride, in a blue swimsuit and matching hat. But look closely and you might just imagine you can make out an almost imperceptible swelling at her belly. It might just be a trick of the light, an optical illusion, but then again . . .

Back home in Medellín, Tata is back at school, and Pablo is back to his womanizing ways, and is always away with 'work'. But at least he has finally bought them a house, in Medellín's Los Colores neighbourhood, where, for the first time, they can live together as a couple. It's not what she dreamed of, but for now it will do. But even this compromised simulacrum of domestic bliss is not to last.

Fewer than three months after their marriage in Cali, things go badly wrong. Pablo's exploits are beginning to bring him to the attention of Colombia's security services, namely the *Departamento Administrativo de Seguridad*, known as DAS. On 5 June 1976, DAS agents stop a truck travelling towards Medellín. Their search turns up coca paste secreted inside the spare tyre and smuggled from Peru. But rather than haul in the driver, they have their sights set a touch higher. The driver is allowed to call Pablo. He tells him he's been stopped – and that the agents are asking for $5,000 to release him and the vehicle. In 1970s Colombia, in the Colombia of Pablo Escobar, this type of petty corruption is not only rife, it is a vital part of his business model, his everyday life, and his past, present and future success. Thinking nothing of it, Pablo grabs the cash – it's far from an amount he cannot spare – and heads out to the handover spot with cousin Gustavo and his now brother-in-law Mario. The 57lb package of coca paste has been intercepted en route to Pablo's very first cocaine 'kitchen' – a two-storey house in Belén (the neighbourhood that a certain Francisco Maturana calls home, but more about him later) which is only the first in what will eventually become an entire industrialized network of secret sites turning coca paste into cocaine ready to export to the USA.

It is dawn, 6am, when Pablo arrives to hand over the wad of dollars. But this is no pay-off, and he is arrested. Pablo is booked and his smiling mugshot, seemingly proudly holding up the card that denotes him as prisoner number 128482, is an image that will become iconic, and will outlive El Patrón himself (see plate section).

Held in a cell in Medellín, Pablo is unable to keep up with the loan repayments on the mortgage. The bank repossesses the couple's home, and Tata is forced to return to live with her parents. Meanwhile, Pablo is sent to Bellavista, an infamous prison in Bello, southern Medellín. And then Tata discovers she is indeed pregnant.

Eventually his contacts and growing pull enable Pablo to swing a transfer to Yarumito Prison in Itagüí, a much lower security 'open' style prison without guards. But Pablo is determined not to spend any longer being denied his freedom and he formulates a plan that is audacious in its beautiful simplicity, and that perfectly combines his flair for improvisation with his love of football.

After just two weeks of his incarceration at Yarumito, during a regular prison kickabout, Pablo has one of his fellow inmates 'accidentally' boot the ball way out of touch and deep into the undergrowth around the prison. Pablo volunteers to go and look for the lost ball, and disappears into the greenery. Seconds become minutes. No ball. No Pablo. He never re-emerges. The ball is forgotten. An inmate has escaped! However, the authorities are spared any major embarrassment, thanks to none other than Doña Hermilda. After only a few hours on the run, Pablo is castigated on a hurried phone call with his formidable mother, and reminded of his responsibilities as a husband. A call to Tata seals the deal: he can't stay on the run, he is going to be a father. He devises a way to return, paying off a doctor to put his name on someone else's x-rays and heading back to the prison to explain he merely absconded for medical tests.

His escape results in a swift, temporary transfer to a nearby, and somewhat higher security institution, in Itagüí. Then, as soon as they are able, the authorities move him to a new prison in Pasto, near the border with Ecuador. But, undeterred, Pablo is soon back to his old ways. Somehow, no doubt thanks to a heavy dose of unmarked US bills, he is able to convince the prison authorities to allow him conjugal leave. Every weekend that she is able, the teenage Tata travels all the way down to the prison – and Pablo is permitted to take her out on the town. He takes a suite at the finest hotel around, the Morascuro, and is even able to celebrate his young bride's 16th birthday in the lap of luxury, while still officially a prisoner. An image from one visit reveals a heavily pregnant Tata, dressed down in dark blue jeans and a pink blouse, and Pablo not in a prison uniform but instead sporting flared trousers and a bright, patterned shirt. When they go out for a special celebratory dinner later, Tata dolls herself up, donning a multi-coloured dress, her hair and make-up impeccable.

Then, after a whirlwind five months of incarceration, the inexplicable – at least for any lesser man than Pablo Escobar – occurs . . . freedom. When the charges against him are suddenly dropped, he is permitted to leave, and walks out a free man. In fact, having manoeuvred to get the first presiding judge replaced he has been able to bribe his replacement and secure his release. Within months the undercover police officers behind his arrest will be assassinated and Pablo is home and dry. At least in theory. For the time being he has nowhere else to stay but with his in-laws, where a heavily pregnant Tata is weak and bedridden. As soon as he can, he rents a small apartment in downtown Medellín. Money is tight, or so it seems to his teenage bride, but soon Pablo is driving around in a new Porsche with lustrous leather seats. At least he does finally invest in a refrigerator for their apartment.

Then, on 24 February 1977 Tata goes to school as usual, sits an

English test, and feels that tell-tale splash and spread of wetness. Her waters well and truly broken, she walks two blocks from school to her parents' home from where they drive her to the apartment, collect Pablo and take them to the El Rosario hospital in downtown Medellín. Barely half an hour later she bears Pablo a son. Within 48 hours they are home with their baby boy: Juan Pablo.

*

By now Pablo has carved out a cocaine niche – he's the only player in town running the full operation, overseeing the trafficking of coca paste from Peru, its refinement in his kitchens and its export to Miami, Florida. He is making more and more money, and as ever he is blazing a trail, innovating. He allows anyone who is able to scrape together enough capital to invest in his enterprise. Not just the rich or the powerful but the regular people of Medellín. Many beg, borrow and steal to take him up on his offer of guaranteed returns. He does not disappoint, and these ordinary citizens are soon very rich thanks to Pablo's 'business'. But no one is getting richer than El Patrón.

In 1978 Pablo buys a huge house in Medellín's up-and-coming Provenza neighbourhood. It costs him no less than three million pesos – and boasts a pool, seven bedrooms and stained-glass windows. He sets up a home office, where he and Gustavo receive a constant stream of visitors. Soon they move operations to an old house on Calle 9 in El Poblado to give Tata and Juan Pablo some peace.

Pablo has a new home, a new-born son and a business that is growing exponentially. But he still yearns for political power, and he still craves the adulation of the crowd, especially in the sporting arena.

While brother Roberto has always loved cycling, Pablo is a petrol head with a need for speed, a man addicted to the adrenalin of motorsports. He had started out driving his 200cc IT motorbike in local races at the Furesa track, and taking part in unregulated time trials on the outskirts of Medellín in his Porsche, but now he upgrades to proper racing – the 'Copa Renault', the Renault Cup. Renault has a special place in Colombian automotive history – the country had been importing the French cars since 1952, and the Renault 4 model since 1966, and in 1970 Renault took the decisive step of opening the Envigado body assembly plant in Medellín. Here the iconic Renault 4 was put together on Colombian soil for the first time.

In 1979, the Copa Renault national racing series opens up to include rookie drivers. Pablo is first in line. He buys a fleet of Renault 4s, rents the top floor of the Bogotá Hilton for the entire year, and begins travelling down to the capital by helicopter every weekend to take part in the rough and ready, spit and sawdust style races and to party with Gustavo. Despite being far from the most talented of the competing drivers he manages to finish the season in second place. If his cars benefit from any extra-legal modifications no one ever complains.

But Pablo is not just living the life of a playboy *narco*. He has bigger dreams, loftier aspirations. He has never taken his eye off the path to political power, and his money and growing influence give him the perfect platform to embark on his career in politics. Meanwhile the treaty just agreed between Colombia and the United States – formally signed in Washington DC on 14 September 1979 – will make drug trafficking a crime against the USA, and an extraditable offence, and that spurs him on to seek the immunity that only comes with political power.

Pablo has been offering help and advice to the poor of the neighbourhood in La Paz, and has become a kind of community leader of sorts. He rails angrily, and publicly, about the state of the poor, and in defence of the striking workers. One of his early initiatives encourages the planting of trees to help shade the hot tin shacks that crowd the poor areas. In Quibdó, 140 miles west of Medellín, he establishes his own form of private social security system for the poor, using a portion of the wealth he is already amassing from the cocaine business to cover their living expenses and help them to find work. He is relentless in appealing to the poor and marginalized, and in positioning himself as their peer, the everyman done good, the benevolent benefactor who is the only one who truly understands their plight and who will fight for them. Soon he is being hailed as a modern-day Robin Hood. Nothing could please El Patrón more.

He stands at a microphone, before the massed ranks of the unruly crowd, many of them young men like him, and speaks with passion: 'With all of your support, we'll crush the political puppets of Colombia's spineless oligarchy!'

Interviewed on camera, hair perfectly coiffed, in a white shirt with the collar open, no tie (as always), and a dark blue suit impeccably tailored, his voice is soft as he speaks: 'I was raised poor, in a family without means to cover our basic needs. Like most Colombians, we struggled through hard times. I'm no stranger to the problems of this country.'

He is the opposite of the Bogotano elite, the buttoned up blue bloods who have controlled the country from their ivory towers for years. Visitors to his offices on Calle 9 often find him, come mid-afternoon, playing football with his brother Roberto on the pitch he has had installed there.

Soon enough he is elected to the Envigado town council. From here he has a platform to campaign for election to Colombia's House of Representatives. If he can secure that seat, he will be immune from the new threat of extradition to the US.

He makes football a cornerstone of his campaign. In his speeches to the Envigado council one of Pablo's regular and most impassioned subjects is the need for the creation and construction of sports facilities that are both well-lit and accessible to the public. He even begins to take matters into his own hands, donating lights for local pitches and kit to local teams. Whatever they need to be able to play their beloved game, he supplies. And, unlike other politicians, there's no delay. If he promises shirts or balls, the next day one of his men turns up with the gear. If he promises lights or stands, within 24 hours a team of workmen arrive to do his bidding. Soon he is travelling from neighbourhood to neighbourhood, building brand-new football pitches in each barrio with his cousin Jaime. Older brother Roberto will later estimate that Pablo created up to 800 new football pitches. For the young boys of Medellín he is a saint. The patron saint of the barrios, and of football.

He arrives at a brand-new football stadium that he has had built in the La Paz neighbourhood, dressed more smartly than he ever did for a council meeting. For once he wears shiny leather dress shoes instead of trainers or football boots – he is turning on the style not for the stuffed shirts in Medellín or Bogotá but for the poor of the slum, for the boys who dream only of football. This is a grand opening, and he poses for photos, taken by the assembled press. He knows the value of this publicity, even if he does find himself occasionally ill at ease when he is so publicly centre of attention. He stands in the middle of the pitch, where he is given a brand-new football to hold, the pristine black and white panels matching his dark trousers and white shirt (short-sleeved and without a tie, as is always his style). On either side of him the two boys' teams stand proudly, holding long banners that proclaim their gratitude to Pablo. Behind, young men and boys smile and goof around, filled with joy at this festival of football. Many of those playing and watching will become so enamoured of Pablo that they will sign up to join him, becoming part of his army of sicarios. Many will end up dying for him. Others though will end up playing for him. He lets the ball drop from his hands and sends it out of the centre circle with a cushioned left-foot volley. Like a queen smashing a bottle of Champagne on the hull to launch a new vessel, the ceremonial act is complete, the pitch has been christened, let the games begin.

In the barrios where his pitches give the space, and where his generosity gives the light, there are regular tournaments. The slums are packed with players and fans, families crowding to support their boys – among them future players of Pablo's beloved Nacional, young men who will carry the hopes and dreams of Medellín deep into the Copa Libertadores, the pinnacle of South American club football; a crop of talented young footballers who will graduate to playing for Los Cafeteros too, and will shoulder the burden of expectation of all of Colombia all the way to the World Cup itself. Players like Luis 'Chonto' Herrera, a tough kid from Medellín's El Salvador slum, and his fellow future footballing stars like Alexis Garcia, Mauricio 'Chicho' Serna and Leonel Álvarez, all grow up on the pitches Pablo built. They sneak out of their homes at night to play in tournaments in celebration of El Patrón, learn to forget their poverty, their worries, and to express themselves on the perfect world of the football pitch. Many of them, most notably René Higuita, will eventually become friends of El Patrón. They watch on as Pablo the (not too) smartly dressed local politician and businessman gives his brief speech at the microphone, and if others whisper about the source of his wealth and success, gossip that he is a *narcotraficante*, a drug lord, these young boys care not a jot. They are just grateful to have a pitch, to be able to play.

Pablo stands, swigging on a bottle of beer, every inch the benevolent man of the people as he signs autographs. His wife and young son are by his side. The game plays out on the dusty pitch, the masses that cover the sloped banks revelling in the spectacle as fireworks burst into a kaleidoscope of colours overhead. The crowd breaks out into a chant of 'Pablo! Pablo!' He is giving Medellín the gift of football, and they will love him for it.

Meanwhile, in stark contrast, the Colombian government, rife with political infighting and financial constraints, is singularly failing to make good on its promise to FIFA. Next to no progress has been made on developing stadia suitable for the planned 1986 World Cup.

Eventually, with his charitable good deeds – from supporting grassroots football in the barrios to creating *Civismo en Marcha* (Public Spirit on the Move), a movement which promotes social and ecological projects in the Aburrá Valley in which Medellín sits – having earned him the ear and support of much of the populace in key areas across Antioquia, he begins to push a new agenda. And he makes his opposition to extradition a matter of national pride for all Colombians, a refusal to be dictated to by *los gringos* in Washington. It is all part of his new campaign to win election to Colombia's House of Representatives. For all that he hates the historic power of the politicians in Bogotá, he knows that if he can join their ranks he will be immune from prosecution – and protected from extradition to America. This threat has become his single biggest fear, the fear of a foreign justice system that hates him, that sees him as alien, foreign, and that he cannot bribe, bully or intimidate. Extradition becomes the hill on which Pablo decides he will die if he must.

As the 1970s end, and a new decade of thrilling opportunity – the 1980s – is ushered in, Pablo is advancing on three fronts. From his new Medellín home, a four-million peso two-storey house on half an acre of land in the El Diamante neighbourhood of El Poblado, he begins to campaign as a serious politician, to gain the power and prestige he craves and to gain the Holy Grail – immunity. He also sets the wheels in motion to create the Medellín Cartel, bringing together the various heads of the key aspects of his holistic cocaine operation to make him the leader of what will become one of the biggest organized crime groups the world has ever seen. And he takes his first steps into the world of professional football – a move that will put him on a collision course with not just the national and global governing bodies of the beautiful game, but with another new, and deadly threat – the Cali Cartel . . .

Chapter Four

The Genesis of Narcoball
(1979–1987)

In 1979, while Pablo is cementing his power in Medellín, 250 miles south – a long, hot day's drive but a veritable world away – the Narcoball era is about to begin in the country's third city, Cali.

Santiago de Cali, to give the city its full name, is a different beast from Medellín. While Medellín's population has now swollen to almost 1.7 million, Cali is home to more like 1.1 million people by the time the 1970s are drawing to a close. But it is the gateway to the Pacific, the only major city in Colombia within striking distance of that coastline. Like Medellín it is big, busy and boasts two rival football teams – América de Cali and Deportivo Cali – who share a stadium. And, like Medellín, it is a growing drug trafficking centre. Here the Rodríguez Orejuela brothers, Gilberto and Miguel, have, like Pablo, made the move from marijuana to the big new drug on the block – cocaine. Their operation will become the now-legendary Cali Cartel. And while up in the mountains of Antioquia Pablo is embarking on a career in politics, down in the Valle del Cauca, the Rodríguez Orejuela brothers are diversifying their criminal wealth – and investing in local team América.

It is an interesting choice. The club has never won a Colombian championship in the modern era. Meanwhile their cross-town rivals Deportivo have amassed five titles in just fifteen years since 1965, and only the year before, in 1978, made it all the way to the final of the Copa Libertadores. Many put América's travails down to the 'Curse of Garabato'. In 1948, the side's star player was club legend Benjamín Urrea. A tiny, fast and skilful player he was nicknamed *Garabato*: 'the scribble'. But, when he fell out with the club over their plans to join the country's professional league, he cursed them. América joined the league despite him, but for 30 years would not win it even once.

Then, in 1979, Garabato is invited back to the bosom of América de Cali. He visits the club's shared stadium and signs an official letter, lifting the jinx. Rumours swirl of a special mass held to remove the curse, of an exorcism carried out to cleanse the club. Whatever the truth, at the same time the club appoints one of the biggest names in the domestic game as their new manager. Gabriel Ochoa Uribe has already racked up seven league titles in Bogotá – six with Millonarios and another with rival side Independiente Santa Fe. With the curse lifted, a new manager and the beginnings of a cash injection from the Cali Cartel, *Los Diablos Rojos*, the Red Devils, as América are known, have a clean slate. But it's hard to imagine that anyone believes their fortunes will change so dramatically, and so quickly . . .

Colombia has had a professional football league since 1948. However, this initially unregulated league, sitting outside of FIFA's jurisdiction, led to Colombian football facing sanctions from the sport's global governing body from 1949 to 1954, including exclusion from the 1954 World Cup. Yet despite that, or in fact because of it, in

the early 1950s Colombian domestic football had a handful of years
of major investment that took advantage of a strike in Argentinian
football to lure players such as Alfredo di Stéfano to play in Colombia
and to help distract the population from the political turmoil and
bloodshed of La Violencia with the spectacle of the beautiful game.
Without FIFA's rules and regulations Colombian clubs, Millonarios in
Bogotá principal among them, were able to offer players from overseas
much higher wages than their neighbours and the domestic game
flourished briefly in what would become known as the *El Dorado*
period – the first golden age of Colombian club football. But after
barely five years, now back under the auspices of FIFA, and with the
political capital of football diminished with the end of La Violencia,
football in Colombia regressed from the mid-1950s.

But over the years the number of professional clubs and the
domestic structure solidified, and the country adopted a version
of the complex two-part league format favoured by much of Latin
America. In 1979 this comprises of an initial *Apertura* league in which
all 14 teams play each other home and away, then a *Finalización*
competition in which the teams are split into two groups of seven
based on the seedings from their final positions in the Apertura.
The results from both the Apertura and Finalización are combined
into a final league table – the *Reclasificación* – which then decides
which sides make it into the two groups of four that make up the
quadrangular semi-finals, in which each side plays the other three
in their group home and away. The top two from each group advance
to play in the four-way quadrangular final which will ultimately
decide the year's champions. Variations on this format will remain
the mainstay of Colombian league football until 2002, when the
governing body began awarding two championship titles per season,

thus making the Apertura and Finalización tournaments independent championships within a single season.

However, despite the ambition shown by the Cali Cartel, who inject what might be the most capital into Colombian football since the 1950s, initially it seems like a case of so near, yet so far for América. Built on the foundations of an almost impenetrable back line, the 1979 side finds itself in a neck and neck race to finish top of the Apertura with none other than local rivals Deportivo Cali.

At the close of the Apertura, there is nothing to choose between the two sides, who sit alongside one another atop the table. A two-legged play-off ensues but, after two 0-0 draws, even that cannot separate the sides. The sport's governing body is forced to go back to the Apertura league standings. Both sides have identical records, with 13 wins, 8 draws and 5 defeats giving them 34 points each. Not only that, they have the same goal difference of +10. In the end Deportivo are awarded the top spot in the standings – on goals scored. América's focus on defence, to the detriment of scoring goals, is their undoing. Perhaps the curse lives on?

But come the second half of the season, and the Finalización tournament, they start strongly and don't look back. They finish the regular season top, four points clear of Deportivo in second place. They do, however, struggle in the four-team group A that forms the league's quadrangular semi-final stage. They squeak into the four-team round robin final by a single point. The tournament going gets tough and they earn two wins and two draws from the first five games, their only defeat a 1-0 loss to Santa Fe in Bogotá. One of those tied games was a 1-1 draw away at Unión Magdalena, and it is this side that they must beat, at home in this final match, to win the title. Ochoa guides them to a 2-0 victory. América are champions of Colombia for the first time in their history. The 'Curse of Garabato' has well and truly been lifted. And the Rodríguez brothers can celebrate their new venture in style.

This moment, perhaps more than any other, marks the true beginning, the birth, of the era of 'narco-fútbol' that will burn bright and deadly for a decade and a half. Another story, possibly apocryphal, from the same year – 1979 – reveals the heights of the ambition of the Cali brothers and the potential sway of this new 'narcoball'. Miguel Rodríguez Orejuela, the younger of the two brothers, meets with a 19-year-old Argentinian, a boy who has grown up in the shanty towns of Buenos Aires. He is small, just 5ft 5in, but stocky – yet despite his youth and stature it is clear that the older man takes him seriously. Miguel wines and dines the teenager – who is none other than rising star of Argentinian football and Argentinos Juniors, Diego Armando Maradona. Miguel offers the teenage Diego a staggering $3 million to come and play the second half of the Colombian league season for the Rodríguez brothers and América de Cali. Maradona turns the offer down. In 1982 he will set a world record transfer fee when he moves to Barcelona from Boca Juniors for 1.2 billion pesetas. But this high-end dinner in Cali is not the last time he will cross paths with a Colombian drug lord.

In truth Cali is not the first club in Colombia to have drug money in its coffers. That dubious accolade may well belong to the team they have just beaten to the 1979 title – Unión Magdalena.

Ironically it was marijuana, the drug which the founders of both the Cali and Medellín cocaine cartels would graduate from, that would first find its way into Colombian football. A group of marijuana smugglers, headed by drug baron Eduardo Enrique Dávila Armenta, invested in Unión Magdalena in the early 1970s. The club had just won its first Colombian championship in 1968, becoming the first side to bring the league title to the Caribbean region of the country. But whatever money the illicit co-operative brought to the club, it failed to have the desired impact. To this day, Unión Magdalena have yet to win a second title, and remain most famous for being the first club of local legend, national superstar and global football (and hair) icon – Carlos *El Pibe* ('The Kid') Valderrama. In contrast, América de Cali are about to show just what 1980s narcotraficante cocaine money can do, and embark on an era of almost total dominance – at least until a certain Pablo Escobar decides to get in on the game and bring his beloved Atlético Nacional to the party.

But in these early years it's not all plain sailing for América and their shadowy patrons. In 1980 they make it all the way to the end-of-season four-way final, only to finish third behind hated rivals Deportivo Cali and winners Junior de Barranquilla. And in 1981 there's a bigger and more enervating upset.

Pablo Escobar has by now taken a vested interest in his favourite club, Atlético Nacional of Medellín. And it will not take long for his money and influence to properly be felt. In the 1981 Apertura tournament it initially seems like normal service has been resumed, as América de Cali finish top – guaranteeing their place in the end-of-season semi-finals despite their finishing bottom of Group A in the Finalización. In fact they finish top of the combined standings, the Reclasificación, two points ahead of Atlético Nacional and Millonarios. América go on to finish top of their semi-final group conceding only one goal and scoring twelve across the six games. But in the four-team final they stutter – and the title is won by Atlético Nacional. For Cali it is a bitter pill to swallow. But for Pablo, it is his first taste of victory. The scene is set for a series of titanic battles to come as the two cartels, and the teams they will end up controlling – Atlético Nacional and Deportivo Independiente in Medellín, Millonarios in Bogotá, and América de Cali – prepare to go head-to-head on the football pitch long before they end up embroiled in all-out war across the country . . .

*

1981, as well as being the year of Atlético Nacional's fourth Colombian league championship, is also the year that Pablo Escobar truly forms the loose co-operative, with him as the de-facto head, that will become known across the world as the Medellín Cartel.

In the Colombian countryside, where La Violencia raged during Pablo's childhood, things have changed. The Latin American debt crisis and its local and international repercussions have led to an implosion of the local coffee industry which has decimated Colombia's biggest cash crop and export. Meanwhile the factions in the nation's bloody conflict have been replaced by new armed groups, with the most active the *Fuerzas Armadas Revolucionarias de Colombia*: the FARC, a Marxist people's army growing in power and influence in the rural areas. In this semi-lawless and impoverished countryside a new, risky but lucrative crop rises to take the place of coffee: Coca.

In the late 1970s Pablo gains access to much of this local Colombian coca supply through the fast-rising narco José Gonzalo Rodríguez Gacha – known as *El Mexicano*, 'The Mexican', not for his country of birth (he was in fact born into a family of Colombian pig farmers) but because he held a love of all things Mexican, including the music, culture, horses – and the overland smuggling routes he has pioneered with the Mexican cartels. Gone are the days when Pablo and Gustavo would travel to Peru and Bolivia and bring back bags of coca paste stashed in hidden pockets sewn into their coats by his mum Doña Hermilda, or drive back in a car with local plates, the coca hidden in the wheel well, the spare tyre or false compartments. Now, with El Mexicano's coca being turned into paste and then cocaine in his growing network of factory-like kitchens in the Colombian jungles, Pablo's smuggling expertise and creativity are channelled into how to supply their product to the market with the greatest demand: *Los Estados Unidos*, the USA, where the appetite for cocaine as the 1980s burst onto the scene becomes insatiable.

Pablo invents a series of ingenious ways for his *mulas*, a near army of human drug mules, to smuggle his cocaine into the US. Some pose as blind, with cocaine secreted in their white canes. Others travel using wheelchairs or walking frames, the drugs stuffed inside their hollow metal. Many use his old trick, with packets of the drug stashed in hidden pockets sewn into their clothes or in their hollowed-out shoes. The riskiest method, at least for the mula, is to swallow condoms or balloons filled with the drug. When they burst, and burst they often do, it rarely ends well for the poor human courier. Then Pablo hits on his most streamlined delivery method yet. With a network of pilots and air stewards on the cartel payroll, Pablo increasingly sends unaccompanied luggage – suitcases filled with cocaine – on flights, to be collected and handed off on arrival at the destination airport in America.

Soon the volume of coke El Patrón and El Mexicano are producing requires a bigger, bolder plan. Before the 1980s arrive, they team up with a maverick Colombian-German pilot and smuggler, Carlos Lehder, who uses his planes and his private island in the Caribbean to fly their cocaine into the US. The triumvirate now has supply and distribution, but is yet to coalesce into the Medellín Cartel that will dominate Colombia and bring bloody war to its streets. That solidification comes in 1981.

In the 1970s, a rival guerrilla organization to the FARC, M-19, is gaining fame. In 1974 they steal a symbol of Colombian patriotism and one of the nation's most priceless relics: a sword belonging to Simón Bolívar, the man who liberated Colombia from the Spanish Empire. In 1976 M-19 kidnap and murder a high-profile trade union leader, and on New Year's Eve 1979 they tunnel into a Colombian Army depot and steal 5,000 weapons. Less than two months later they take 14 ambassadors hostage in a siege during a cocktail party at the embassy of the Dominican Republic. Then, in 1981, it is M-19 who unwittingly help to formalize the Medellín Cartel.

It is 13 March. M-19 guerrillas, including their leader Iván Torres, drive up to the university in Medellín just as a young woman, Martha Ochoa, is walking out with a friend. She is snatched off the street, bundled into a car and driven away. Martha is the sister of three of the richest men in Medellín – the Ochoa brothers: Jorge, Juan David and Fabio. M-19 demand a ransom for Martha's release. But they have miscalculated. Badly. The Ochoas are not only drug traffickers but are increasingly partnering with Pablo and his associates. Pablo rallies the Ochoas behind a new cause: *Muerte a Secuestradores* (MAS), 'Death to Kidnappers', and with money, men and guns from Pablo and his fellow narcos, an MAS army of some 2,000 men wage swift, bloody war on M-19. United against this common enemy, the Ochoas become the final piece in the jigsaw that is the Medellín Cartel. M-19 are forced to withdraw to lick their wounds, and Martha is soon returned.

With the Ochoas now joining Pablo and Gustavo (who has remained a vital partner to his cousin throughout) alongside El

Mexicano and Carlos Lehder, the nascent Medellín Cartel is primed and ready. The money rolls in, in ever-increasing quantities – and one of the biggest challenges for Pablo and 'The Accountant', his brother Roberto, is how to launder it all.

The decision to funnel funds through football, and specifically through Pablo's team – Atlético Nacional – is a masterstroke. The brothers take control of the club and stadium finances, and also take a stake in the rival Medellín side, run by fellow local gangsters Hector Mesa and Pablo Correa Ramos, who also share the ground, and for whom Roberto can often be found cheering at the Atanasio Girardot: Deportivo Independiente (DIM). It is a money-launderer's dream, the perfect machine for washing dirty cocaine cash. Tickets are sold for cash, and it doesn't take much for Roberto to ensure gate receipts are falsely inflated. With 40,000 fans a game, this alone helps the cartel wash millions of dollars. But football clubs are big, complicated businesses with an array of expenditures, all of which are ripe for the kind of creative accounting that facilitates the laundering of ill-gotten gains. Player transfer fees, player wages, staff salaries, construction costs – football is the gift that keeps on giving.

But football is more than just a mechanism for legitimizing the cartel's cash profits. For Pablo, football has always been much more. From playing on the dusty Medellín streets to championing the building of new pitches, and opening stadia – it is a game he loves, and a sport that he knows can sway the hearts and minds of the people. And so he doesn't just wash his money through Atlético Nacional, he invests in the club. This is his city, and his team. These are his people. Like a Roman Emperor, proclaiming bread and circuses, he will bring them glory, and they will love him for it.

In the same period, Santa Fe, one of Bogotá's big clubs, is also under the influence of drug money. Their debts have been paid off by their new chairman Fernando Carrillo. But in May 1981 he and his Inverca Group are charged over cocaine shipments to Florida. His removal does little to clean up the club's situation though – as it is taken over by two brothers Silvio and Phanor Arizabaleta-Arzayus, who are also drug traffickers.

However, in the first half of the 1980s, it is the América de Cali of the Rodríguez brothers who rise to dominate football in Colombia, while Pablo is busy with his number one priority: getting elected to Congress and earning immunity from extradition. For now, it will take a change in his fortunes for football to become his focus, and for Atlético Nacional to reap the generous but tainted rewards of his patronage.

*

In 1982, after two successive third place finishes in the domestic league, América de Cali embark on one of the greatest runs of footballing success in the modern era. Coach Ochoa is a former goalkeeper who had started his playing career with América before moving to Bogotá where he won four league titles playing in a Millonarios team that boasted none other than the great Alfredo di Stéfano. As a coach he has already won seven league championships with Millonarios and Santa Fe, his victory with América in 1979 making it eight. But, supercharged by the financial support of the Cali Cartel, he is about to make history.

He has built a side that is strong all over the park. Argentinian Julio César Falcioni is a dominant 6ft goalkeeper, signed in 1981 from Vélez Sársfield in Buenos Aires. Ahead of the 1982 season, he is joined by his fellow countryman Roque Alfaro, a striker who cut his teeth at

Newell's Old Boys before a stint in Europe at Panathinaikos. And also arriving on the scene in 1982 are two youngsters graduating to first team football for the first time: Humberto Sierra, and a new, young striker who stands at only 5ft 3in – Antony de Ávila.

The blend is intoxicating. In 1982 América pull off a rare feat – they sweep the board, winning the Apertura, topping their group in the Finalización and then winning the now eight-team octagonal season finale. It is only their second title, but it will not be their last. In fact they will go on to win the league championship in 1983, 1984, 1985 and 1986 – a record-breaking five times in a row. In Colombia, no one is their equal.

Each season Ochoa is able to strengthen and evolve his side, his coffers swollen by Cali's cocaine cash. In 1983 it is one of the stars of the league, the wily goalscoring midfielder Willington Ortez, who is prised away from local rivals Deportivo. Nicknamed *El Viejo Willy*, 'Old Willy' may be 30 years old but he helps turn América from a defensive side into a free-flowing attacking team, his 'unknown' transfer fee perhaps hinting at the Machiavellian forces that are bankrolling the side and their ulterior motive in funnelling money into the club. América march to the title once more. In 1984 Ochoa signs 'The Left-Footed Poet', Peruvian midfielder César Cueto. The end result is the same – as América claim their third successive championship.

By the start of the 1985 season América have added yet more firepower – in the form of the New York Cosmos prolific Paraguayan international forward Roberto Cabañas and Argentinian international striker Ricardo Gareca of River Plate. The season is to be hard-fought however, and will bring a bittersweet combination of joy and heartbreak, a recipe football fans across the globe will recognize. At every stage, Apertura, Finalización and the eight-way octagonal final, they are pushed all the way by neighbours Deportivo Cali. In the end, a late victory over Deportivo in the penultimate match proves decisive, as they pip their city rivals to the title by just half a point.

But the 1985 season is notable for one further aspect. While América will also win the 1986 league championship to set a record in Colombian top flight football, 1985 marks the beginning of a new obsession for the team, and one that will soon transfer to Pablo and Nacional – winning the Copa Libertadores. At this point no Colombian side has ever won the Copa, the biggest club tournament in South America, the continent's equivalent to the European Cup or Champions League as it is known today. The only side from Colombia ever to reach the competition's final is, of course, their city rivals Deportivo, who made it all the way to the showpiece in 1978 only to lose 4-0 to Boca Juniors. In 1985 América follow in their footsteps and reach their first ever Copa Libertadores final. Full of confidence from their incredible run in the domestic league, América fly to the final by way of an unbeaten group stage and then topping their semi-final mini-league. They too face Argentinian opposition in the guise of Argentinos Juniors, who are also contesting their first final. However, the cup has been won by an Argentinian side on 13 of the previous 25 occasions.

In the first leg, in Buenos Aires, América suffer a narrow 1-0 away defeat. But in the return fixture they triumph – by the same score. With the final tied, the two teams face off in a play-off final in Asunción, Paraguay. Argentinos take the lead on 37 minutes, but América strike back almost immediately, as *El Tigre*, their very own Argentinian Ricardo Gareca, pounces in the 42nd minute to make it 1-1. And so it stays, as the clock ticks down for the entire second half. Eventually Chilean referee Hernán Silva blows his whistle, and the teams prepare for penalties. Both sides trade goals, as Gareca, Soto, Herrera and Cabañas match the successful strikes of their Argentinian counterparts. When Mario Hernán Videla makes it a perfect five from five for the team from Buenos Aires, the burden of keeping his side in the tie, after three full matches have failed to separate the teams, falls on the diminutive shoulders of *El Pitufo*, 'The Smurf', Antony de Ávila.

By now an established member of the team and well on his way to becoming the club's all-time most prolific goalscorer, de Ávila places his shot to Argentinos goalkeeper Enrique Vidallé's right. But the keeper guesses correctly, and dives to palm away the Colombian's shot. América have fallen at the final of all final hurdles. The cup is once again on its way to Argentina.

Even winning the league again in 1986, at the expense of Deportivo Cali, cannot fully assuage the pain América once more endure – as they again lose in the final of the Copa. This time they even knocked out Deportivo on their run to the final. But once again they faced Argentinian opposition – and not the diminutive first-timers Argentinos but instead Latin American powerhouse River Plate. A 2-1 home defeat for the Cali side gave them too much to do, and they lost the away leg 1-0, and the tie 3-1. At least there were no penalties this time.

The Copa has become such an obsession that they allow Millonarios, now under the control of Pablo's Bogotá partner El Mexicano, to finally wrest the league title away from them in 1987 as they endeavour to break their Libertadores hoodoo. This time the omens look to be favouring them. First, they finish joint-top of their group with none other than Deportivo Cali – and with the sides locked on the same points, goal difference, goals scored and goals conceded, a one-off tie-breaker game is needed. A 0-0 draw is finally decided in América's favour by a 4-2 penalty shoot-out victory over their rivals. Then they qualify from their semi-final group by virtue of having scored a single goal more than Cobreloa of Chile. And then, in the final, they are for once not up against Argentinian opposition but instead must face Peñarol. However, the Uruguayans are four-times winners of the Copa. Can América, fresh from making domestic history with five league wins in a row, go one better and bring the Copa to Colombia for the first time?

The Estadio Pascual Guerrero is crammed with 65,000 spectators to see their team earn a healthy 2-0 home win, thanks to goals from Battaglia and Cabañas, to take to Montevideo. When Cabañas strikes again to give América a 1-0 lead after only 19 minutes in the Estadio Centenario it looks as if the team from Cali will succeed where none of their Colombian rivals have. But a goal from Diego Aguirre for Peñarol midway through the second half changes the complexion of the game. And then, with 87 minutes on the clock, the Uruguayans score a vital second to make it 2-1 on the night. There is no time for América to mount a comeback. The game ends 2-1, and with both teams on two points each awarded for their respective wins, and the aggregate score across the two ties not playing a part in the cup's equation, they are headed for yet another play-off final.

If Ochoa, América and their fans in Cali and across Colombia thought they had suffered heartbreak before, nothing could prepare them for what was about to unfold. At the Estadio Nacional in Santiago, Chile, the two sides battle to a 0-0 draw over the 90 minutes. Still, as extra time ticks away, neither team can find a winner. Another penalty shoot-out looks inevitable. And then, in the final seconds of extra time, Aguirre scores the most last-gasp of 120th-minute winners to seal the tie and yet again deny América the Copa. It will be nearly a decade before América reach another Libertadores final – which they again lose, in 1996, to River Plate.

But in the early 1980s, while América have been winning the league, and before he can bring glory to Atlético Nacional, Pablo has been preparing to launch his political career . . .

Chapter Five

El Patrón, El Politico (1982)

In 1979 Pablo had been elected to Envigado's town council. In 1981 he had seen Atlético Nacional win the league. Now, in February of 1982, he is back on the campaign trail, his sights set on election to Congress.

Congress is due to be replaced in March, with the new Presidential election to culminate in May. He is on the ticket for the Liberal Renewal Movement (MRL), who are allied with the New Liberalism party. New Liberalism are surging behind their presidential candidate and founder, Luis Carlos Galán.

Pablo's first rally is at the main park in La Paz. A crowd of 500 gather as he addresses them, standing on the bonnet of a Mercedes-Benz. He promises to work for a better future for the poor of Envigado and Antioquia. Standing in opposition to the old guard, the elite, the 'Men of Always', his slogan is 'Pablo Escobar: A Man of the People. A Man of Action! A Man of his Word!'

This is a man who has brought electricity to the poorest neighbourhoods of Medellín, for when Pablo says 'let there be light' there is indeed light. He has not just built football stadia and pitches, but planted trees, helped cure cleft palates, given support to job seekers. He has brought schools, hospitals, jobs, wealth. When he has promised it, the people have become used to it being delivered. He makes promises in his speeches, from floodlights for the football pitches to painting the church or providing new books for the schools, but, unlike normal politicians, within just a few days his men turn up and follow through on his campaign pledges. His admirers compare him to the charismatic former presidential candidate Jorge Eliécer Gaitán, the leader of the Liberal Party, whose assassination in 1948 led to La Violencia. Of course, it also doesn't hurt that, always dressed down like a true man of the people in jeans and trainers, Pablo hands cash out to the crowds, or that he rains down 'Vote for Pablo' campaign flyers and bank notes from planes overhead.

In particular, Pablo plays to the long-entrenched divisions inherent in Colombian society that are in such stark relief in Medellín. He stands on the side of the *pobresitos*, the poor, the marginalized, the working class. Although the cost of his charitable work, if it can be called such, is but a drop in the ocean that is the flood of money he is amassing from his criminal empire, the very fact that he spends any money, any time, any effort, courting this poor and working class vote does wonders for his campaign.

Pablo is at a local football match with his cousin Jaime. During the game he hears of a disaster unfolding in another part of Medellín. The Moravia dump, a landfill site where nearly a thousand families live in a makeshift shanty town and scavenge the enormous rubbish piles, is on fire. He leaves the game and rushes there. The site is one of the many forgotten dark corners of Medellín, ignored by anyone with the power to help. Finally, the inevitable has happened: toxic gases escaping from the rotting detritus piling up in the dump have been ignited by a spark, or an open flame. The slum is ablaze, the chaos total. Over 60 shanties are burning, their flimsy walls of scavenged wood and cardboard collapsing in flames. Families are walking the rubbish-strewn streets, barefooted, soot-stained, carrying their children and meagre possessions. Whether or not it reminds Pablo of his escape from La Violencia, he springs into action. He orders his men to bring blankets, mattresses, food, medicine. The destruction inspires him to create *Medellín sin Tugurios*, 'Medellín without Slums', a charitable organization to provide homes not just for all the residents of Moravia but for the poor of the whole city. He buys a huge plot of land in the Buenos Aires neighbourhood and plans an initial phase of 500 houses, with the ambition of creating 5,000 within just two years. This development will become the infamous Barrio Pablo Escobar.

But Pablo's criminality, overlooked by the poor to whom he was well on the way to becoming not just a 20th century Robin Hood but indeed sanctified as a modern-day saint, is something that is becoming increasingly hard to ignore for those higher up in the campaign. His life as a narco is just too toxic, no matter his votes.

Galán, the leader of New Liberalism, is giving a speech in downtown Medellín's Berrío Park. He begins to rail against the morality of his supposed ally, Pablo Escobar. His attack on Pablo is brutal, and extremely public. Galán disavows not only Pablo but the entire MRL, distancing himself and his party from them and openly rejecting their support for his campaign. It is a slap in the face for Pablo, in fact a potentially fatal punch to the gut of his political aspirations. But all is not lost. Pablo switches his allegiance to a rival party, Liberal Alternative, who welcome him into the fold. His cash, and his fervent supporters, make him an attractive proposition to anyone prepared to look the other way when it comes to the source of his wealth and power. Liberal Alternative even celebrate the defection of this valuable candidate with a full-page ad in the local press. It reads:

'We support Pablo Escobar's candidacy for the House because his youth, his intelligence, and his love for the most vulnerable make him deserving of the envy of cocktail-party politicians. He has the support of all the liberals and conservatives in the Magdalena Medio, as he has been the Saviour of this region.'

Pablo uses the attack from Galán to pivot, and go further on the offensive against all that New Liberalism represents. He attacks the aristocracy, calling out the hypocrisy of their fake morality, and branding them as mere political puppets manufactured by the Colombian oligarchy. As he begins to believe he may well succeed in his aim of getting elected to Congress, he devotes more and more time to his speeches; memorizing the texts, practising his arm movements and gestures, he becomes an increasingly powerful orator. His dream of a life in the Casa de Nariño, as President of Colombia, is still alive . . .

But the immediate necessity of winning a seat in Congress is the first key aim. With the US–Colombia extradition treaty originally signed in 1979 coming into effect on 4 March 1982, Pablo knows his time will soon be up if he cannot secure the diplomatic immunity that comes with political office. For him, extradition is a death sentence. He will win this election, or get the treaty repealed, or die trying.

Growing more confident in his support and in his oration, and ever more desperate with extradition on the cusp of being enshrined, his campaigning focus shifts. At a rally in Caldas he urges President Julio César Turbay to withdraw from the treaty with the US. As his entreaties fall on deaf ears in the corridors of power he seeds the idea of repealing the extradition treaty. His campaign team pays for full-page ads in local and national newspapers to promote his anti-extradition stance, and position it as a patriotic duty to stand against the over-reaching jurisdiction of the Americans. It is an issue of national pride.

It is 5 March 1982, the day after the extradition treaty has come into effect and the day of Pablo's final campaign rally. The party has chartered buses and shuttles in supporters and voters from all over the region. The crowds are massed in front of the Liberal Alternative HQ in Envigado, the Medellín suburb where Pablo grew up. Pablo, the local boy seemingly done good, urges his supporters to buy Colombian, to support domestic industry. He whips them up into a patriotic fervour. It is not hard to see why, in the Medellín of 1982, his message strikes a chord with his fanbase. But will his popularity be sufficient to sweep him to victory?

Pablo must wait for over a week, under the prospect of looming extradition, to find out if he has triumphed in this next, vital moment for his political aspirations. On 14 March Pablo heads to the offices of his party, the Liberal Renewal Movement, the MRL. Surrounded by his campaign colleagues he spends the afternoon there as the votes are counted. At 8pm the National Civil Registry is finally able to confirm the results. Pablo has won. The lower classes have turned out to vote and have helped their man to victory. He will be sworn in as a *suplente*, a stand-in or alternate, in Colombia's House of Representatives. He will be granted the full diplomatic immunity that comes with the office. He is safe from prosecution, and from extradition, for the full four years of his term. And he is one step closer to taking a run at the presidency. But first he must travel to Bogotá to be officially sworn in. And, Pablo being Pablo, even this becomes a moment of tension.

On Tuesday 20 July 1982, Pablo paces the bedroom in Bogotá where he is dressing for the swearing-in ceremony that day. He refuses to listen to Tata, he *will not* wear a tie. He is determined to follow his self-imposed dress code, to publicly portray himself as one of the people, in opposition to the Bogotano stuffed shirts. He is obsessed. Eventually Tata convinces him to forego his usual short-sleeve shirt. But the tie? That is a red line Pablo refuses to cross. Tata thinks to snatch one from the rack and stuff it in her bag but, distracted by Pablo's exhortations, forgets the thought just as swiftly. She's left to curse her oversight when Pablo arrives at the halls of Congress and is refused entry without the requisite neckwear. An irate Pablo fails to bluster and bully his way in, and with the clock ticking he is in danger of missing this vital ceremonial moment. Eventually a guard offers him his own tie and, with immunity at stake, Pablo takes him up on his offer. Finally granted entry, he walks in, tie clashing garishly with his suit, and takes his place among the great and the good, the rich and the powerful, a wolf among the sheep.

*

It seems Pablo is now safely ensconced in the political machinery of Colombia, safe from prosecution. But he is right to fear extradition to the US.

By 1981 the tide of Colombian cocaine pouring into Miami, and the money, crime and violence accompanying it, has made the formerly sleepy Florida town the world's deadliest city. In New York a special task force begins to join some of the dots, tracing the coke that has become endemic in the clubs of the city to communities like the predominantly Colombian Jackson Heights, and from there down to Florida, where the drug appears to be entering the country. The Drug Enforcement Agency, the DEA, which already has a Colombian headquarters in Bogotá, finally opens a Medellín office. The city is already a dangerous and deadly one. Pablo's ever-increasing expansion of his criminal empire is far from bloodless, and the bodies his sicarios are leaving on the streets are piling up so quickly the city morgues can't process them fast enough. But the DEA are determined to root out the source of the drug that is sweeping the United States.

In 1982 Pablo, long a fan of Miami and of the United States, at least as a holiday destination, buys a mansion in North Bay, Miami Beach. The huge ranch-style property boasts a pool and cabaña and sets him back a cool $700,000. His new neighbours in Miami? The Bee Gees. The same year, in fact on the same day that Pablo is giving his final campaign speech in Envigado, actor John Belushi dies in his bungalow at the Chateau Marmont in Los Angeles, after a 'speedball', a potent combination of heroin and cocaine, is administered by dealer Cathy Smith.

Just a few days later the DEA carries out its biggest ever bust, intercepting 3,750lb of cocaine arriving into Miami on a Tampa Colombia Airlines cargo plane from Medellín. Cocaine, Colombia and Medellín, and Pablo Escobar himself, are increasingly on the DEA's radar.

But on Pablo's home turf, the DEA struggle. Colombia's equivalent of the FBI, the Directorate for Administrative Security (DAS), hand over their file on Pablo to their US guests. But El Patrón's tentacles extend into every part of Colombia's state machinery – and one of his people inside DAS has already swapped his photo for one of a total stranger. They finally manage to get up to date images of him when they surveil and photograph him at a bullfight. Without legal jurisdiction, they are reduced to observing him from a distance. The DEA agents get the best chances to see Pablo in the flesh at the Atanasio Girardot, watching his beloved Atlético Nacional. Here they find him, blending into the crowd, dressed down as always, flanked by his sicarios. The only clue to his identity, the moments when the stadium announcers call him to a pitch-side or press-box interview via the stadium public address system. He strikes the interested American agents in the crowd as low-key, quiet, certainly not overly ostentatious. A man watching his team play football.

In 1982 it seems like every dream is still a possibility for Pablo. As yet not fully aware of the strength of the DEA's focus on him and his cartel, he is able to enjoy the fruits of his labours. To watch football matches. To buy mansions with the wealth his cocaine is providing. To bask in the protections afforded by his newly secured political status. He has even helped to influence the presidential election, using his money and power to support the two key rivals to his now sworn enemy, Luis Carlos Galán. While these candidates are rivals, on opposite ends of the political spectrum (Conservative and Liberal), both share one key policy that is dear to Pablo's heart – an opposition to extradition. His efforts in playing both sides ensure Galán is beaten into third place. For Pablo, the revenge is sweet.

And in October 1982, when a committee is sent by Colombia's Congress to observe the Spanish elections, a certain Pablo Emilio Escobar Gaviria is chosen as one of the travelling party. Pablo even has the opportunity to meet, greet and celebrate with the winner, Felipe González of the Spanish Socialist Workers' Party (PSOE).

For Pablo things appear rosy. But for Colombia the future seems less certain. 1982 may be the year that the country's most famous novelist, Gabriel García Márquez, is awarded the Nobel Prize for Literature – but it is perhaps telling that he has long since moved to live in Mexico. And the Colombia of 1982, with coca and cocaine replacing coffee, and narcos like Escobar and the Rodríguez brothers on the rise, is very different from that of 1974, when the country was awarded hosting rights for the 1986 World Cup. Successive governments have failed to make good on their promised plans for the stadia and infrastructure required for football's showpiece tournament. And, as the 1982 World Cup ends in Spain, a tournament won by an Italy side led by the deadly, golden boot of Paolo Rossi and dominated by teams from the home continent (West Germany, Poland and France are the other three semi-finalists), FIFA are preparing a new special investigative delegation. The purpose of this hand-picked group is to confirm their fears – that Colombia is in no position to make good on their promises and host the next tournament. In Bogotá the Colombian FA get wind of this. With the writing on the wall, they decide to act pre-emptively in a desperate bid to save face.

And so 1982 is also the year when, after nearly a decade of political uncertainty and financial constraints, Colombia is forced to begrudgingly concede defeat – and hand back to FIFA the hosting rights for the 1986 World Cup. Pablo's Estadio Atanasio Girardot will not be hosting a World Cup match any time soon . . .

In the end it is Mexico which controversially wins out over an impressive US pitch in the new bid process. Even the tragic Mexico City earthquake of 1985 that claims 12,000 lives and destroys large swathes of the city's infrastructure fails to derail plans and they successfully host their second tournament in fewer than 20 years. That tournament will be won by an Argentina side inspired by a certain Diego Maradona, and despite the best efforts of Gary Lineker and England. Colombia, meanwhile, will fail to qualify.

Chapter Six

A Very Political Assassination (1983-1984)

With the DEA yet to properly fix their crosshairs on him and uncover the extent of his Medellín Cartel, and protected by his immunity, Pablo seems as secure as he has ever been. But appearances can be deceptive. And the risk he has taken in making himself a public figure, in entering the lion's den of national politics in Bogotá, is about to spectacularly blow up in his face. The consequences will be brutal and deadly, and will shake Colombia to its very foundations. Nothing will be the same again . . .

But during the first half of 1983 Pablo seems both relaxed and proactive. He promotes his charity 'Medellín without Slums' in television appearances, and Tata arranges an exclusive and upmarket art auction that raises half a million dollars for the cause and seems to mark the family's entry into polite society.

In April of 1983 Pablo is holding court in his favourite Medellín nightclub, 'Kevins'. But it is no ordinary night on the town. This is the first gathering of the 'National Forum of Extraditables'. And while the crowd does contain some of Pablo's most high-profile fellow 'businessmen', it is also packed with priests, former magistrates and a plethora of interested parties with vested interests. Pablo has gathered them all to join him in his crusade against extradition. It is a big enough occasion to bring Pablo to the attention of the national press, and the movers and shakers in Bogotá. The leading Colombian magazine *Semana*, for its 50th anniversary edition, runs a story on the event, and a profile on Pablo himself which is entitled 'An Antioquenian Robin Hood'. It seems Pablo has now managed to co-opt even the national and mainstream media into disseminating his myth. Pablo believes ever more fervently that he is indeed on the path to becoming El Patrón of the whole country, El Presidente. When his fall comes, it will hit him all the harder for it . . .

The following month Pablo is in the Tejelo neighbourhood in Medellín, where a crowd of 12,000 watch him take the ceremonial kick-off to open the new football stadium he has funded. Three weeks later he is doing the same – this time back in Moravia. Here he has not only built the stadium but provided it with floodlights, and the match is a night game between reserve team players from his own Atlético Nacional and local Moravia boys.

Pablo is living the life of Riley, as the narco king of Medellín. As well as investing in football, he uses his money to buy up swathes of land and property. He has already snapped up the land in the Magdalena Medio, in rural Antioquia, that will eventually become his famous Hacienda Nápoles. He has farms in the countryside, and penthouses in the city. He brings women back from Medellín's newest, trendiest nightclubs to party with him, cranking up his favourite song 'Eye of the Tiger', from the big Hollywood blockbuster *Rocky III*, on his bachelor pad stereo.

In a contrast that speaks once more to the strange contradictions of this singular man, he also likes to travel in disguise, not unlike the Robin Hood of English legend, to be among the 'common folk', the regular people of his city. He frequently heads out to Guayaquil, a dangerous and impoverished area of downtown Medellín, to trawl the streets; visit the low, dim local bars; drink cervezas and listen to tango. These mournful songs remind Pablo, despite his new fortune and city life, of his paisa upbringing, of the hardship and poverty he had faced growing up.

But that existence is long gone. And, in August of 1983, his new life comes under threat. President Belisario Betancur, the Conservative candidate who won out over his liberal rivals, including Galán, begins a cabinet re-shuffle. On 8 August, in a bid to appease the opposition, Betancur appoints Rodrigo Lara Bonilla to the post of Minister of Justice. Lara is not only the first member of New Liberalism, the party that so publicly shunned Pablo, to enter the Colombian administration, but he is also the closest ally of the party's leader, Galán. If a furious Pablo has any doubts as to the new minister's intentions towards him it does not take long for them to be dispelled, in no uncertain terms. Barely a week after Lara's appointment, and in Pablo's first open congressional session, the new Justice Minister calls Pablo out as a criminal.

In the House's debate over what is termed 'hot money', the dirty money infiltrating Colombian society thanks to traffickers like Escobar, Pablo strikes a blow – presenting to the House a copy of a cheque for one million pesos, donated to Lara's campaign, and signed by one of the country's most notorious drug lords. This acutely damaging accusation stings Lara into a swift and brutal response. He brands Pablo Escobar a drug trafficker, a backer of paramilitary groups, a member of the Colombian 'mafia' and a wanted man in the USA. All of these things may be true, but Pablo's position in government has up until now depended on the powers that be conveniently ignoring these facts. Lara attacks Pablo openly, and without mercy. He proclaims: 'the mafia has taken over Colombian football', claiming drug money is now supporting the majority of Colombia's professional league teams. In a prepared speech, and sporting a smart, business-like dark suit and with impeccably combed hair, the young firebrand states: 'this drug lord aims to debase our nation's morals'.

Soon the story is front page news. Lara's friends at *El Espectador* newspaper join the attack. Articles appear revealing the dirty money in both politics and football, and referring to shady and morally dubious characters in Colombian politics and 'business', especially in Antioquia. Pablo isn't yet directly named but it is clear who they mean. Then they dig up his 1976 arrest, and publish the story. In calling Pablo out, Lara has threatened El Patrón's position and the immunity it affords, and thus by extension his freedom, his very life.

It is open war between the pair, as Pablo attacks Lara in Congress and on the pages of his own paper *Antioquia al Día*. He gives press conferences and speeches in which he attacks Lara directly. In one of the first, sitting at a low table in his typically relaxed garb and surrounded by his team of minders, he gives a statement in which he insists that 'the Minister of Justice has 24 hours to produce evidence that supports his accusations made in the House of Representatives'. But Pablo's bluffs, threats and bluster won't work this time. The cat is out of the bag, the genie has fled the bottle. In the world of Bogotá politics, mud sticks – and he is tainted. Doubly so as everything Lara is claiming is true, and Colombia knows it.

Then Lara, setting his stall out as the administration's new crusader, begins to use all the power afforded him as Minister of Justice to take Pablo and his fellow narcos down. He grounds numerous aircraft, including Pablo's, under suspicion of their use for drug trafficking. Then a senior judge reopens an old case involving the deaths of two DAS detectives – in which Pablo is implicated. Soon afterwards his US visa is revoked. For Pablo, his political aspirations, his dreams of the Casa de Nariño, are collapsing around his ears. And fast. In the middle of the chaos, Pablo learns that, after years of miscarriages, Tata is pregnant again.

Then, the dagger blow. Lara convinces his colleagues to revoke Pablo's immunity from prosecution. On Wednesday 26 October 1983, the plenary session of the House of Representatives votes to revoke Pablo's parliamentary immunity, effectively ending his political career after just fifteen months and six days. Pablo's underbelly is exposed. He can be arrested, can be extradited, if Lara can bring sufficient charges. For Pablo, this is the end of his life in politics. Forced to give up his seat, he quits Liberal Alternative and leaves Congress, never to return.

Pablo has learned his lesson the hard way. In a line that could be plucked from the movie *Scarface*, the film released in the US on 1 December 1983 (the day of Pablo's 34th birthday), a chilling blend of drugs, crime and paranoia that perfectly encapsulates the modern Miami Pablo has helped create, he states: 'I know they're coming for me. For trying to put them in their rightful place.'

On 20 January 1984 Pablo releases a public letter in which he resigns from politics, and from public life. He once more seeks to position himself on the side of the poor and of justice, the billionaire drug baron seemingly oblivious to, or uncaring of, the hypocrisy inherent in his statement, which reads:

'I will continue to battle against oligarchies and injustices, and against partisan backroom deals, which continually work to undermine the people, and especially against political intriguers, who are fundamentally indifferent to the people's suffering and opportunists when it comes to bureaucratic wrangling.'

With this parting shot, and with his dream of political power removed, Pablo instead prepares to devote all his energies to his other two priorities: money and the love of his people. He still believes that if he can amass sufficient wealth, and court enough popular support (especially through the sport that the people of Colombia love above all else, el fútbol), he will essentially make himself untouchable. But first he needs to take care of Lara . . .

*

But before Pablo can strike, Lara lands one more painful blow. He has been working closely with America's DEA since becoming Minister of Justice. By 1983 the US authorities have cottoned on to a vital, trackable component of the cartel's supply chain: the drums of industrial ether needed to cut the coca and make cocaine. They are able to set up a complex, slow-burn sting operation – arranging the sale of a cache of ether in the US, and secretly attaching miniature satellite tracking transponders to the drums. For months, they are able to track the drums as they make their way from the US to Colombia and out into the deepest jungle.

In March 1984 the DEA and the Colombian National Police launch a raid on the final destination of the ether shipment. In the jungles of Caquetá their combined forces uncover the Medellín Cartel's *Tranquilandia* operation: a giant network of nineteen cocaine labs and eight runways hidden in the dense rainforest, created by the cartel's processing mastermind El Mexicano. The Colombian troops round up and arrest the workers and proceed to destroy the entire facility – and its stash of nearly 14 tons of cocaine, valued at over a billion US dollars. It's like something out of the hottest new television drama series to premier that year in the USA: *Miami Vice.*

An apoplectic Pablo declares war. He puts a bounty of $700, a fortune for the poor teenage sicarios of Medellín but not even walking around money for El Patrón, on the head of each and every Colombian police officer. It's open season. Kill a cop, and prove it to Pablo, and you get paid.

But beyond the regular cops, Pablo has one target above all others: the Minister of Justice, Rodrigo Lara Bonilla. Ever since he called out Pablo, and especially once he started meddling with Pablo's involvement in football, and Atlético Nacional, his card has been marked.

On 30 April 1984 the 37-year-old Lara is told he will move from his post as Minister of Justice to take up the role of Colombia's ambassador to Czechoslovakia, to get him away from Pablo's mounting threats against his life. That evening he is driven back home as usual, a passenger in a white Mercedes, the middle vehicle of a three-car convoy. It is 7:30pm. The sun has long since set over Bogotá. A motorcycle buzzes up behind the follow car. Lara glances at the bulletproof vest that sits on the seat beside him. Despite the repeated protestations of the men charged with protecting him, he has refused to put it on for the drive home.

But before he can don the flak jacket, and before the minister's security detail can do anything to stop it, the bike races up alongside the right flank of the middle vehicle. Through his window Lara can see a hunched driver, clinging on behind him a pillion passenger, something cradled in his arms. The passenger turns to the car, and opens up with a 0.45 calibre Ingram MAC-10 machine pistol. The rear windshield of Lara's car explodes in a shower of glass. Bullets shred the side of the vehicle. A second later, the bike is gone. Lara's men pursue, and as they chase down the bike it skids, and flips. The *parrillero*, as Escobar's pillion riding sicarios have become known – they are so ubiquitous they not only have their own name but their increasing frequency leads to the seeming madness of a ban on motorcycle helmets in Medellín – is thrown off. He somehow manages to stand, and raise his gun. Lara's men don't hesitate. The man, the assassin, they gun down is in fact a boy of just 16. The driver of the bike, whom the bodyguards overpower and subdue, is 19. They are just two more of the desperate, grasping kids of the Medellín barrios of whom Pablo has, for years now, made killers.

Meanwhile Lara's driver steers the car the last few yards back to the minister's house. Jorge Lara, Rodrigo's six-year-old son, is at home and, hearing the noise of an approaching engine, runs to the front door. When he opens it and steps out he is greeted not by a big hug from his father but instead a scene he will never be able to wipe from his memory. The white Merc is pulled in at an angle, and riddled with bullet holes. He sees the bodyguards dragging his father from the car. Jorge doesn't know it yet, but his dad is already dead. Pablo has his revenge. And all it cost him was two million pesos – less than 2 million pesos – a pittance to Don Pablo. He is never charged with the crime.

In fact, Pablo is at the Hacienda Nápoles as the bullets tear through Lara, the one man who dared to call him a gangster to his face, and in public. He is accompanied not by his pregnant wife Victoria (Tata) and their son Juan Pablo, who are instead at her mother's apartment in Medellín, but by a young pageant queen he is attempting to woo despite the chaperoning of her mother.

When, at 9:30 that night, the TV show *Hoy* reports that Lara has been assassinated, their footage showing a dead gunman on the ground, another in handcuffs, and a car, a white Merc, with its rear windshield shattered, no one is in any doubt who gave the order. Pablo has executed a Colombian government minister. The Rubicon has been crossed.

The next day Colombian forces raid the Hacienda Nápoles, but Pablo has fled. This is war, and it will not truly end until Pablo is dead or behind bars.

Rodrigo Lara Bonilla, the man who lasted barely eight months as Colombia's Minister of Justice before he was killed by the country's criminal kingpin, is given a hero's funeral. His coffin, draped in the Colombian flag and bedecked with garlands of bright red flowers, is carried through the streets crowded with throngs of people.

Chapter Seven

The Power of Narcoball
(1984–1985)

The brutal slaying of Lara has shocked the nation. President Betancur responds immediately, signing the official extradition papers for all of Colombia's most wanted criminals. This includes many of the top dogs from Pablo's Medellín Cartel, but not El Patrón himself. Thus far, the combined might and intelligence gathering of Colombia's DAS and the DEA have failed to make a case against their number one target.

However, the raid on Nápoles has left Pablo in no doubt. He is Colombia's most wanted man, and the government is hot on his heels. He is forced to go into hiding, and eventually on the run.

Growing ever more fearful of the US, and of the DEA presence in Colombia, Pablo had begun to put in place plans to intimidate the gringo interlopers. When the DEA had got wind of a plot to kidnap the children of US Embassy staff, to snatch them from their schools in Bogotá, the Embassy had flown all non-essential family members of their staff out of the country on an Avianca jet. But now the boot is on the other foot. Pablo knows his family is at risk, and is also his biggest weakness. Twenty-three-year-old Tata is heavily pregnant, and Juan Pablo is still just seven.

Pablo stashes them somewhere safe, then sends a helicopter to get them out of the country. His pregnant wife and young son are flown low over the jungle canopy of the lawless Darién Gap, invisible to radar, on an illegal, unscheduled flight across the border with Panama. The chopper is eventually forced to land at a remote airstrip in the middle of the Panamanian jungle. Tata and Juan Pablo have no idea where they are. Eventually a car arrives and drives them to a safe house in Panama City, where Pablo joins them. He claims he stayed behind in Colombia in order to arrange for keys to be delivered to 300 families from the Moravia landfill: the first wave of houses built by Medellín without Slums had been completed and were ready for them to move into.

Whatever the truth, he does soon succeed in moving his own band of exiles to more salubrious surroundings. As honoured guests of the regime, the Escobars take up residence in a house owned by the country's leader, General Noriega. Their escape to Panama buys Pablo some breathing room. Safe from both the Colombian state and the US security forces, he is able to relax. He has managed to get his brother Roberto out of Colombia too, and the siblings spend the hot days lounging by the pool, working out in the gym and even sneaking into the neighbouring golf course – not for a quick round but instead to play football on the perfectly manicured greens and fairways.

In fact, Pablo has a plan. Panama is about to have national elections. A delegation of senior Colombian officials arrives to observe the process – and Pablo gets word to them. When they meet, he is able to open a channel of communication with the Betancur administration back in Bogotá. Pablo's offer? The cartels, not just Medellín – for he boldly claims to speak for all of them – will dismantle their illegal operations, pay off Colombia's entire national debt and invest in programmes to replace the coca and marijuana trade with other crops in return for the abolition of extradition. But whether or not the Conservatives would have considered such an offer, the proposed deal withers on the vine – there's just no way the Liberals, the supporters of Lara, or the country as a whole, will accept a backroom deal that gets Pablo off the hook that easily.

The deal is dead in the water. Then Pablo gets wind of rumours that General Noriega might be finding sheltering him to be bringing too much heat, and may even be negotiating with the DEA to hand him over in return for wiping his own slate clean. A hasty exit is required. But on Friday 25 May 1984, in Panama City, Tata gives birth to her second child, Manuela. Pablo arranges for his new-born baby daughter to be taken back to Colombia, but then sends Tata and Juan Pablo not back home but instead on to Managua, Nicaragua. The family have merely jumped from the frying pan into the fire, however. Pablo may be on good terms with the anti-American Sandinista regime, but the city is under siege by Contra rebels funded, with money from secret arms sales to Iran, by the US regime.

Eventually Pablo allows Juan Pablo, for whom the only moments of happiness in these weeks on the run have been the occasional chances to listen to football matches taking place back in Colombia, to return home. Tata he tries to keep close, but she refuses to be kept from her children and escapes, flying back to Medellín via Panama City. She is reunited with the children and takes refuge in the Altos del Campestre building, a private block of apartments.

Pablo's self-imposed exile is about to be cut short too . . .

It is Tuesday 17 July when television news breaks the story that the *Washington Times* has just published photos of Pablo Escobar that finally prove he is indeed a drug trafficker.

On 24 June, before Tata had fled Nicaragua, Pablo had been nowhere to be found. He had in fact been at an airstrip, loading cocaine onto a plane with his partner El Mexicano, and the help of several Nicaraguan soldiers. The pilot of the plane was an American, Barry Seal. Seal was a former TWA captain turned drug smuggler, who had been a key component in the Medellín Cartel's operation for several years, flying their cocaine into the US. However, unbeknown to Pablo, he had been caught in a DEA sting operation and turned into an informant and undercover operative. The DEA had fitted his plane with remote cameras, and now they had their proof – Pablo Escobar himself, loading coke onto a plane – in irrefutable black and white.

Two days after the photos hit the news, Herbert Shapiro, a judge in the Florida Southern District Court, issues an arrest warrant for Pablo for conspiracy to import cocaine into the USA. The threat of extradition has now become a very real probability. It's a potentially deadly blow against Pablo, and a betrayal he will not forget – eighteen months later two of his men will track down Seal and kill him in a Salvation Army car park in his home town of Baton Rouge, Louisiana.

No longer safe in Nicaragua or Panama, at the end of July 1984 Pablo secretly returns to Colombia. Once more in hiding, he is only able to visit his family fleetingly. Then he hears that his father, Don Abel, has been taken hostage. It takes more than two weeks of negotiating but, realizing it is a gang of common criminals who have snatched his dad, Pablo is eventually able to secure his release from captivity in a remote mountain farm for $300,000 – far less than the original demand of $10 million.

As 1984 draws to a close, Pablo is hiding out in a country estate in Guarne. With New Year's Eve on the horizon, he brings his family to him to celebrate. But before they can start the festivities, a dawn raid from the police sends Pablo running for the hills – he escapes the noose by the skin of his teeth, losing his beloved white ruana as he flees. Pablo seems to be lurching from one disastrous near-miss to another. But beware the wounded lion.

*

1985 is a year of turmoil. And it is only five days old when the Colombian authorities strike their next big blow. On 5 January, Hernán Botero Moreno, a leading member of Pablo's cartel and the president of Atlético Nacional, is extradited to the US on charges of drug trafficking and money laundering. The claim is that he has laundered $57 million of Pablo's drug money. It's unclear if this is even a crime in Colombia at all, let alone an extraditable one – but Botero is on a plane and in the USA before anyone can stop it. Pablo is fearful, and furious. And he's not the only one. The Cali Cartel, too, now perceive the threat posed by the DEA, extradition and the attentions of the authorities on their involvement in Colombian football.

El Patrón calls an emergency summit. He summons all the Colombian cartels and the bosses of their football teams to a meeting at one of his properties – a farm known as 'The Circle'. As is his wont, Pablo holds court. And, in his impassioned oration one sentence in particular strikes home, and will become the slogan for this common cause that binds the assembled narcos: 'I would rather have a grave in Colombia than a jail cell in the United States.' Spurred on by their mutual fear of extradition to Los Estados Unidos, the assembled group listen carefully to the plan Pablo lays out for them.

They will go on strike. Refusing to allow their teams to play, they will force the suspension of the league. They will use football to force the issue, and to pursue their political agenda. Once more Pablo is banking on the support of the people, of the masses, of the fans. He believes if the supporters of Nacional, of DIM, of América de Cali, know that their beloved teams are refusing to play in protest against the extradition of Botero – that the clubs are united in their patriotic stance against the threat of extradition that hangs over the heads of the men who are pouring cash into their sides – then they too will join the cause. And he is hoping that by holding football to ransom, he can force the Colombian government to rescind extradition. The cartels agree, their clubs will join Pablo and Atlético Nacional in their strike.

But, later that night, Colombian forces raid The Circle. Pablo's guests have left, but he and the key members of the Medellín Cartel are still there. Pablo's men defend the property, and a shoot-out ensues. Pablo, his brother Roberto and his cartel partner Gustavo are forced to flee into the dark. It's another narrow escape, and raises some suspicions. Are the Cali Cartel trying to do a deal behind Pablo's back? Have they offered up El Patrón to save themselves from extradition?

Whatever the truth of it, América de Cali does join all the other teams in the Colombian top flight on strike, and the league is suspended for a week. And, just like that, the power of 'narcoball' is revealed. With so many of the top clubs in the Colombian league now inextricably entwined with cartel money, Pablo has succeeded in pulling off an extraordinary feat. He brings football in Colombia to a grinding and total halt. It will not be the last time that his actions will have the same effect.

*

At the same time, Pablo and *Los Extraditables* go on the offensive. The group he created with the sole purpose of fighting his war against extradition have adopted Pablo's mantra as their slogan: 'better a grave in Colombia than a jail cell in the United States', but Pablo, as ever, remains the power in the shadows – the unnamed leader of this violent organization. And he and The Extraditables are about to strike at the very heart of the government, and the issue.

During 1985, the Colombian government continues to extradite Colombian citizens to face justice in the US. League football has long since resumed, with América de Cali in the middle of their extraordinary run of domestic success and the strike having failed to force the political agenda. Pablo is angry and scared. The Extraditables and the Medellín Cartel are combining to push the murder rate in Medellín through the roof, as the standard targets of judges and policemen are joined by journalists and sports reporters who dig too far into the links between the narcos and their football teams. No one is safe.

It is 6 November. In Bogotá the Supreme Court is about to begin deliberations on the constitutionality of the Colombia–United States extradition treaty. Meanwhile, Pablo is hiding out at La Pesebrera farm in Loma El Chocho, Envigado. He brings his family out to join him, but although he has hardly seen them all year, he sends them almost immediately back to Medellín. Then the news breaks. A gun battle is raging in downtown Bogotá. M-19 guerrillas have occupied the Palace of Justice, the building housing the Supreme Court.

The guerrillas had driven into the basement just before midday and opened fire, shooting their way inside to join up with colleagues who had taken the ground and first floors. The building shakes from a series of explosions that mark their progress as they work their way up from floor to floor, leaving armed guards to control the access points.

Soon they are able to reach the fourth floor and locate and capture the President of the Supreme Court, the Chief Justice. They demand those hiding hand themselves over – and the first hostage they call for is the Supreme Court Justice and President of the Constitutional Court, Manuel Gaona Cruz. Interestingly, he is the justice in charge of delivering the opinion of the court on the constitutionality of the extradition treaty between Colombia and the United States. Soon M-19 have taken 300 people hostage – including all 24 judges.

After a few hours the combined might of the Colombian police and army forces are able to free around 200 of the hostages and take control of the lower floors. Trapped above, but with a hundred hostages as collateral, the guerrillas use a telephone to call and demand President Betancur arrive and stand trial for the death of one of their commanders. He refuses, and a stand-off ensues.

The conflict drags on into a second day. M-19 release a hostage and ask for Red Cross aid and the chance to establish a dialogue with the authorities. They are refused, and the army prepares for a siege.

As rockets are launched at the building, a fire breaks out. The wood-lined walls of the library that houses Colombia's legal archives catch alight. Finally, after some 27 hours, the army wrests control of the building from the guerrillas and brings the siege to a bloody end. Around a hundred lives have been lost, including a dozen magistrates, hostages (including Gaona Cruz), soldiers and much of the M-19 senior command.

But the fire crews struggle to put out the blaze that is still raging. Over 6,000 documents, the criminal records, proof and warrants against many of the country's most wanted criminals, Pablo Escobar included, all of the Supreme Court's extradition requests, burn to ash. Years later, claims and counterclaims will continue to swirl as the true motive for the attack, and the source of the money, weapons and vehicles that facilitated it, are debated. Did Pablo give M-19 a million dollars? Did he provide the supplies they needed to carry out the raid? Was the destruction of his criminal records and extradition papers the true aim? Was the timing of the attack deliberate?

In the 1970s Pablo had admired M-19 and their hijacking of milk delivery trucks and their handing out of the bottles to the poor of Bogotá. When they had put him on their kidnap list in a bid to raise funds however, he had been less sympathetic, and their snatching of Martha Ochoa in 1981 had inspired him to create his 'Death to Kidnappers' group. But had he found a way to use them to wage his anti-extradition war, and carry the fight right into the heart of Bogotá, into the Palace of Justice?

President Betancur is chastened, and is forced into a very public apology for the deadly debacle. Only a week later he is once again seeking to reassure the public after the Nevado del Ruiz volcano erupts and wipes out the town of Armero in Tolima. More than twenty thousand Colombians lose their lives. Pablo sends one of his own helicopters to deliver drinking water, and enlists his men to take supplies to the survivors.

But 1985 has ended as it began, with a bold move to force the end of extradition coming to nothing.

Chapter Eight

The Rise of Narcoball
(1986–1987)

In the mid-1980s Pablo is at the height of his fame and wealth. Despite being on the run for much of the decade, he is still able to enjoy the numerous fruits of his ill-gotten gains. And his biggest joy remains the beautiful game. In 1986, with América de Cali sweeping all before them for season after season, and with Los Cafeteros absent from the World Cup in Mexico which had once been earmarked for Colombia, he adopts his own uniquely narcoball version of Fantasy Football.

Pablo had always taken pleasure in combining his money with football. At his infamous ranch, the Hacienda Nápoles, he had regularly made outrageous spot bets with Gustavo. One of them challenging the other with offers like '$100,000 says Nacional will have the ball when there's 1 minute and 27 seconds on the clock in the first half'.

Nápoles was his pride and joy. He had bought the initial 2,000-acre plot of land, the Valledupar estate, for 35 million pesos. In 1979 that was a small fortune, nearly $1 million – and it was just a rustic house in the forest, surrounded by jungle and with no electricity. But Pablo knew that the worn-out old road that cut through the region was about to be upgraded to an *autopista*, creating a major new national highway to connect Bogotá to Medellín. Property and land values in the area would skyrocket. Soon he spent over $2 million buying up nine more surrounding properties – another 4,700 acres. He merged them all into Nápoles – named after the Italian city that was home to the parents of his favourite gangster, Al Capone. In bringing his dream property to life he spared no expense. Hacienda Nápoles had walk-in fridges; a gas station, helipad and runway; a games room filled with arcade game cabinets; a bull ring; a water park – even Latin America's largest motocross track. He created his own version of Jurassic Park: 'Aventura Jurasica' – a dinosaur theme park boasting life-size steel and concrete models designed by top artists. Then he got obsessed with creating a zoo. He read *National Geographic* to research the animals best suited to the Nápoles habitat, ruled out lions and tigers as too dangerous, then travelled to Dallas to buy his first consignment. The operation to bring the various beasts back to Colombia was like something out of *Fitzcarraldo* – the Werner Herzog film in which a mad opera lover attempts to haul a riverboat over a mountain in order to build an opera house in the jungle.

In the end his menagerie boasted the biggest herd of hippos found outside Africa, along with rhinos, elephants, ostriches, emus, monkeys and even Amazonian pink dolphins swimming in a man-made lake. Two of his favourites were a kangaroo that liked to kick footballs, and a parrot named Chinchón that could recite the names of Colombia's most famous football players. And, in another grand gesture, the brutal narcotrafficker and self-styled Robin Hood offered up the whole thing to local families – his zoo was open to the public, and completely free. The only casualties were the six giraffes, who quickly got sick and died.

But as Pablo had become Colombia's public enemy number one, his ability to enjoy Nápoles had been drastically reduced by raids and seizures and the ongoing battle over ownership with the government. However, this did nothing to stop El Patrón from entertaining at his other ranches and properties.

Since the early 1980s José Gonzalo Rodríguez Gacha had been the not-so-secret owner of Millonarios, and over the years Pablo challenges his friend, rival and Medellín Cartel associate El Mexicano to put up sides to beat one of his. They wager one or even two million dollars, and recruit their dream teams from their club sides – El Mexicano from Millonarios and El Patrón principally from the Atlético Nacional squad. They hand-pick their sides, supplement them with the occasional overseas all-star, and fly them out to one of Pablo's ranches, almost all of which have their own high-spec football pitches and facilities. The players are handsomely rewarded. And many of them know Pablo of old, having grown up playing on the Medellín pitches he built, long before they became the star players at Nacional and beyond. They are his employees, some are even his friends.

Such is the power of this new era of narcoball in 1980s Colombia that El Patrón and El Mexicano are able to put on some of the most elaborate private exhibition matches in history.

But there is trouble on the horizon, and its source is another sport, in another country . . .

*

In the summer of 1986 a 22-year-old, 6ft 7in, 221½lb black American has the world at his feet. Len Bias is widely regarded as the best college basketball player in the US. On 17 June 1986 he is picked second in the NBA draft by the defending champions Boston Celtics, led by Larry Bird. Two days later he is dead – from a cocaine overdose seemingly taken while celebrating. The death of this bright young sporting talent shakes America to its core, and presses President Reagan and the nation's policy makers into action. Soon cocaine is the hot button topic, and the War on Drugs becomes an issue that will turn the focus of the US and the world on Colombia, on Medellín and on Pablo.

Before the year is out the war Pablo is waging on a rejuvenated DEA presence in Colombia is under threat from a new enemy. The *Bloque de Búsqueda*, or Search Bloc, has been created by Colombia's President Virgilio Barco with the prime directive of tracking down and ending Pablo Escobar. The new unit staffs up with only the very best of the best of Colombia's elite police and military forces. It contains not a single member from Medellín – insulating its ranks from infiltration and corruption and with the added benefit that the families of its recruits live hundreds of miles away from Pablo's stronghold, even if not quite out of reach of his influence.

As the year draws to a close, Pablo feels the heat increasing. On the run and forced into hiding, he is unable to attend his son Juan Pablo's first communion. But he uses The Extraditables as a mouthpiece to increase the pressure on the government and this, combined no doubt with a healthy dose of his *plata o plomo*, 'money or bullets', approach, seems to work – as on 12 December 1986 the Supreme Court, barely a year after the M-19 siege, rules against the extradition treaty. But within 48 hours his dreams are thwarted once again as the government rejects their ruling and issues its own, new decree, reinstating the policy.

Not content with waging war on the police and the government, Pablo carries out his most overt action yet against the nation's media. At 7pm on 17 December 1986 Don Guillermo Cano, the editor-in-chief of *El Espectador* ('The Spectator'), the national paper founded almost a hundred years earlier, leaves the newspaper's offices in Bogotá. The 61-year-old is driving his family's Subaru Leone away from the building when a man approaches his car as he makes a U-turn on the busy street. It is one of Pablo's sicarios. Cano is shot four times in the chest with an Uzi submachine gun. The gunman jumps on a motorbike and disappears into the night.

Cano, who fewer than two weeks earlier published an editorial entitled 'Raining on the Mafiosos' Parade', was the seventh journalist killed for his stance against the cartels in 1986. His murder sparked a 24-hour news blackout as his colleagues across the entire country, in print, on radio and on television, refused to report the news in protest, in mourning, in defiance.

As the year ends, Pablo has become more nervous than ever. The government is refusing to bow to his pressure, extradition is still on the table, and his increasingly overt war is bringing more and more attention on him. He is now not just top of the hit list in Colombia but is a focus of the US 'War on Drugs'. He begins a new security measure – from now on even his own family are blindfolded when they are brought to visit him.

*

However, one of the hallmarks of Pablo's career as a billionaire drug lord is that, even while on the run and in hiding, he is able to continue to oversee his illegal empire, to bring in millions of dollars and to live at least some of the life of a man of wealth and privilege.

But even the high life can turn sour. In early 1987 Pablo is hosting a massive party. Just one of many, it is however notable for the attendance of a certain Carlos Lehder – Pablo's number one drug running pilot and partner in the cartel. Lehder is back in Colombia on the run after the US authorities got a bit too close to his base in the Bahamas, and is seemingly even more erratic than usual. During the debauched party, Lehder gets in a row with one of Pablo's loyal henchmen, 'Rollo'. The night ends with Lehder reportedly shooting him dead. Pablo shows rare leniency, and allows his friend to leave. But days later Lehder is pinned down in a gunfight, taken alive and extradited to the US. We may never know for sure whether the Colombian police were tipped off by Pablo, but it's clear that extradition is a serious threat for any and all in Pablo's close circle. If Lehder attempts to do a deal and give up Pablo, his offers fall on deaf ears and he disappears into the US criminal justice system, the very fate that Pablo most fears. Pablo watches the news report footage of his associate being thrust into a plane to be sent to America. He would rather throw himself into the propellers and die on the tarmac than get on that plane.

Then, after a tense six months, a sudden change brings blessed relief. In June the Supreme Court rules in favour of a lawsuit brought against the extradition policy. The law is overturned. Over a hundred arrest warrants and extradition orders, including Pablo's, are overturned by the Minister of Justice José Manuel Arias. However it came about, Pablo has his victory. He is 37, one of the richest men in the world and, after three years of being almost continually on the run, is able to return home to be with his family. He takes up residence with his wife and children in their swanky Mónaco apartment, and plays the role of dutiful dad, taking Juan Pablo to school and Manuela to her nursery. Even so, he still favours his trainers, often sporting his preferred cleats, just in case he needs to make a quick getaway.

And so, in this brief hiatus in overt hostilities, Pablo is finally able to give some much-needed attention to his passion project: Atlético Nacional. América have just won the league for his cartel rivals in Cali for the fifth season in a row. Someone needs to put them in their place. To this end, Pablo embarks on a bold strategy. He identifies a new manager, a man if not plucked from obscurity then certainly a left-field appointment that hints at El Patrón's aptitude for lateral thinking, problem solving and creativity, a man who might just help Nacional turn the tide. That man is Francisco 'Pacho' Maturana. Pacho is a former player, known and loved by the fans. He is, however, no managerial heavyweight. But, like Nacional goalkeeper René Higuita – who Pablo first identified on the pitches he had built in the Medellín slums and brought to the attention of the professional scouts – he has a certain something. A talent. And Pablo has built his reputation on spotting talent, judging characters and exploiting opportunity.

Having moved to Belén in Medellín as a child, Maturana had played for a decade for Nacional, making 359 appearances between 1970 and 1980 and had won the league with them twice while also obtaining a degree in dentistry from the university. Capped six times by his country, his playing career was impressive. But when, in 1987, Pablo hires him as the new manager of Atlético Nacional, he has just a single league season under his belt as a manager, and that at the minnows of Once Caldas. Although his rapid escalation from youth team manager to head coach of the Colombian national men's side at the same time, and their impressive third place finish in the 1987 Copa América, suggests his is a star in the ascendant. The appointment of

Maturana is a bold move, classic Pablo – and one that will change the fortunes of Atlético Nacional, and of Colombian football, forever.

Pablo has helped to put in place the building blocks of an Atlético Nacional side that will go down in history for all the right, and wrong reasons. A new coach, with a philosophy of football that embraces freedom and expression, who celebrates creativity on the pitch. The same coach now also the manager of the national side – and, in sync with Pablo and Nacional, seeing the patriotic benefit of a squad full of Colombian players rather than foreigners. A team of young, talented players, many of whom have grown up on Pablo's pitches in Medellín – from eccentric star goalkeeper Higuita to breakout centre back Andrés Escobar, who after making his first three appearances for the club in 1986 will become a vital part of Pacho's side in 1987 after a row between Pacho and Norberto Molina gives the kid from the reserve team the chance to shine.

With Pablo's money behind them, the ability to retain and incentivize these players, rather than lose them to rivals at home or abroad, the platform is set. Success is not instantaneous, however. América are indeed deposed – but it is a new challenger who initially ascends.

In Bogotá, Pablo's partner in the Medellín Cartel, José Gonzalo Rodríguez Gacha, aka El Mexicano, is also a major player in the narcoball era. In 1982 Colombian footballing heavyweights Millonarios had fallen on hard times. The 11-times league winners were, like many of the country's professional sides, strapped for cash and facing an uncertain future. Enter, stage left and carrying bags of narco cash just begging to be laundered: El Mexicano. Along with his partner Edmer Tamayo Marín, El Mexicano became a majority shareholder in the club, but when Rodrigo Lara Bonilla began the crusade against Pablo, the cartels and the onset of narcoball that ultimately got him killed, Rodríguez Gacha stepped back into the shadows, his involvement removed from official records.

Then, in 1986, Tamayo dies. And, with Lara long gone, El Mexicano is free to exert greater influence over the side once more – albeit still insulated from prying eyes by the use of his lawyers as the official chairmen of the club. Emboldened, he ploughs funds into the squad, and reaps the rewards. Millonarios take the title in 1987, and again in 1988. If anyone is in any doubt as to whose team this really is, at every home game the crowds at the Estadio El Campín in Bogotá are treated to a joyous spectacle: the performance of a full mariachi band.

El Mexicano, like Pablo, rules with a 'plata o plomo', money or lead, carrot or stick, approach. And this extends to his team. He holds lavish feasts for the players, and showers them with cash – extending the same generosity to his manager and coaching staff, to fan group leaders, even journalists. But woe betide you if you cross him. And as a player, no matter what another team might offer you, there is no leaving Millonarios until it benefits El Mexicano.

Coach Luis Alberto García and a team featuring the likes of Argentinian midfielder Mario Vanemerak and Colombian strikers Arnoldo Iguarán and Carlos Estrada dominate the 1987 season – with Millonarios topping the Apertura and Finalización tables and losing only five times in 56 games to take the title. The three teams below them in the final standings? Miguel Rodríguez Orejuela's América de Cali, a Santa Fe side bankrolled by fellow narco Phanor Arizabaleta-Arzayus, and Atlético Nacional. Colombia's top four sides are all narcoball teams. In 1988, the influence of the drug lords will become impossible for the fans, and the players, to ignore. But first, war is about to break out . . .

Chapter Nine

War on Two Fronts (1988)

In Medellín, the normal chaotic, bloody order of things has resumed. Pablo has been in hiding since the assassination of politician Jaime Pardo Leal in October 1987. It was most likely El Mexicano rather than El Patrón who ordered the hit, but any high profile political assassination increases the heat on Pablo. He has been forced to leave his family in the Mónaco apartment, his time doing the school drop off at an end. Then a ghost of his former life reappears, with disastrous consequences.

When Pablo had spent time in prison in 1976 one of his most trusted lieutenants, Jorge Pabón, had helped look after El Patrón when the two men were stuck behind bars. The pair had been friends since the early 1970s, and Pabón – nicknamed *El Negro* – was soon a key part of Pablo's criminal organization. In late 1987, El Negro reappears in Medellín, having just finished a two-year stint in a New York prison on drug trafficking charges.

El Negro, like Pablo, has a deep passion for football – but his team is Medellín's Deportivo Independiente (DIM). One day, after the local derby in which DIM have achieved a rare victory over their local rivals Nacional, he drives home from the Atanasio Girardot. His joy is short-lived. Stuck in post-match Medellín traffic in his convertible

Mercedes, he is shot a dozen times by motorbike gunmen. But El Negro survives, and with Pablo's help he discovers who has dared to attempt to take his life in his own town.

They track down the would-be killers, who reveal that an intermediary, a *burro*, hired them. The burro tells Pablo and El Negro that it was a man called Alejo Peña who ordered the hit. It is this shocking discovery that will cause open war between the cartels – as Peña is not only a member of the Cali Cartel but the man El Negro had just spent his US jail time looking after. This explosive intel is kept under wraps by Pablo and the cartel, and only becomes public knowledge when Popeye dishes the dirt on the true story of El Negro in an interview a full quarter century after the death of El Patrón.

When it is revealed that the killers knew to look for El Negro after the game, and that he would be driving his convertible, Pabón is finally able to put the pieces together. His wife is the only person who had that information. And when Peña had been released ahead of him, El Negro had agreed to allow him to visit his wife, to check on her and help her out if needed – as a thank you for the protection the Medellín man had given his Cali compatriot in prison. Clearly Peña has been giving Pabón's wife more than a helping hand.

Up until this point, the Medellín and Cali cartels had been allies and (mostly) friendly rivals, united in their pursuit of wealth through cocaine trafficking and in the common fight against extradition. But now El Negro wants blood. Pablo allows him to move into the Mónaco building while he calls in a favour with the Rodríguez Orejuela brothers. But his request to have Peña's superior in the Cali Cartel, none other than their top man Pacho Herrera, handed over, falls on deaf ears. If Pablo has his doubt about his relationship with Cali, what happens next will push him into all-out war with his former criminal allies . . .

On 13 January 1988, Pablo visits his family at the Mónaco building. Juan Pablo is now nine, and is being home-schooled – as the danger inherent in attending a regular school, even with armed protection, has become too great. Rather than risk staying over, Pablo opts to leave during the night. At 5:30 in the morning a car rolls up towards the front of the apartment block. It is packed with 1,500lb of dynamite. When the car bomb goes off every window in the Mónaco building shatters, an entire frame exploding onto the cot where the three-year-old Manuela is sleeping.

Pablo is in no doubt. It was Cali. And this is war. Whether it was an attack aimed at him, or just possibly at El Negro – who was also absent from the building at the moment of the bombing – either way it cannot be allowed to stand. Three people die in the attack and a hundred more are seriously injured, but Pablo's family somehow survive in one piece. The uneasy alliance between the Medellín and Cali cartels does not.

But now Pablo is fighting a war on two fronts. In January alone he first has a candidate for Mayor of Bogotá kidnapped, and then the Attorney General is killed when Pablo's men botch his kidnapping. Both were vocal proponents of extradition. The Colombian authorities respond by raiding raiding La Manuela, Pablo's farm in the Peñol, looting the property, destroying his football pitches there, and blowing up the building. Meanwhile Pablo strikes back at Cali – by embarking on a bombing campaign against the Medellín outlets of the La Rebaja chain of pharmacies owned by the Rodríguez Orejuela brothers. And in response the rival cartel blows up Pablo's mother's house. The gloves are well and truly off. *Time* magazine declares Medellín the most dangerous city ever. Not just of the year, or in Colombia, but the most dangerous city that has ever existed.

The tit-for-tat battles are taking their toll on Pablo, and on 22 March he has one of his closest shaves yet. He is in hiding in a farm on his Hacienda El Bizcocho property when the Colombian army launch their biggest operation yet. Nearly a thousand soldiers encircle the farm, their movements co-ordinated by their general in one of several attack helicopters circling overhead and supported by tanks. As dawn breaks they move on the farm. Tata is captured, along with many of Pablo's men. Guns, radio equipment and multiple tapes of illegally recorded phone calls, including several with the former President Belisario Betancur, are seized. But they miss Pablo. His bed is still warm to the touch, but El Patrón is nowhere to be seen. He has been tipped off, a silent alarm triggered by loyal locals on the road up to the farm.

A handful of soldiers are approached by a group of men. It is Pablo and his most trusted inner circle. But as some of the cartel men move forward, feigning surrender, they block the soldiers' view of El Patrón himself and, quick as a flash, he turns tail and runs. Realizing their mistake, the soldiers unleash a volley of gunfire at their principal target. Pablo feels something warm, wet, sticky spatter his cheek. Has he been hit? Is this the end, shot as he runs through the fields? He wipes his face, and his fingers come away streaked not with crimson blood but with rich, brown earth. The bullets have struck the mud at his feet and splattered his face, nothing more.

But Pablo and his men have not yet broken through the army lines. A photographer from the Medellín newspaper *El Colombiano* is hovering around the farm's perimeter, observing and documenting the historic raid on Pablo. He snaps a line of men as they walk in single file across the fields. Soon the line reaches a soldier, and the man at the front of the group explains he is a member of the secret police, an undercover plain clothes operative. His captives are some of Pablo's men, and he is escorting them to the nearest police station. The young soldier lets the group pass. Only later will he, and the rest of the world, discover that the supposed undercover policeman was in fact Pablo Escobar himself. Pablo has bluffed his way out from under the very noses of his would-be captors.

The operation to hunt down and capture Pablo continues for days. The first wanted posters of him begin to spring up, a 100 million peso reward is offered, and a tip hotline number given. But Pablo continues to evade the authorities. And the hotline is bombarded with a deluge of fake tips and false leads, as the local Antioquenians rally in support of El Patrón.

*

While Pablo is struggling to cope with the combined attentions of both the full might of the Colombian police and military and the cold, calculating killers down in Cali, the footballing project he has built is starting to blossom.

On 24 May 1988, Pacho Maturana's Colombia side are over 5,000 miles away, in London. They are on a mini tour of Europe in preparation for their imminent World Cup qualifying campaign back in South America, and are in the UK to play in the Rous Cup against Scotland and England. The previous year it had been global footballing heavyweights Brazil who had been chosen as the guest side in the three-team tournament. It is a huge opportunity for Pacho's still little-known team to show what they can do at the home of football – Wembley Stadium. They have already battled to an impressive 0-0 draw at Hampden Park despite having only arrived on the continent 36 hours earlier and fresh from a 2-0 win over the USA in Miami. At Wembley, however, they are facing an England side preparing for the 1988 European Championships under the stewardship of Bobby Robson. It is only the second time the two countries have ever met on the football pitch – the first was the 4-0 humbling Colombia suffered in Bogotá in 1970.

England are keen to end the tournament with a statement win ahead of the Euros. Many of those watching at home, and among the 25,000 spectators in the stadium, believe it will be a routine victory for a team boasting Peter Shilton, Bryan Robson, Peter Beardsley, Chris Waddle, John Barnes and Gary Lineker. England even have Glenn Hoddle on the bench.

But Colombia have as their captain the 26-year-old South American footballer of the year, Carlos Valderrama. El Pibe is the midfield maestro in Pacho's new-look Colombia, the creative force in the centre of the park capable of casting a spell over the pitch with his passing. His talent has meant he is on the cusp of becoming Colombia's highest profile footballing export, with a transfer from Deportivo Cali to top French side Montpellier agreed for a fee of around $4 million.

England may be the home side, and Wembley far from full, but this is the first time any of London's Colombian community have had the chance to see their country play in England. Early in the game a cluster of brightly coloured fans high up in the stands begin their chant: *¡Colombia! ¡Colombia!'* It's not long before cult hero Higuita comes miles out of his penalty area to chest down an England long ball and bring a chorus of appreciation from the crowd. The English commentator will later call him 'a bit of a Dave Beasant this boy' in the televised highlights. In the middle of the pitch, England captain Bryan Robson, socks pulled up high, is the dynamo, all energy and endeavour. In stark contrast his opposite number, Valderrama, strolls around with his socks around his ankles. The game is open, and even.

Then the ball breaks to Steve McMahon on the edge of the Colombian penalty area and his volleyed drive stings Higuita's palms, the Colombian keeper turning the powerfully struck shot acrobatically behind for a corner. The initial set piece is cleared, but after a scrappy period of play England manage to work the ball back out to the right. Waddle turns inside his man and crosses the ball left-footed into the box – where the predatory Lineker steers a glancing header beyond Higuita and in off the far post. With a quarter of the game gone, England have the lead. But, in a keenly contested game, the away side refuse to wilt. Some typically slick one-touch passing from Colombia leads to a 20-yard effort from Bernardo Redín that forces a flying save from Shilton. The Colombians visibly grow into the game as the first half progresses, quick flicks and backheels, probing passing from El Pibe, a well-drilled back line and Higuita sweeping up. But Lineker remains a threat for England.

The second half begins as the first ended, with the quick feet and deft one-twos of the Colombians opening up England around the edge of their penalty area, but without managing to find that final shot to trouble Shilton. Then, with an hour gone, Lineker wins a free kick just outside the Colombian box. John Barnes shoots from distance, and has Higuita scrambling to paw the effort away. England seem more or less in control, holding their 1-0 lead – and Higuita's skills in evading Peter Beardsley's attentions bring a cheer from the crowd and smiles from the England bench. As the home fans sing 'we love you England, we do' Bryan Robson ghosts into the box and his header comes off a Colombian defender and flashes just wide. It looks like England might drive home their advantage and double their lead imminently. Then Valderrama and the pacy substitute John Tréllez stretch England and win a rare corner for Los Cafeteros. Up trot the two tall centre backs from Atlético Nacional, Andrés Escobar and Luis Perea. With 66 minutes gone, it is Andrés Escobar who leaps highest in the box, and sends his header over Shilton and in off the crossbar. On the bench, Maturana, impeccably dressed in a white shirt, slim black tie and grey sports coat, smiles. In the stands, the pocket of Colombian fans are overjoyed. As he runs back into position after celebrating with his teammates, Andrés makes the sign of the cross. At just 21 years of age he has just scored his country's first ever goal at Wembley. It is the least the boys in yellow deserve.

England are rattled. The Colombians draw a series of fouls, their quick feet too much for the defenders in red. The introduction of Hoddle gives England fresh impetus, however, as they up their tempo and press for a winner. In the end Valderrama helps Colombia keep possession for the final minutes and, as the ref blows his whistle, the yellow, blue and red flags wave in the crowd to celebrate a famous point for Pacho's men. The England players are impressed enough by the performance of their opposition that they swap shirts with their South American counterparts ahead of the presentation of the Rous Cup to England – and earn a barracking from Bobby Robson into the bargain. For many neutral fans, Colombian football has finally arrived.

And it's telling that nine Atlético Nacional players featured in the game – seven as starters and two as subs. With three from Deportivo Cali, including the captain and heartbeat of the team

Carlos Valderrama, and just one from Millonarios, it means that not a single Colombian player from a team owned by one of Pablo's rivals takes to the field that night, while the majority of the side, including its manager, have their salaries paid by the world's biggest narco.

*

Back in Colombia, the overseas sojourn of Los Cafeteros now over and the league season resumed, fans of the beautiful game are about to be reminded of the dangers caused by the influence of the cartels in Colombian football.

Millonarios, the side bankrolled by Pablo's Bogotá partner José Gonzalo Rodríguez Gacha, are bidding to win back-to-back titles. El Mexicano is reluctant to leave anything to chance, he is desperate for his side to triumph over his friend Pablo in Medellín and especially over their new enemies in Cali. He is not the first to attempt to bribe, or to threaten, referees. But his actions tip the balance. First a referee rules out a perfectly good América de Cali goal, a 30-yard strike, against Millonarios. A week later and another referee waves away Santa Fe claims for a penalty before gifting Millonarios a spot kick following a foul that clearly took place outside the box. The Bogotá side might be on the verge of their second successive league title but the game ends in violence and disorder and no one watching can ignore the invisible hand of El Mexicano in all this – and the corruption the growing tide of narco dollars has unleased on the game. The season's nadir, which is saying something, comes in November 1988.

First, on 31 October the referees go on strike, refusing to officiate the third round of matches in the octagonal final, seemingly against the advice of their association, which appears to be under the influence of the cartels. They have had enough of the bribes and the threats, the incessant plata o plomo offers that Pablo and his ilk have introduced to the sport.

Then, on 2 November, Colombian top-flight referee Armando Pérez is kidnapped in Medellín. Six armed men snatch him, bundle him into a vehicle and spend the day driving him around the city at gunpoint. The gunmen claim to represent the men in charge of the country's leading clubs and, when they finally release him, remind Pérez that any officials who give the wrong decisions on the pitch will be killed. On his release his colleague, fellow referee Jesús Díaz, remarks that the only thing missing from the cartel's intimidation of officials is a dead man. Tragically, he won't have long to wait.

Eventually, El Mexicano's Millonarios do indeed triumph. They win the league, but only just – taking the title on goal difference from Pablo's Atlético Nacional. The stage is set for a blockbuster season in 1989 . . .

PART TWO

NOBODY WRITES
TO THE COLONEL

(1989–1992)

When I die, I want my coffin
To be painted green and white like my heart
When I die, don't cry for me
Because I was born green, and green is happiness
The crowd jumps, the heart beats
Come on, Verdolagas, I want to be a champion
Come on, El Verde, I will always be there for you
Because not even death will separate us.

'*When I Die*'
A favourite song among the supporters of Atlético Nacional,
sung at their Estadio Atanasio Girardot in Medellín.

Chapter Ten

The Curse of Narcoball (1989)

Having only just lost out on the 1988 league title to Millonarios, Atlético Nacional are primed and ready for a huge season in 1989. Pacho Maturana has had the time, and money, to forge a perfectly balanced side. With his footballing philosophy drawing inspiration from Colombian music and dance, he has created a 4-4-2 system in which the two defensively minded central midfielders give the rest of the team the freedom to express their footballing creativity. With their nucleus of local Medellín lads, and an entirely Colombian line-up, Nacional are ready to dazzle.

But 1989 starts badly, for Pablo Escobar at least. On 20 January 1989 George HW Bush is inaugurated as the 41st President of the United States of America. Reagan's former vice-president was once the Director of Central Intelligence, the head of the CIA. He is likely to be at least as tough in the ongoing 'war on drugs' as his former movie star predecessor in the White House.

Medellín is still the most dangerous city in the world, with over 4,000 murders every year. But, with somewhere in the region of 200,000 acres of Colombia now planted with coca, Pablo and the cartels are making more money than almost anyone else on the planet. *Forbes* magazine estimates Pablo's wealth at $3 billion, placing him seventh on their list of richest men in the world. It is his third year in a row in the coveted list, and his highest placing so far – thanks to the fact he now supplies 80 per cent of the world's cocaine. Insiders estimate that a single weekend's take from his Miami operation might be $50–70 million. He is not just the biggest criminal in Colombia, he has risen to be *el capo de capos*, 'the king of kings', boss of all bosses, of the global underworld. And the king has his eyes trained on one very specific bauble, the trophy that has eluded not just his hated rivals América de Cali but every team in Colombia – the Copa Libertadores.

The 1980s has seen the gradual rise of Colombian football, after nearly three decades in the wilderness. Led initially by América de Cali, the nation's club sides have been threatening to finally get one over their South American rivals and win the Copa Libertadores. And now, under Pacho Maturana, the national team are looking like they might qualify for their first World Cup since 1962. The cocaine money of the Cali and Medellín cartels has finally given teams like Atlético Nacional and América de Cali the chance to recruit and keep top players, and to challenge their Argentinian and Brazilian rivals. And Los Cafeteros have benefitted as a result. A golden age of Colombian football is about to break out thanks to the era of narcoball – but, like everything Pablo touches, it will end in blood and death, irrevocably tarnished.

In February 1989 the 30th edition of the Copa Libertadores kicks off. Each nation is represented by two sides – the two top-placed teams in their nation's domestic league in the previous season. In 1988 El Mexicano's Millonarios had won the Colombian championship for the second year running, with Pablo's Atlético Nacional the runners up.

And so, as the tournament begins, the Medellín Cartel control both of the sides carrying Colombia's hopes.

The group stages are organized into five mini leagues, each containing four teams from two countries. Millonarios and Nacional share Group D with the two Ecuadorian entrants – Deportivo Quito and Emelec. But the first game for the Colombians is contested between the two of them – as Millonarios host Atlético Nacional in Bogotá on 15 February. A 1-1 draw ensures honours are even. But after Nacional can only manage two more draws on the road in Ecuador – a 1-1 in Guayaquil against Emelec swiftly followed by a third consecutive 1-1 draw, this time in Quito and thanks to a penalty scored by their goalkeeper René Higuita – they are left with just three points from their opening three games.

The visit of Millonarios to Medellín comes next. On 7 March, Nacional fall to a potentially catastrophic 2-0 home defeat to their rivals, courtesy of two second-half goals from Arnoldo Iguarán. They have given themselves it all to do if they want to make it out of the group. By the end of the month, Millonarios have thrashed Deportivo Quito and Emelec in their final two games. El Mexicano's side top the group, unbeaten, securing their berth in the round of 16.

Meanwhile Nacional must take full advantage of playing their final two matches at home if they are to avoid the ignominy of a first-round exit. On 13 March they welcome Deportivo Quito to the Estadio Atanasio Girardot in a must-win game. The match starts well for Pacho's boys, as Jaime Arango squeezes in a shot at the back post that gives them the lead after just two minutes. Everything seems to be going to plan until just before half time, when all hell breaks loose. On 40 minutes Quito's Adelberto Angulo and Nacional's goalscorer Arango are both sent off. As half time looms both sides are down to ten men, but before Pacho can get his men together and regroup, and with the dust barely settled after the pair of red cards, Quito snatch a 43rd minute equalizer through Álex Aguinaga. It's 1-1, and ten men apiece, at the break.

As the second half ticks away the crowd's nervousness grows. Yet another 1-1 draw would put a major dent in their hopes of reaching the next stage of the competition. For almost 40 minutes of the half Nacional are unable to find a way through the Ecuadorian side's defence. And then, a corner. The ball is swung over, and there, unmarked eight yards out, is Andrés Escobar. His header is straight at the middle of the goal, but the pace and power are enough to beat the keeper. Nacional have the lead, and with just six minutes left. In the end, there's enough time for a second red for Quito, shown to Leandro Pérez, but not for an equalizer. The dream is still alive.

In the final game Nacional host Emelec. With only the bottom team set to be eliminated, the Medellín side know anything bar an unexpected thrashing at the hands of their visitors and they are through. In the end a comprehensive 3-1 victory means they finish second, behind Millonarios. Pacho Maturana and his team have qualified for the knockout stages, and dodged the anger of El Patrón.

On 5 April, in the first leg of the round of 16, Millonarios are in La Paz, Bolivia, taking on Club Bolívar while at the same time in Medellín, Atlético Nacional are facing off against Argentinian heavyweights Racing Club. In La Paz the side from Bogotá fall to a second-half goal from Jorge Hirano, leaving them 1-0 down ahead of the return tie. In contrast, Pablo's Nacional run out 2-0 winners.

Exactly a week later, and El Mexicano's Millonarios side are struggling to find the breakthrough they need. When the whistle goes for half time the game is still 0-0. Ten minutes into the second half and the Bogotá side are given a mountain to climb – as Hirano strikes to give Bolívar the lead. But three minutes later Rubén Hernández pulls a goal back for Millonarios. And three minutes after that a Nilton Bernal effort gives them the lead on the night. But the pendulum swings again on 76 minutes when Carlos López restores Bolívar's advantage. The game is tied 2-2. Unless Millonarios can score they will be eliminated. With just seven minutes to go Hernández gets his second, and Millonarios's third. The tie will go to penalties. Millonarios score their first four spot kicks, while Bolívar miss once, leaving fifth penalty taker Carlos Estrada with the chance to send the Colombian team into the quarter-finals. But he can't convert. Rafael Cuevas has the chance to take the shoot-out into sudden death. But he too misses – and Millonarios are through.

In Argentina, Atlético Nacional stumble. A goal shortly before half time for Racing Club is followed by a second midway through the second half. At 2-0 down, the Medellín side are staring defeat in the face. Then, with just four minutes remaining, one of the young Medellín lads in the team, Felipe 'Pipe' Pérez, controls a pulled-back cross around the penalty spot. As defenders throw themselves in front of him to try and block his shot, he arrows a strike into the top corner with virtually no back lift. Nacional hang on, and the 2-1 defeat is enough to see them through 3-2 on aggregate. And guess who they will face in the quarter-finals? That's right, none other than Millonarios. It will be Bogotá versus Medellín, Pablo versus El Mexicano, for a place in the semi-finals of the Copa.

The first leg takes place in Medellín on 19 April 1989. At half time it's all square, but six minutes into the second half Albeiro Usuriaga, the 6ft 4in striker nicknamed *El Palomo*, 'the Pigeon', gives the home crowd what they've been waiting for – the lead. Found just inside the box, he gets the ball out from under his feet, swings a long right leg at the ball and, as his standing foot gives way under him and sends him to the turf, guides his shot between the keeper's legs and into the net.

The game ends 1-0, and Pacho and his men can only hope their slender advantage is enough to defend when they travel to the capital. Exactly a week later, and the Estadio El Campín in Bogotá is rocking as Millonarios take a 25th minute lead through Carlos Estrada. Having seen El Mexicano's side win the Colombian league twice in a row, surely Pablo is not going to have to face being knocked out of the Copa by his cartel partner's team too? The tie is on a knife-edge as the clock ticks down. It's 1-0 Millonarios at half time. And still, with an hour gone. Then, on 67 minutes Nacional keeper René Higuita brings down Millonarios striker Iguarán inside the penalty area. But the impassioned pleas of the home side are ignored. The Chilean referee, Hernán Silva, fumbles and drops his whistle, then recovers to signal a corner. The Millonarios bench and players are furious. The stadium is seething. Eventually order is restored, and the game continues. As the clock ticks past 70 minutes, then 75, still Nacional can't find a way to score the vital goal that would tip the balance of the tie in their favour. Then, on 80 minutes, John Tréllez finds half a yard of space in between two converging Millonarios defenders, and jabs a shot goalward. The deflection from the diving keeper can only help the ball spin up and over the line. The Bogotá crowd is stunned. Maturana's men hold on, seeing out the draw and winning the tie. They're into the semi-finals.

Pablo Escobar's beloved Atlético Nacional must overcome Danubio of Uruguay to reach their first Copa Libertadores final and have the chance to become the first side from Colombia to lift the famous trophy and be proclaimed the best team in South America. He is desperate for his team to triumph where América de Cali have failed for three agonizing seasons in a row. On 10 May 1989, at the Centenario stadium in Montevideo, Nacional grind out a respectable 0-0 draw. Any kind of a win, at home in Medellín, will see them into the final.

Less than a week later, and three Argentinian men leave Medellín's airport. They get into a taxi and are driven into town. But as they are taken into the heart of the city, their cab driver becomes increasingly chatty. In fact, he revels in the telling of a series of gruesome and bloody tales, in particular pointing out the spots along the road where the dumped bodies of referees and linesmen who had refused El Patrón's bribes had been found. The taxi driver is almost certainly one of the many in the city who are loyal to Medellín's crime kingpin, Pablo Escobar. The three men are the match officials Carlos Espósito, Abel Gnecco and Juan Bava, who are due to oversee the second leg of the semi-final. The chillingly 'educational' tour is no coincidence.

In the hours before the game, the officials decline an invitation to dinner and decide to stay in their room at the Hotel Dann. When there's a knock at the door, Bava answers it expecting a room service delivery of mineral water. Instead, he is barged out of the way by four men, trailing behind them a fifth in a suit and tie – Pablo's baby-faced assassin, Popeye. The Argentinians take in the scene, a machine gun pointed squarely at them. One of the thugs moves to press the barrel of a 9mm pistol to Gnecco's head. Popeye produces a suitcase, and addresses Espósito. He opens the case. It is stuffed with US currency.

'Here is $250,000. Take it, don't worry, you're going to leave Colombia without problems.'

When the officials tell Pablo's top sicario that they intend to do their jobs properly he closes the briefcase, before telling them 'your life here is worth nothing. And in Buenos Aires it will only cost us $1,000 for each of you.'

On 17 May, Atlético Nacional romp to a 6-0 home win over Danubio, with four goals from El Palomo – the pick of them an outside of the right boot 40-yard lob from a long goal kick. Whether Popeye and his entourage had visited the Danubio team with a similar offer we may never know, but the record books will forever show that Nacional were in the final.

To lift the trophy, Nacional must triumph over Olimpia of Paraguay. They are not one of the Argentinian, Brazilian or Uruguayan heavyweights who have dominated the tournament since its inception – but unlike Nacional, in fact unlike any Colombian side, they have won the Copa Libertadores previously, in 1979.

On 24 May Pacho Maturana's men face the biggest moment of their footballing lives, as the first leg of the 1989 Copa kicks off in front of 50,000 spectators inside El Estadio Defensores del Chaco in Asunción. The players are nervous, and it shows. Away from home and before a partisan crowd the pressure on them builds. It takes a remarkable goal-line headed clearance, and a string of typically athletic saves from Higuita, to keep them on level terms. Then the Nacional defence fails to track Olimpia midfielder, and former Millonarios player, Rafael Bobadilla – who steals in between defender and goalkeeper to nod his side in front. Maturana, impeccable as ever in his textured light suit, white shirt and dark tie, looks down at the ground wryly.

On 60 minutes comes a dagger blow. Olimpia's Vidal Sanabria gets to a bouncing ball on the edge of the penalty area just before the raised foot of a Nacional defender . . . and hooks an unerring strike past the despairing dive of an outstretched Higuita and into the top corner.

It's a brilliant goal, seemingly conjured out of nothing. And with that moment of magic the Medellín side find themselves 2-0 down. The travelling Colombian fans can't believe it.

When the tie ends with the score unchanged, many could be forgiven for thinking Atlético Nacional might have already fluffed their lines and passed up their chance for footballing immortality. But, as with anything involving Pablo Emilio Escobar Gaviria, this story has many more a twist in the tale . . .

*

The offer, when it comes, and come it surely does, is neither the first nor the last of its kind. And yet it feels like now, at this time, in this place, a threshold has been crossed. Plata o plomo. The words themselves are not uttered, or maybe they are, by one or other of the parties there present, either way the meaning is clear. Silver or lead. Cold, hard cash or an ignominious death in a hail of bullets. Or perhaps just a single one, to the back of the head or through the eye. Carrot or stick, bribe or brutality, the choice is an illusion – not even an ultimatum, but a fait accompli. No one ever chooses plomo.

The man, well-dressed, or perhaps expensively dressed is a better description, appears unannounced beside their table as they dine among the great and the good, the prim and the proper of Bogotá, Colombia's bustling capital city nestled in its fertile basin high in the Andes. There is no mistaking what he is. The clothes, the stance, the attitude, give him away as clearly as a red or blue bandana might reveal an Angeleno as a member of the Bloods or Crips. Colombia, and especially Bogotá, has more than its fair share of wealthy citizens, of rich and powerful men in expensive suits, clothed in a fog of supreme self-confidence like cigar smoke in a gentlemen's club. But this is a new breed of vulgar upstart, lacking in education, sophistication . . . breeding. Neither blue blood nor thrusting industrialist, but instead the fastest growing class in 80s Colombia: the narco. And this man is a sicario, sent by Pablo Escobar himself. Perhaps he is even the infamous Popeye.

With just his appearance, the threat is implied, the message already clear, the three seated men in no doubt as to who this interloper is, or why he is here. And yet he spells it out, as if the trio dining together that night need it. Another example of the vulgarity, the lack of class and subtlety, of his kind . . . of his master. A suitcase each, stuffed with US dollars.

'If Atlético Nacional de Medellín does not win, you will go home in coffins.'

As offers go, it is at least lacking in ambiguity. The message may not be delivered at literal gunpoint, although the man is doubtless armed (in fact is that the muzzle of a submachine gun glimpsed beneath his jacket?), but it might as well be. Nothing is lost in translation for the three outsiders.

For the three diners are not cops, nor judges or politicians, are not even Colombians, but Argentinians. More than that, they are match officials. The referee and his two linesmen are guests of Bogotá on the eve of the biggest game in the history of Pablo's beloved Atlético Nacional.

It is 30 May 1989, the night before the final game of the tournament, when referee Juan Carlos Loustau and his two colleagues and compatriots, his linesmen, have their meal interrupted. And the trio are in Bogotá not Medellín as the return fixture of the two-legged final is to be played in front of a 50,000 capacity crowd at the city's Estadio El Campín rather than the smaller Estadio Atanasio Girardot in

Nacional's, and Pablo Escobar's, hometown. But El Patrón's tentacles spread far and wide. Wherever the match is to take place, Nacional must win. There is to be no avoiding his will in this. Except this time the three officials turn down the money. They stick to their sporting principles. Surely this will not end well . . .

*

31 May 1989. The Estadio El Campín, Bogotá, Colombia. The players of Atlético Nacional take to the pitch for the second leg of their side's first ever Copa Libertadores final. Can they overcome a 2-0 deficit from the first leg? Can they succeed where every other Colombian team has previously failed, and bring the Copa to their homeland? Neither they, nor their coach Francisco 'Pacho' Maturana, may well have any idea that their infamous and not-so-secret benefactor could be looking to tip the odds in their favour. But what follows has, for better or worse, become football folklore . . .

Nacional's opposition, Olimpia, travel to Colombia's capital city full of confidence. With a healthy lead from the first leg in Asunción, they arrive in Bogotá having taken part in three previous finals – and having even won the whole shebang ten years earlier. The odds seem stacked in their favour.

And yet, as El Patrón takes his place in the stands he is happy, confident even. With extradition still nullified thanks to the actions of the Supreme Court he feels safe enough to watch his side in their greatest hour. Beside him stands his infamous hitman and lieutenant Jhon Jairo Velásquez Vásquez, his top sicario Popeye. Pablo cheers as his friend *El Loco*, Nacional's maverick goalkeeper René Higuita, emerges. The young keeper's gloves are an impossibly bright white, his trademark mass of black shiny curls bounce around his shoulders, his moustache twitches nervously. Andrés Escobar, still just 22, clean-shaven and baby-faced, skips onto the pitch. Nicknamed *El Caballero del Fútbol* – 'The Gentleman' – his defensive odd-couple pairing with Higuita, the calm and the storm, has been pivotal to Nacional's rise. In midfield, Leonel Álvarez – sporting a mullet even more spectacular than Andrés Escobar's, and with a thin black moustache lining his top lip – is the man Pacho Maturana relies upon to pull the strings and dictate play. Up front, the dangerous goal machine John Jairo Tréllez brings the Medellín side pace and unpredictability. From back to front, and including coach Maturana himself, the team is 100 per cent Colombian. The stadium is packed with more than 35,000 Nacional fans who have travelled down to the capital from Medellín in a raucous, joyous caravan of coaches. It feels like all of Medellín has gone to Bogotá. For those watching, for Pablo in the stands, Nacional, in this moment, *is* Colombia.

The first half is a tense, cagey affair. Maturana decides his side need more control of the ball, and the game, and makes a crucial tactical switch, sacrificing one of his strikers to bring on an extra midfielder. The impact is immediate. On 46 minutes, the inexplicable – a low ball fizzed across the away side's six-yard box by Usuriaga causes chaos. The Olimpia defenders slide in to try and deal with the danger and, in a comedy of errors, the ball eventually cannons onto Olimpia captain Fidel Miño – and into the unguarded net. Nacional are in front.

Nineteen minutes later and the fervent home crowd dare to dream. Alexis García sends a cross into the opposition box and somehow the diminutive figure of Luis *'El Bendito'* Fajardo leaps and heads it back into the danger zone. There El Palomo rises, more like a phoenix than a pigeon, to lever his giant frame up and over the defender, to get his head on the high, looping ball six yards out. He connects, getting there just before the despairing punch of the Olimpia goalkeeper. And 50,000 hold their breath as the ball loops up, then down, and somehow squeezes under the crossbar. 2-0 Nacional. The volume in the stadium reaches an almost deafening crescendo. El Palomo wheels away, then slides to the turf with arms outstretched as he is mobbed by his teammates.

In the stands, Pablo cheers, jumping and screaming along with his 35,000 fellow fans as the goal goes in. Never before has Popeye seen his boss, normally a block of ice, so animated, so euphoric. On TV screens across the country fans at home hear a repeated refrain shouted over and over by the commentator: '*Gol de Colombia! Gol de Colombia! Gol de Colombia!*' Not 'gol de Nacional', 'gol de Colombia'. Is Pablo's dream of unifying the country, his country, behind football – and his beloved Atlético Nacional – finally coming true?

But as the clock ticks on, a winner fails to materialize. The home crowd begin to get restless, their nerves transmitting through the stadium, El Patrón growing more and more angry and agitated. As the minutes and seconds roll by he struggles to contain his infamous rage.

The referee blows his whistle to signal the end of the 90 minutes. With no extra time, a 2-0 win for Nacional has left the two sides facing football's equivalent of Russian roulette: the dreaded penalty shoot-out. A lottery from 12 yards. For the crowd the tension is unbearable, for the players the pressure unparalleled, and for Pablo it is a unique form of torture.

As the teams huddle, Pacho Maturana grabs Higuita and tells him to dive right on the first penalty. When his keeper asks him for his tips on the others he can only laugh and tell him the first one is his gift, but the rest are up to him. And, sure enough, when the away side's

Uruguayan goalkeeper Ever Almeida takes the first Olimpia penalty his scuffed low strike heads to El Loco's right. Nacional's keeper has heeded his coach's advice. He dives, and makes the save. First blood to Higuita in the battle of the keepers. He trots off like a show pony, flexing his thighs beneath his short, tight shorts. Almeida skips nervously on towards the goal, to face the first Nacional spot kick. On the touchline the tall, handsome, smartly-dressed figure of coach Maturana watches on, hugging his arms across his chest to keep his emotions at bay.

Next, it's one of Nacional's youngest but calmest players, Mr Cool himself, Andrés Escobar. El Caballero makes no mistake, slotting his penalty left-footed into the bottom left corner with Almeida going the wrong way. He jumps for joy, pointing skywards, then turns and pumps his fist as he runs back to his teammates. 1-0 Nacional.

The sides proceed to trade goals from 12 yards – a series of almost perfect strikes giving both keepers no chance as the tension ratchets up with every long walk to that tiny, white painted circle, surely the loneliest place on a football pitch. But Nacional, indeed all of Colombia, know that if they can continue to score with their remaining attempts the trophy will be theirs.

Then, tragedy. The ever-dependable Alexis García, Maturana's captain, misses the fourth Nacional spot kick, his strike far too close to Almeida, who guesses the right way and makes the save look easy. García looks down and kicks the turf as he turns away. When Raúl Amarilla steps up to take the final attempt of Olimpia's five, Higuita, ever the showman, ever the psychological warrior, does his best to put him off – twitching and bouncing on the line, faking to dive. But to no avail. Amarilla strides up and smashes his kick into the corner with the minimum of fuss. Suddenly it is 4-3 to Olimpia. The momentum has shifted, and Nacional are left needing to score with their final attempt to avoid defeat. One man remains: René Higuita. If there is ever a goalkeeper you want taking a clutch penalty kick for your team, surely it's the Colombian ...

Where others had fired their efforts into the corners, or scuffed them and seen their shots saved, Higuita just strolls up and smashes his kick with such power that both his feet end up off the ground – and sends it rocketing straight down the middle of the goal. It flies beyond a despairing Almeida, who can only watch the net ripple as he falls to the turf. The Nacional icon, unlike the Olimpia goalie, has shown no nerves, and made no mistake. Now, after five penalties apiece, it is 4-4, and sudden death, and the pressure of the occasion seems to infect both teams ...

First, Higuita makes a crucial save from Olimpia substitute Gabriel González, and the Colombian crowd starts to spill onto the pitch, sensing the moment of victory. Maturana remains calm on the touchline, but his sideways glance, the gleam in his eyes, hints at the hope bubbling up beneath his otherwise unflappable exterior. Surely this is it? But Felipe Pérez fluffs his lines. Leaning back, his strike flies too high, glancing the crossbar and soaring into the seats behind the goal with a well-beaten Almeida skidding across the turf on his knees in relief. The Olimpia keeper leaps up to celebrate, arms spread wide. Will those millimetres haunt the Colombians?

Not if the symbol of Nacional, the hero of Medellín, the friend of Pablo, René Higuita is to have anything to do with it. He seemingly has the Indian sign over the opposition, and tricks the next taker, Jorge Guasch, with a subtle twitch of the hips – feinting to go one way before once more picking the right side to dive, and making yet another save. But for every Higuita save it seems there is now a Nacional miss – as

Gildardo Gómez too feels the intense pressure and screws his shot wide of the upright.

Surely Higuita can't do it again? Incredibly he does, pulling off yet another strong diving save, this time from Fermín Balbuena. But yet again his teammate will miss. This time Luis Perea sees his penalty, blasted down the middle, tipped up and over the bar by Almeida's rigid left hand. It is a rare save from the Olimpia keeper, but will it turn the tide once again?

Then it is finally Olimpia's turn to miss the target – Vidal Sanabria, the man who had scored that wondrous second goal in Asunción that had seemingly put the Paraguayans in such a strong position, leaning back and ballooning his strike miles over the bar. Somehow it is still 4-4. The crowd in the stadium hold their breath, the millions across Colombia utter their silent (and not-so-silent) prayers, Maturana paces the line, and Pablo Escobar clenches his fists.

Up steps Leonel Álvarez knowing he has the chance to write a new chapter in Colombian football history. The English speaking commentator too senses the enormity of the situation as he speaks:

'This is a moment for the history books. Flirting with fate. One shot will decide the prized Copa Libertadores of America. Leonel Álvarez . . .'

Coach Maturana has been watching aghast as his players have resolutely ignored his tactical advice. He has told the penalty takers to stop short, to see which side Almeida will dive, as he is going down very early. None have listened. Until now.

A stuttering run up convinces Almeida to start to dive to his left, before Álvarez calmly slides the ball to the other side of the goal. The unthinkable has happened. After two ties, two 2-0 home wins, 18 spot kicks, and over three hours of tense, gruelling football, Nacional has won 5-4 on penalties. It is the first time a Colombian club side has ever won South America's equivalent of the Champions League or European Cup – the Copa Libertadores. Álvarez wheels away, knee-sliding towards the corner of the pitch before being hoisted aloft by his joyous teammates.

The team celebrate, holding the giant silver trophy aloft as fireworks explode from the stands and the home fans get the party started. Interviewed on the pitch Andrés Escobar tells the TV camera that 'yes, our team has won this for the whole country'. Then, seemingly acknowledging the rumours that have dogged their progress through the competition, he looks straight into the camera, addressing us all down the lens as he states: 'We had to beat the best teams on the continent, but we've won it all, fair and square.'

The crowd in Bogotá, and those watching back in Medellín, celebrate with wild abandon. But, unnoticed by those in the stadium, one man who you might expect to be as ecstatic as anyone, if not more so, is seemingly far from happy. And he is not a man on whose wrong side you want to find yourself . . .

*

After the game, linesman Francisco Lamolina sees a ghost. It is the same man from the previous night, the man in the suit. Popeye. He watches on in horror as Pablo's sicario grabs his colleague, referee Loustau, by the hair and drags him away before bundling him into a waiting car.

Lamolina is shocked, and pleasantly surprised, when his friend reappears at their hotel sometime later, visibly beaten but miraculously alive. Loustau tells his colleague of all that had transpired. That he had been driven around the streets of Bogotá as fireworks were set off and celebratory gunfire exploded into the night sky (that night 20 people would die in the celebrations). That Pablo Escobar himself had called him a schmuck – that El Patrón was angry that he had not given Nacional more decisions and made sure they won inside the 90 minutes. Pablo was furious that the match, the tie, the whole competition, had been decided by spot kicks, that it had all boiled down to a game of Russian roulette from 12 yards. The Argentinian duo are left in no doubt that the only reason that they are even both still alive to have this shocking conversation is that somehow Nacional had triumphed without their intervention. If the match, the shoot-out, had gone the other way, and Nacional had failed at the final hurdle, it was an absolute certainty that an enraged Escobar would have had all three officials killed.

His ire quenched, his anger sated, Pablo is finally able to enjoy his moment of personal glory, of triumph. He – Pablo Escobar – has given the fans of Nacional, the people of Medellín, of the whole of Colombia, the greatest moment in their footballing history. He invites the entire Nacional squad to his ranch for the kind of epic celebration only a narcotraficante can engineer. The whole team attends, are paid their extravagant bonuses by an ecstatic Pablo, and are even given the chance to win a new truck in an impromptu raffle he holds. Pablo is in his element, surrounded by the young men who he sees as friends, to whom he has gifted fame, fortune and football. But it is not long before the taste of victory sours, if not for Escobar then certainly for all true fans of Colombian football . . .

CONMEBOL, the South American Football Confederation, take the extraordinary step of banning all Colombian clubs from playing any of their home matches in the 1990 tournament in Colombia, due to (perhaps understandable) security concerns. As a result, all except

Nacional are forced to skip this next edition of the Copa Libertadores. For the public, the people, the hearts and minds Pablo so desired to win over, the 1989 victory is forever tainted, a stain in Colombian football where once, however briefly, there had been the silvery glint of victory, of pride, of joy, of the Copa.

But Pablo's Nacional, desperate to defend their trophy, agree to play all their home games in the competition abroad, in Chile. For the fans it is a disaster and a source of shame that remains to this day. To Escobar it barely matters. His reach extends easily beyond the border, and he will have no trouble still influencing matches.

In fact, in 1990, following a 0-0 draw in the first leg of their quarter-final tie against Vasco de Gama of Brazil, Pablo offers his plata o plomo, $20,000 or death, to Uruguayan referee Juan Daniel Cardellino. Nacional win the second leg 2-0, but the home side's protests lead to a replay. Nacional win that match 1-0, and progress to the semis regardless – but are knocked out, in a twist of fate, by Olimpia. The Paraguayans go on to lift the trophy and exact some measure of revenge over Pablo and Nacional. The referee in the second leg of the final is none other than Juan Carlos Loustau.

Chapter Eleven

All Out War (1989)

Pablo has just achieved the pinnacle of his footballing ambitions, he has brought the Copa Libertadores, the most prestigious club trophy in Latin America, to Medellín. The team he has supported since he was a boy, Atlético Nacional, are the champions of all of South America. But victory on the pitch is one thing, victory on the streets, and over his enemies in the corridors of power, is quite another. Pablo decides to up the ante in his war, in his own words: 'We will create such chaos, they will beg for peace.'

It is Tuesday 30 May 1989, the day before the second leg of the final. At 7:25am the Carrera Septima (Seventh Avenue), one of Bogotá's key arterial roads, is packed with rush hour commuters. School children group together in clusters at the bus stop near the junction with Calle 56 (56th Street). A five-car motorcade drives by. The armoured Mercedes-Benz in the middle contains General Miguel Maza Márquez, the head of Colombia's Department of Security, the DAS. The secret service boss has attracted the Medellín Cartel's anger; in April he accused Pablo and El Mexicano of operating 'death squads' and being responsible for the rise in drug-related killings and political assassinations in Colombia.

Maza's cavalcade cruises past a parked car, and seconds later the street explodes; 220lb of dynamite blow a crater in the road. Five people unlucky enough to be in the vicinity of the blast lose their lives. A mile away windows are blown out, shattered by the force of the blast. Up and down Carrera Septima, for a ten-block radius, pedestrians are knocked to the ground. A hundred will suffer wounds from the attack, including ten school children. Two of the support vehicles in the motorcade are destroyed, along with six other civilian cars. The general's reinforced Merc avoids the brunt of the impact, however.

Taxi driver Ricardo Martinez is driving down Carrera Septima when the blast produces a six-storey blaze, and his windshield is sprayed with dust and fragments of shrapnel and debris. Through the smoke and chaos, he can hear shouts and screams. He's flagged down by one of Maza's security detail, who helps the stunned general into the cab and asks Ricardo to drive him and two DAS agents, one of whom appears seriously wounded, to a nearby military hospital. Two hours later General Maza is discharged, having suffered nothing more than a series of cuts and bruises.

The attack has failed, but it is only the start of an escalation of violence perpetrated by Pablo and the cartel. Over the coming months judge María Helena Díaz and magistrate Carlos Valencia García will be gunned down by motorcycle riding sicarios, and the governor of Antioquia, Antonio Roldán Betancur, murdered by a Medellín car bomb.

Just days after the Carrera Septima bombing, Luis Carlos Galán, the man who publicly refused the support of Pablo in 1982, announces he will once more run for president. And, like his friend Rodrigo Lara Bonilla, whom Pablo had killed when he was Minister of Justice, he makes extradition the key policy in his campaign, a campaign that is aimed squarely at taking down the cartels. A powerful, emotive orator, he lays out his vision, looking more like Pablo than Lara in a bright red polo shirt tucked into cream chinos, as he proclaims 'from today forward, if we remain organized, we will reclaim our country and blaze a new path to a new society!' If he is in any doubt as to the risk he is taking, it is made clear when, while in Medellín, on Pablo's home turf, a rocket-propelled grenade (RPG) attack narrowly fails to kill him.

It is 18 August 1989. Colonel Valdemar Franklin Quintero, commander of the Antioquia police and the man who had helped thwart the RPG attack on Galán, sits in his chauffeur-driven car, waiting for a Medellín traffic light to change from red to green. Before his vehicle can pull away, a car blocks its path. Six gunmen emerge and open fire. They don't stop shooting until their clips are empty, the car is riddled with bullet holes, and the colonel is dead.

The same evening, 250 miles south, Luis Carlos Galán is preparing to speak at a rally in the main square of Soacha, a working-class suburb just outside Bogotá's city limits. Ten thousand have gathered to hear the 45-year-old firebrand speak. Under his shirt he is wearing a bulletproof vest, insisted upon by his *Jefe de Debate*, his 'debate chief', César Gaviria. The RPG attack was a close call, and the candidate is all too aware of the fate of his friend Lara. Gaviria had, however, failed to dissuade Galán from visiting Soacha altogether, despite his insistence that it was dangerous, and a serious security risk.

As he steps up onto a low platform, takes his position behind the microphone and raises his arms to address the crowd, the vest rides up beneath Galán's shirt. Simultaneously, there's the hint of movement out among the masses, a poster ripples, a man steps forward, and then a shot rings out. And another. Galán goes down. The crowd surges, and in the ensuing chaos, to the percussive sound of machine gun fire, a photographer beside Galán hears him call to his men to get him to hospital.

He is carried to a car, the bullet wounds in his stomach, where the flesh was left exposed as the vest lifted, leaking blood. His men lift his legs and swing him in, his leather shoes shiny and clean. Ten are injured in the shooting. Luis Carlos Galán dies from his wounds.

Maza and the DAS will later claim it was El Mexicano rather than Pablo who ordered the hit. And, many years later, leading Liberal politician Alberto Santofimio Botero will be convicted of involvement in the assassination. Whatever the truth, Galán was a crusader who, like John F. Kennedy in the USA, had made some enemies in high and dangerous places. But in 1989 the general consensus is that it was the Medellín Cartel, and most likely Pablo himself, who had Galán killed. Now it is open war between the Colombian State and Pablo and the narcos.

President Virgilio Barco calls a national state of emergency and uses his extraordinary powers to reactivate the extradition treaty, which had been suspended by the Supreme Court, without the need for congressional approval. In his own words:

'This is not an isolated incident. We have learned the hard lesson of tolerating this criminal organization and its deranged leader. The Colombian government will dedicate all resources to dismantle Pablo Escobar's drug cartel.'

Barco has already appointed Colonel Hugo Martínez (known as *Flaco*, 'Skinny') to lead El Bloque de Búsqueda, the Search Bloc, the highly trained unit of 700 of the most trusted Colombian police, trained by members of the US Delta Force and tasked with taking out

Pablo and his cartel. Now the Colombian president goes one further, and finally relents and openly welcomes US support, which comes in the form of a renewed appetite from George HW Bush to wage, and win, the War on Drugs.

In response, Pablo's terror attacks ramp up again. The Medellín Cartel threaten to kill ten judges for every person extradited. Pablo's bombing campaign intensifies. He pushes the government, demanding a truce and a chance to take extradition off the table. Barco refuses and immediately sanctions a major raid on the Hacienda Nápoles, with intelligence and support provided by the DEA.

It is the early morning of Saturday 2 September 1989. Two men in a 1987 Chevrolet panel truck branded with a ladies' underwear logo pull into a petrol station in Bogotá. Beyond the pumps they can see the back of the two-storey *El Espectador* building – Colombia's oldest newspaper, whose editor was gunned down by Pablo's sicarios three years earlier.

When the attendant approaches, they let him know that they're going to grab a coffee while he fills her up. But, as soon as he turns to grab the pump, they sprint over the road to a grey Mazda sedan that is idling nearby. The car drives off. Across the street early morning commuters are clambering onto two buses. It's 6:40am when 220lb of dynamite in the truck are ignited by a timing device and explode, setting alight 11,000 gallons of fuel stored beneath the petrol station. The immense explosion is felt 18 miles away, and the blast blows out windows in a 2-mile radius and shatters every pane of glass in *El Espectador* office building. The truck is almost completely vaporized; all that remains is the transmission that sits smouldering in the bottom of a crater 10ft deep, and the bumper that lands 50ft away in the newspaper's car park. A part-time reporter and paper delivery driver who is unlucky enough to be close to the blast is killed. Nearly a hundred more are injured, many of them the bus passengers over the road from the petrol station.

The explosion has caused $1 million of damage at *El Espectador* but, just like after the assassination of their editor Guillermo Cano in 1986, the paper refuses to bow to the intimidation. That same evening the staff have sufficiently repaired the damaged presses and electronic editing system to enable them to run off the first copies of Sunday's paper, featuring a page 1 editorial headlined 'Over the Rubble'.

But it is not the last bomb. Over the coming days explosions rock the *Vanguardia Liberal* paper, the Cartagena Hilton and numerous other sites across Bogotá. A man dressed as a nun plants a bomb that explodes outside the Banco Popular in Medellín.

Then, with President Bush's promised aid, both financial and material, beginning to arrive in Colombia in earnest to assist the local forces in the war on drugs, Pablo's attacks increasingly target US interests in the country. He has a US military plane firebombed when it is on the ground for maintenance. Another bomb is found and defused at the Colgate-Palmolive offices in Cali.

On Sunday 17 September two bombs explode in bank offices in northern Bogotá. Less than 45 minutes later, at 8:55pm, there's a loud bang and thud as something strikes the wall of the US Embassy. It is a homemade rocket, and thankfully the damage it causes is minimal and no one is seriously injured. Police later find an identical device discarded, unfired, in a park half a mile away.

Up until now Pablo's terror attacks have focused on Medellín, but now, as he brings his war to Bogotá and threatens US citizens, he only succeeds in galvanizing the efforts to stop him at all costs. Less than a week after the Embassy attack, Pablo is almost captured. When the

Colombian authorities track him to the El Oro farm in the Magdalena Medio he escapes by the skin of his teeth, running for his life through a muddy, unplanted field. But one of the circling army helicopters guns down his brother-in-law Mario as he flees. Tata's beloved brother is dead, and Pablo and Popeye are forced into several weeks of escape and evasion.

While on the run Pablo is at least able to enjoy Colombia's qualification for the 1990 World Cup, due to be held in Italy the following summer. In October Los Cafeteros are victorious in their two-legged play-off against Israel, a 0-0 draw in the second match in Tel Aviv, largely thanks to a string of saves by the inspired René Higuita, enough to see them win 1-0 on aggregate. Across the cities of Colombia the streets are filled with the celebrations, fans waving flags and drivers tooting their horns. President Barco even invites the squad to the palace to hail their sporting achievement. But before the joy of a first World Cup campaign in almost thirty years, and barely six months after Atlético Nacional win the Copa Libertadores, El Patrón will bring Colombian football to its knees . . .

Left Pablo Escobar's infamous 'smiling' mugshot, taken after his 1976 arrest.

Below The arch marking the entrance to Pablo's beloved Hacienda Nápoles.

Above Pablo relaxes with his son Juan Pablo.

Above Pablo – the 'Paisa Robin Hood' – taking the ceremonial kick-off to open a football pitch he donated to the impoverished and young of Moravia in Medellín.

Above President George HW Bush lauds a successful operation in the 'war on drugs'.

SE BUSCA

PABLO EMILIO ESCOBAR GAVIRIA

SOLICITADO POR LA JUSTICIA

A quién suministre información que permita su captura, se le ofrece como recompensa

$ 2.700´000.000.oo
DOS MIL SETECIENTOS MILLONES DE PESOS.

JHON JAIRO VELASQUEZ VASQUEZ (Alias POPEYE)

LUIS CARLOS AGUILAR GALLEGO (Alias EL MUGRE)

OTONIEL DE JESUS GONZALES FRANCO (Alias OTTO)

JHON JAIRO ARIAS TASCON (Alias PININA)

y por cada uno de estos prófugos la suma de

$ 100´000.000.oo
(CIEN MILLONES DE PESOS)

Right A Pablo Escobar 'Wanted' poster, promising a reward of 2.7 billion pesos – and also offering rewards for his inner circle including 'Popeye'.

Above Fans line the streets of Medellín to celebrate Atlético Nacional's controversial triumph i the 1989 Copa Libertadores, the fi ever for a Colombian side.
Left Francisco 'Pacho' Maturana.

Above Atlético Nacional (in their famous green shirts) take on European giants AC Mila in the Intercontinental Cup in Tokyo. Alberico Evani is pictured curling in the extra time free kick, past 'Chonto' Herrera (number 4), that won the game for the Italian side.

Above The Estadio Atanasio Girardot in Medellín today, home of Atlético Nacional and Deportivo Independiente (DIM).

Right Colombian captain Carlos 'El Pibe' Valderrama on the ball in the 1990 World Cup round of 16 game against Cameroon. Colombia would lose 2-1 and be eliminated from the tournament.

Below La Catedral prison complex, perched on the hillside above Medellín.

Above A crowd gathers around the prone form of Pablo Escobar on a Medellín rooftop in the moments after his death.

Left Just some of the estimated 20,000 who went to the cemetery on the day of Pablo Escobar's funeral in Medellín.

Opposite top left Andrés Escobar moments after scoring the fateful own goal in a 1994 World Cup match against the USA.

Top right Fans mob the funeral car containing the body of murdered footballer Andrés Escobar as it drives through the streets of Medellín.

Right René 'El Loco' Higuita wows the crowd with a new, unique trick move – dubbed the 'scorpion kick' – in Colombia's friendly game against England at Wembley, clearing the ball (out of shot)

Above Miguel Rodríguez Orejuela is escorted off a plane in Bogotá following his capture in Cali.

Above A riot of colour: Colombia fans at the 2001 Copa América – the first and only time they have won the tournament.

Chapter Twelve

Pablo's War on Football (1989)

On 26 October 1989 the other giant of Antioquenian football, Deportivo Independiente Medellín, are playing an away game in Cali. Like Nacional, DIM are a side bankrolled by Pablo and his cartel. And, in this 42nd edition of the *Campeonato Colombiano*, they are looking the most likely of the trio of Medellín Cartel teams (Nacional, DIM and Millonarios) to challenge the América side belonging to the Cali Cartel.

The referee at the Estadio Pascual Guerrero is 32-year-old father of two Álvaro Ortega. With just two minutes left, América are leading Medellín 3-2. Then, in the 89th minute, teenage striker Carlos Castro, in his debut season, scores what looks like a late, late equalizer for DIM. Pablo, following the game from afar, is ecstatic. But moments later Ortega chalks off the goal for a foul in the build-up. Pablo is apoplectic with rage. He is convinced his side have been robbed, that the ref has been bought by the Cali Cartel. He tells Popeye he wants Ortega dead.

Three weeks later Ortega is due to be one of the linesmen in the return fixture, with DIM taking on América at the Atanasio Girardot in Medellín. The other linesman was to be his close friend, and his fellow touch judge in the controversial 3-2 match, Jesús Díaz. It was Díaz who, after the kidnapping of Armando Pérez, had famously said 'all that remains is for them to kill a referee'. In fact, Díaz – Colombia's leading referee, a national celebrity who fans asked for autographs and who had officiated at the World Cup and the Olympics – had tried, and failed, to convince Ortega to refuse to officiate the match after the late drama in Cali.

At midday on Wednesday 15 November Ortega receives a call in his hotel room. He seems distressed but, when pressed by his friend, tells Díaz he will tell him what it was about after the game. Instead, the pair head out to a nearby shopping centre to buy clothes for their families back home.

The game kicks off at 8:30pm. With neither team having anything serious to play for it is to all intents and purposes a 'dead rubber'. And, true to form, it is an uneventful 0-0 draw, with no contentious refereeing decisions.

By the time Ortega and Díaz are clear of the stadium it is nearly 11pm. They are dropped off near their hotel, but at their restaurant of choice, Dino, they are told the cook has already left for the night. They each have a drink and then decide to walk the few yards up the street to another restaurant, Sorpresa ('Surprise'). As they walk, Díaz asks again about the call. Before his friend can reply, they hear the squeal of tyres behind them and turn to see a gunman getting out of a car. Ignoring Díaz, he fires at Ortega as he attempts to flee, and a bullet catches the official in the leg and puts him down. Pushing past Díaz, the shooter closes on Ortega, grabs him by the throat and fires nine rounds into him from point-blank range. As he leaves, the killer assures Díaz he is safe, at least for now.

Díaz carries the bullet-riddled, bleeding body of his friend across the street, but no one will stop for them. Eventually a homeless man helps him get Ortega into a car, but not without surreptitiously stealing the wounded man's wallet. Only minutes later Díaz is in the nearby Soma Clinic being told his friend and fellow referee has not made it. Álvaro Ortega is dead, killed on the orders of Pablo Escobar. It is not yet midnight when the national radio stations are reporting the news – they have killed a referee in Medellín. DIM's star midfielder Oscar Parejo hears the news. He feels numb. He knows the club's ownership is shady but, as a footballer, he doesn't ask too many questions. But now he knows the whole country will be in no doubt as to what is going on in Colombian football. It is surely a point of no return for the era of narcoball.

Díaz feels compelled to write to João Havelange, the President of FIFA, to withdraw from refereeing at the upcoming 1990 World Cup in Italy. His family begs him to retire, fearing that he too will be killed. The Colombian Football Federation has finally had enough and a week later the Colombian referees' association, Dimayor, takes the extraordinary step of cancelling the 1989 Campeonato with the following statement:

'The law of the bullet is killing our sport. We cannot allow a competition to continue that is dominated by psychological coercion and physical threats . . . no more deaths, no more massacres, and no more blood.'

It is the first and only time that Colombian football will not have a league champion. In just a few months Pablo has gone from seeing Nacional win the Copa Libertadores for Medellín and all of Colombia, to causing the total suspension of football in his country.

Four months after the slaying of Álvaro Ortega, the head of Dimayor resigns. In 2009, due to Colombia's 20-year statute of limitation, the still unsolved case relating to the murder is officially closed. And yet despite, or in fact because of, the tragic fate of his uncle, a young man by the name of Carlos Ortega decides he too wants to be a professional referee. He will eventually rise to become one of Colombia's top officials.

*

Pablo's actions have had one further, very specific and unforeseen immediate consequence, however. Atlético Nacional, as winners of the 1989 Copa Libertadores, have for the first time in their history, indeed in a first for Colombian football, qualified to play in the Intercontinental Cup – a trophy pitting the best club side in South America against the champions of Europe. Nacional are due to play the winners of the European Cup: Italian giants AC Milan. With the game set for 17 December, Milan are keen to find out more about their little-known Colombian opposition. Chairman Silvio Berlusconi and manager Arrigo Sacchi dispatch scouts to Medellín to keep tabs on Maturana's side – but Ortega's murder and the subsequent suspension of the domestic league means they have no chance of watching Nacional play any competitive football.

And so, while Pablo's war rages in Colombia, his beloved Nacional leave Medellín and fly nearly 9,000 miles to Japan where, in Tokyo's National Stadium, they will face off against AC Milan in a bid to be crowned the best club side in world football. Sixty thousand pack the ground, built in Shinjuku for the 1958 Asian Games and 1964 Summer Olympics, to bear witness to a match that has become a political hot potato – following Berlusconi's inflammatory comments about the Milan side's opposition, the Italian vowing that his side 'would fight Nacional to defeat the dirty part of the world'.

Without the distraction of domestic competition, and the risk of injuries caused by competitive matches, Pacho Maturana is able to field a strong Nacional side. In goal, as ever, the maverick sweeper-keeper and penalty scoring and saving specialist René Higuita. At the back the likes of Chonto Herrera are marshalled by the calm, elegant centre half Andrés Escobar. Captain Alexis García and Leonel Álvarez are a strong, potent midfield duo. Up front is the prolific John Jairo Tréllez, with cult hero El Palomo – Albeiro Usuriaga – ready to make an impact from the bench. As ever, Pablo and Pacho's side is 100 per cent Colombian.

But their Milanese opposition for this, the greatest moment in the Medellín club's history, is one of the best club sides ever to grace a football pitch. Sacchi's team boasts two foreign players – and they are two of the most gifted footballers the Netherlands has ever produced, Ballon d'Or winning striker Marco van Basten and midfielder Frank Rijkaard. The rest of the team is made up of Italian players who will go down in the history books as some of the finest to play the game. Paolo Maldini, still only 21, forms an impenetrable back line with Alessandro Costacurta and club captain Franco Baresi. And in the middle of the park Rijkaard is joined by Diego Fuser, Roberto Donadoni and future managerial legend Carlo Ancelotti. New signing Marco Simone offers goals and creativity from the bench – a testament to the squad depth of the European champions.

If the game is a boxing match then Nacional edge the first half on points, without creating any clearcut openings. The biggest cheers from the Japanese crowd are reserved for the quirky but effective goalkeeping antics of Higuita as he sprints from his goal, or dives at the feet of an attacker, or palms the ball away from the opposition before starting a counterattack with a quick throw out. There are some oohs and aahs from the stands as the skilful Colombians are on the wrong side of some rugged tackling from the Italians. For Milan, both Rijkaard and van Basten come close with snatched half chances from the edge of the Nacional box. The Colombians threaten, their combination of possession and pace and trickery putting the Milan midfield and back line under pressure. But, after 45 minutes, the two sides are still locked at 0-0. Maturana is the first to blink, the Nacional coach throwing on two subs at half time, El Palomo among them, in the search for a breakthrough.

Milan start well, pressing the Colombians back and peppering Higuita with crosses, high balls and long range strikes. But Nacional continue to threaten on the break with the pace of the fresh and long-legged Usuriaga. Still neither team can find the net. On 65 minutes, Sacchi makes a change to the left side of his midfield, bringing on Alberico Evani for Fuser. Not long after, he introduces Simone from the bench too. But no goals come. The best chance of the match falls to van Basten, but Higuita throws himself bravely at the striker's feet to prevent a certain goal. At 90 minutes it's still a goalless draw.

And so the two teams prepare for extra time. The clock ticks down. Half time in extra time comes, and still there is nothing to separate the sides. Locked in mortal combat they parry and thrust, Milan gradually gaining the ascendancy, van Basten coming within inches of giving his side the lead with a volley on the turn. But with just two minutes left before penalties the deadlock remains unbroken. Having won the Copa Libertadores in a shoot-out, inspired by the exploits of Higuita between the sticks, Nacional must surely be optimistic about their chances. But then, disaster.

Van Basten breaks with the ball, turning and powering away from the defenders towards the Nacional box. A despairing lunge from a green shirt brings him down. For a split second it's unclear whether a penalty has been given, but no, a direct free kick barely a yard outside the penalty area is correctly awarded. Wearing number 14, the second-half substitute Evani steps up and curls a left-footed free kick around the outside of the Nacional wall. Partially unsighted by his own players, and with the ball taking a faint deflection off the thigh of one, Higuita is only able to watch it spin just inside his right-hand post and into the net. With 119 minutes gone, there is no time for Nacional to find an equalizer. The Milan players run to the centre circle, punching the air, certain now of their victory. For Higuita, for Nacional, and for Pablo back in Colombia, it is a heartbreaking way to fall agonizingly short.

But for two hours, in the Tokyo sunshine, a team made up entirely of Colombians has gone toe to toe with a truly great football team and come within moments of besting them. Colombian football wins many a new admirer. And one player in particular catches the eye of the AC Milan hierarchy – the calm young defender known as El Caballero, Andrés Escobar. And they will not forget the potential they have seen in him . . .

Chapter Thirteen

Pablo the Narcoterrorist (1989)

The murder of Álvaro Ortega in mid-November rocks Colombia, but Pablo's next major assassination attempt will shock the entire world. And it comes in the same month, and only 12 days later.

At 7:13am on 27 November 1989 Avianca flight 203, a domestic flight from Bogotá to Cali, takes off from the El Dorado airport in Colombia's capital. The Boeing 727 has 107 passengers and crew aboard. It climbs steadily away from the Andean plateau across which the city spreads, its distant streets, far below, still coming to life as the morning arrives. By 7:18am it is travelling at nearly 500mph, at an altitude of 13,000ft.

One of the passengers is a 19-year-old lad from Medellín, who sits uncomfortably in his rather too expensive clothes in a seat that happens to be directly over the Boeing's fuel tanks. Unbeknown to anyone else aboard, this young man is actually a recently-recruited member of the Medellín Cartel. Over the course of the preceding weeks and months Pablo's men have trained and tested him, having him take packages for them and blindly follow their orders, and rewarding the impressionable teenager with money and clothes. For he is to be the *Suiza*, the 'Swiss' – and their patsy.

The young man, travelling as 'Alberto Prieto', has boarded alone, carrying a black nylon suitcase given to him by one of Pablo's men who, at the last minute, had declined to take the flight. It is this confusion that leads to a small delay to take-off for the plane, which had been scheduled for 7am. The flight attendant offers coffee to the passengers, as some of those in the rear smoking seats light up their cigarettes. Next to 'Prieto' is the empty seat that was due to be occupied by his compadre, the man with a ticket in the name of Mario Santodomingo.

Five minutes into the delayed flight, at 7:18am, 'Prieto' opens the case and flicks a switch on the recording device within. But he is not on board to covertly capture the conversations of a fellow passenger, as he has been told. And what is secreted in the case is no tape recorder. He is the unwitting trigger man for a bomb. As the plane flies over the town of Soacha on the outskirts of Bogotá, the very place where Pablo has recently had Luis Galán gunned down at a rally, 11lb of dynamite explode, blowing the plane in half. It crashes to earth, killing three innocent bystanders on the ground. All 107 aboard perish.

News camera crews arrive on the scene to find debris scattered across the rocky mountainside, blackened pieces of the plane still smoking, the giant white Avianca letters still visible on one side of a section of the red body of the plane that has somehow remained in one piece. The landing gear and wheels are still on fire.

Two of the dead hold US passports. Initially the American Embassy, and the news teams on the ground, believe a faulty fuel tank might have exploded and caused the horrific accident. But it soon becomes clear that the plane was blown up with explosives. The death certificates of the two Americans give their cause of death as 'blunt trauma due to falling from aircraft'. Now Pablo can be charged with terrorism – and with killing US citizens. It's all the impetus George

HW Bush needs to ratchet up the war on drugs. And finally, the whole world knows Pablo for what he truly is – the planet's first, and most brutal, narcoterrorist.

One passenger who is meant to be onboard the ill-fated plane, but is not, is César Gaviria Trujillo – the leading liberal candidate in the upcoming Colombian elections. Gaviria stepped into the breach, filling the role left open following the assassination of his friend and colleague Galán. It is Gaviria who Pablo wants dead, and he had devised the entire attack based on the candidate's planned itinerary. More than one hundred innocent people have perished, but the one person Pablo wanted killed is still alive. As ever, Pablo's strategy when faced with disappointment is to double down, to press on at all costs rather than relent.

*

It is 6 December 1989, barely more than a week since Pablo blew a commercial passenger plane out of the sky and killed 110 people. At 7:28am General Miguel Maza Márquez has just arrived at his desk, in his partially-reinforced office, on one of the upper floors of the 11-storey DAS headquarters in Paloquemao, in the southwest of Bogotá. The surrounding streets and buildings are already thronging with commuters and workers in this busy industrial, commercial and administrative part of Colombia's capital city. A huge explosion rocks the DAS building, blowing away much of its façade, ripping through its interior, and bringing the ceiling crashing down on Maza. He miraculously escapes unharmed, but as he makes his way through the dust, smoke and rubble he sees a body, trapped and lifeless. It is one of eight victims killed inside DAS HQ. The calls of injured and scared secretaries echo through the building.

Outside, the carnage is even worse. A 1961 Chevrolet truck, loaded with over 1,000lb of dynamite – from the same stash of the explosive imported from Ecuador, kept in a secret warehouse in Bogotá and used by Pablo and the Medellín Cartel to blow up Avianca flight 203 and also in their previous attempt to kill Maza himself with a car bomb on the Carrera Septima – has been detonated.

An entire complex of two-storey commercial buildings collapses. Well over 50 people in the neighbouring buildings, and out on the street, are killed. Over 2,000 are injured. The blast leaves a crater 10ft deep in the road. Windows shatter in a 26-block area around the epicentre. Hundreds of commercial properties, spanning more than a dozen city blocks, are destroyed, with losses of close to five billion pesos. The wounded stagger through streets strewn with rubble, destroyed cars and the bodies of the dead.

Pablo has just detonated the single deadliest car bomb attack in all of Latin America up to this point. But Maza is still alive. Once more Pablo has failed, but yet again scores of innocent victims perish, collateral damage in his war.

And, with war raging, there is another man, a key figure in the Medellín Cartel, who the authorities on both sides of the Atlantic are almost as desperate to stop as they are Pablo: his fellow billionaire drug lord, and the power behind Millonarios, José Gonzalo Rodríguez Gacha, aka El Mexicano. Up until now, the Colombians have managed to confiscate properties and assets belonging to Pablo and El Mexicano, and have come within minutes of capturing both of them, but they have resolutely failed to apprehend any of the top tier of the cartel. One person they do have under lock and key is El Mexicano's teenage son, Freddy. In December 1989 the young man is released, the authorities finally admitting they have insufficient evidence to prosecute him on a weapons possession charge. But Freddy is being freed for one reason only – to act as bait. Days later, unaware his every move is being watched by undercover Colombian police, Freddy finally goes to visit his father.

On 15 December, two days before Nacional play AC Milan in Tokyo, two Colombian military helicopters packed with members of the Search Bloc buzz over a farm in the village of El Tesoro, on Colombia's Caribbean coast. It is here, not far from the historic port town of Cartagena, but far north of both Pablo's base of operations in Medellín and his own adopted home turf of Bogotá, that El Mexicano is hiding out. Freddy's return to the paternal bosom, and the intel of a police informant within the Medellín Cartel known as *El Navegante*, 'The Navigator', have helped the authorities zero in on the location. But as they circle, and demand on their loudspeakers that Rodríguez Gacha give himself up, the farm workers below ignore them. It is only when the choppers refuse to withdraw that the labourers bolt for a red truck nearby, and it is revealed that they are in fact El Mexicano and his men, in disguise.

Pursued by the helicopters, eventually Freddy and some of the bodyguards jump out of the truck and run for a stand of trees, shooting at the aircraft. Several are killed by fire from the mounted machine guns on one of the choppers, which lands to allow members of the Search Bloc to get out and pursue on foot. They catch up with Freddy and gun him down in the ensuing firefight. Meanwhile the second helicopter is still pursuing El Mexicano in the truck. When the fugitives are blocked off on the road by police vehicles they are forced to run for it. El Mexicano almost gets caught in barbed wire and, bleeding and desperate, he fires off his machine gun at the helicopter overhead. Having given away his location, he's a sitting duck. The machine gun mounted on the chopper fires away, bringing him down with a shot to the leg before the kill shot rips through his skull.

The Colombian authorities have their biggest scalp yet in the war against Pablo and the Medellín Cartel, and El Patrón has suffered the single most damaging blow to his organization and his survival thus far. Two days later, on 17 December – the same day that Nacional fall to a 119th minute goal by AC Milan in the Intercontinental Cup final in Tokyo – 15,000 mourners pack the streets of El Mexicano's hometown of Pacho for his funeral.

Meanwhile, Pablo learns of El Navegante's treachery. This is a man close to the centre of the cartel's power, who knows a lot not just about how Pablo runs his operation but also his elaborate security protocols. Pablo knows his safety is dangerously compromised. He is forced to change up all his vehicles, safe houses, bodyguards and messengers. Now no longer living on the run but living in fear, he will barely see his family for the first six months of 1990.

Chapter Fourteen

A New Hope (1990)

But 1990 starts promisingly for Pablo. The unrelenting pressure his terror campaign has put on the administration is looking like it might bear fruit. In January he hands over three high profile hostages. President Barco softens his rhetoric, suggesting the government might lessen the sentences of any narcos who willingly hand themselves in. In February, to coincide with the visit of George HW Bush to Colombia, Pablo – under the guise of 'The Extraditables' – hands over a cocaine lab in Urabá, a school bus stuffed with dynamite and a helicopter. The symbolic gestures hint at a de-escalation in the bloody war.

On 22 March presidential hopeful Bernardo Jaramillo Ossa is about to take a break from weeks of intensive campaigning. He has received numerous death threats but refuses to wear a protective vest. Waiting for a flight to Santa Marta in the Puente Aéreo terminal of the capital city's El Dorado airport he walks past a pharmacy with his wife when a young man approaches the couple. Before his bodyguards can intercede, the teenager draws a Mini Ingram 380 machine gun and fires on Jaramillo. The politician dies on his way to the operating room of the nearby police hospital.

Although the candidate had an anti-extradition stance, Pablo is blamed for Jaramillo's assassination – although much later many will feel it more likely Jaramillo was killed on the orders of paramilitary leader Fidel Castaño. Next the press leak the suggestion that the government has been secretly negotiating with Pablo – and that he released the hostages in order to gain exemption from extradition. Deal or no deal, the damage is done. The government are forced to publicly deny any such agreement – and aggressively reaffirm the need for unconditional surrender.

Pablo retaliates. Car bombs rock Bogotá, Medellín and Cali. He openly attacks the Search Bloc wherever possible. And he launches the infamous 'Operation Pistol' – offering two million pesos for every police officer killed. Being a policeman in Medellín becomes the most dangerous job in the world, hundreds are killed. At the near-constant funerals, DEA agents share the front rows with their senior Colombian counterparts in the police. The US Embassy considers pulling out the chief of the DEA office in Colombia as he now has a bounty on his head.

Soon it is open warfare. President Barco marshals the state's forces of the army and police against Pablo the narcoterrorist and his Medellín Cartel. On the streets of Medellín, narcos arrive in columns of armoured cars to battle the authorities. Helicopters buzz the sky and tanks block the roads. Troops rappel down onto rooftops and engage in gun fights with sicarios. The injured are dragged on stretchers down the streets as their allies return fire with submachine guns. Pablo and Popeye are Colombia's two most wanted men. Then, in the May election it is Galán's successor, César Gaviria, who wins out.

Pablo fears for his family, and decides he needs to get his 13-year-old son Juan Pablo as far away from Colombia as possible. His beloved football gives him the answer: Italia '90. Pablo packs his boy off to Europe in advance of the opening game of the World Cup, with a passport in a fake name and visas for a plethora of the surrounding countries too. Far from the threat of kidnapping, assassination or arrest, Juan Pablo is able to support Colombia in their first campaign for nearly 30 years.

The tournament starts on 8 June 1990, with a shock win for Cameroon over Argentina. Juan Pablo, unable to find a hotel room in Italy, is staying in Lausanne, Switzerland, and travelling across the border in disguise to attend games, following his dad's advice by sporting dark glasses with his face painted in the colours of the Colombian flag.

On 9 June, Italy start their campaign against Austria at the Stadio Olimpico. The home side squeak a 1-0 win, the goal introducing the world to the wild card in the Italian team, a certain Salvatore 'Toto' Schillaci. On the same day, in Bologna, Colombia are playing their first game in a World Cup since 1962, against the United Arab Emirates. For Pacho Maturana's side, all of them playing in a World Cup for the first time, it is a must-win game. They know anything less than victory will dent their hopes of escaping from a group that also contains Yugoslavia and West Germany. Their nerves threaten to get the better of them, but the sight of El Loco Higuita rushing way out of his penalty area to head clear galvanizes them. At half time, however, it's 0-0. Colombia know their tournament hopes rest on the next 45 minutes at the Stadio Renato Dall'Ara. Just five minutes after the restart, Leonel Álvarez carries the ball inside the UAE penalty box, gets to the by-line and pulls his chipped cross back to near the penalty spot – where Bernardo Redín nods powerfully home to give Los Cafeteros a precious lead. But the minutes tick on and Colombia can't find the crucial second goal to calm their nerves and put the match to bed. On 75 minutes, with the score still 1-0, Maturana makes a change, refreshing his front line by replacing Iguarán with Carlos Estrada. And then, just when it looks like they'll have to hold on for a priceless but unconvincing win, on 85 minutes, the substitute Estrada picks up the ball deep inside his own half. Spotting Valderrama racing towards the halfway line, he curls a raking 40-yard cross-field pass into his captain's path. El Pibe races towards the UAE goal before cutting inside onto his right foot and stroking an unerring 25-yard shot into the bottom corner. As the players hug each other in relief, the joyous fans wave their flags proudly in the stands.

Juan Pablo Escobar is in the crowd, camouflaged among his fellow fans, for the remaining two group games for Los Cafeteros. First comes a tight, tense game against a well-regarded Yugoslavia – where a sumptuous piece of chest control followed by a swivelled volley from Davor Jozić on 74 minutes is the difference. Five minutes later a trademark penalty save from Higuita bails out his teammate Perea, who had committed a needless handball inside the area. The game ends in defeat for Colombia, but the 1-0 scoreline is at least a huge improvement on the 5-0 drubbing Los Cafeteros had endured against the same opposition in the 1962 tournament. And their hopes of continuing in the tournament are still alive. Then comes the result that puts Colombia back on the footballing map . . .

Two days before Colombia's final group game, a letter from Pablo arrives in Lausanne for Tata, who has flown out to join her son in Europe. In it, El Patrón seems far more optimistic than previously. Gaviria, the president-elect, is not, it seems, a hard-line advocate for extradition. He is no Lara, no Galán, perhaps far more of a pragmatist than an idealistic firebrand. Pablo is growing increasingly confident that the new National Constituent Assembly members will write an article prohibiting extradition, and as a result he is considering de-escalating his war to help ensure extradition is taken off the table. Things are looking up, at last.

It is 19 June 1990. Over 70,000 fans, a teenage Juan Pablo Escobar hidden among them, are in Milan's famous San Siro stadium to see the mighty West Germany take on relative unknowns Colombia. The West Germans have already dispatched Yugoslavia 4-1, and the UAE 5-1, with Lothar Matthäus, Rudi Völler and Jürgen Klinsmann running riot, and Franz Beckenbauer's men are heavy favourites. Colombia know they must avoid defeat if they are to guarantee their escape from Group D.

And, for 88 minutes, René Higuita, Andrés Escobar, Luis Perea, Leonel Álvarez and company keep their lauded European opposition at bay. Their high defensive line draws a series of offsides, and when the Germans do find a way through they are met with rugged challenges from defenders, or Colombia's sweeper-keeper extravagantly mopping up behind. One shot seems destined for the top corner but Higuita leaps to fingertip it away. The Colombians begin to grow into the game, with Valderrama releasing his teammates with clever passes only to see their snatched efforts fail to trouble Bodo Illgner in the German goal. As the Europeans resort to roughing up El Pibe, Valderrama exhorts his midfield enforcer Leonel Álvarez to protect him, to strike back. He duly obliges, flying into a challenge on Matthäus that earns him a yellow card but ignites the fire in the bellies of the Colombians at last. In the stands, is the colourful 'Birdman' – *El Cole*, aka Gustavo Llanos, the law student from Barranquilla who quit his studies to become Colombia's number one fan, sleeping on the streets of Italy dressing as a brilliantly-coloured condor complete with giant wings.

He orchestrates the South Americans in the crowd, who can sense their team might be in with a chance. By half time tempers are already fraying on the pitch.

In the second half the sides trade chances without making the vital breakthrough. If anything, Colombia are edging the contest, creating the more clearcut opportunities but, as the minutes tick by, and knowing that a draw will see them qualify for the knockout stages, they try to shut the game down. It all seems to be going to plan until the diminutive Pierre Littbarski, on as a half-time substitute, receives the ball outside the Colombian penalty area with 88 minutes on the clock. A touch to steady himself, and he unleashes a left-foot shot from just inside the box that flies past Higuita. Germany lead.

The 90 minutes are up, and Colombia have only injury time left to salvage something. Then, with 92 minutes gone, a brilliant interchange of passes in the tightest of spaces beats the German press, and Valderrama threads a perfectly timed and weighted pass through the West German line for Freddy Rincón to run onto. Illgner rushes out, spreading himself wide and narrowing the angle. But Rincón calmly slots the ball between the keeper's legs. The net ripples. The Colombian players leap on each other's backs for joy, the colourful red, yellow and blue flags of their distant homeland waving in the crowd. One of the fans holding the rope that suspends the Birdman over the crowd below lets go, El Cole momentarily forgotten in his ecstasy. Luckily the rope is tied around another fan's waist, and Llanos's sudden plummet is halted before he is hurt. Moments later the final whistle is blown, and Colombia are into the knockout stages of a FIFA World Cup for the first time in their history.

For the round of 16, Colombia travel to Naples. Here, at the Stadio San Paolo, where another South American, Argentina's Diego

Maradona, is the footballing hero, Maturana's men will take on the tournament's surprise package. To make it to the quarter-finals, Colombia must overcome the Cameroon side who shocked the football-watching public with their opening day victory over Maradona and the defending world champions. Like Colombia, the African side have never made it out of the group stages of a World Cup before. With both teams in uncharted waters, the pressure unsurprisingly gets to them.

The game is scrappy, but Colombia edge the first half, creating more goalscoring opportunities and even rattling the frame of the goal with a thunderous free kick which cannons back off the junction of post and crossbar. The second half is equally stop-start, but the introduction of legendary Cameroon striker Roger Milla from the bench – at 38 the oldest outfield player in the tournament – leads to one of the clearest openings yet, but his shot is smothered by the alert Higuita. Cameroon grow into the game, and soon Colombia are increasingly relying on the last-ditch defending of Andrés Escobar and Luis Perea. Higuita is by far the busier keeper. But as the game inches towards the 90-minute mark, it's still an edgy, fractious and only occasionally entertaining 0-0.

In the first half of extra time, Colombia find a new gear, their subs injecting more pace and threat into their attacks. But still, no goal comes, and after 105 minutes it's all square. Then, moments after the restart, Milla skips past an outstretched Colombian leg, darts into the box, and slams a shot high past Higuita and into the net. Cameroon have the lead. Milla runs away to dance by the corner flag. Less than two minutes later Higuita is 20 yards outside his own penalty area when, struggling to control a first-time return pass from Perea, he decides to attempt a drag back to keep the ball away from the predatory Milla. The Cameroonian tackles the goalkeeper, drives towards the box and rolls the ball into the unguarded net from 18 yards out. Milla dances once more, as the Cameroonian tricolours wave in the crowd. 2-0 Cameroon, two goals for super sub Roger Milla, and surely that is goodnight Colombia.

Then Valderrama finds one last inch-perfect pass, and Colombia's own striking substitute Bernardo Redín tucks the ball home. There are four minutes of extra time remaining. Colombia pile forward, desperate to repeat the last gasp heroics that earned them a point against West Germany and a place in the knockouts. But it is not to be. The whistle blows, and Colombia are eliminated.

Higuita bravely volunteers to face the media at the post-match press conference, and selflessly shoulders the blame. But, in a tournament that will be remembered for Pavarotti's *Nessun Dorma*, for David Platt's 119th minute volley, for Gazza's tears and the goals of Roger Milla and Toto Schillaci, Colombia have made their mark. Few will have failed to see the potential in a side boasting Higuita, Escobar, Valderrama and Rincón, and when West Germany lift the trophy Maturana's side are able to hold their heads high knowing they drew with the team that would become world champions. In their first World Cup for 28 years, Los Cafeteros and their colourful fans have done their homeland proud. And Maturana's squad, packed with Atlético Nacional players, return to a Colombia where there is renewed hope that Pablo Escobar and a new president might just be able to bring an end to the violence at last.

Chapter Fifteen

A Gilded Cage (1990–1991)

On 7 August 1990, César Gaviria, Luis Carlos Galán's former campaign manager, is sworn in as the 28th president of Colombia. Pablo and the cartel have called a truce as they attempt to negotiate the removal of extradition from the Colombian constitution. But Gaviria refuses to stop the crackdown on the narcos, and it doesn't take long for the wheels to come off the peace process . . .

Just four days after César Gaviria takes office, Gustavo, Pablo's cousin, friend and key partner in the Medellín Cartel, is killed in a Search Bloc raid on a luxury apartment – complete with bulletproof glass windows – in southern Medellín. While the authorities decide not to trumpet their highest profile win in the war on drugs for fear of reprisals, it does little to placate a distraught Pablo.

Over the coming weeks, El Patrón arranges the kidnapping of numerous high-profile journalists and the relatives of senior political figures in a bid to turn the screw. At the same time he has not forgotten his war with Cali and, on 25 September 1990, 20 of Pablo's men attack the rival cartel, opening fire on them as they play football on a farm in Candelaria in the Valle del Cauca. Fourteen players are gunned down on the pitch, five more are slain on the touchline. But the key cartel members, including Hélmer 'Pacho' Herrera, Pablo's nemesis, escape. Newspapers report it as revenge for a failed plot by Cali to use a helicopter to drop a bomb on Pablo at the Hacienda Nápoles.

Pablo's kidnappings ramp up but, as he is once again engaged in a struggle on multiple fronts, he begins to fear that he might become the victim for once. His suspicions grow that Tata, Juan Pablo and Manuela, still hiding in Switzerland, might have been discovered, and that they might be at risk of a kidnap attempt. But then, just as it seems he might have bitten off more than he can chew, all of Pablo's devious work behind the scenes finally pays off.

The bargaining power afforded him by his high-profile hostages, and the incessant bribes and threats he – and even his rivals in Cali, who despite everything support his anti-extradition stance – have levied against the country's policy makers, have swayed the mind of the president. In December of 1990 Gaviria makes an extraordinary concession. He announces a new policy, an amendment to the pivotal Decree 2047, that allows for any narco to surrender, hand themselves in, confess to just a single crime, and avoid extradition. It is everything Pablo and his Extraditables have hoped for. The government will willingly surrender its most potent weapon in the war against the cartels. He immediately summons his family back to Colombia, and they go into hiding together in Medellín as he prepares the next stage of his plan.

However, the war is not over just yet. Search Bloc – known to many Colombians as the Elite Force – continue to hunt out and kill senior members of the cartel, among them David and Armando Prisco Lopera, two of the four brothers who led the armed group within the Medellín Cartel known as Los Priscos, and to rescue hostages still held by Pablo's men. Their efforts are not always successful, however. In late January 1991, a botched operation to free leading journalist, and daughter of a former president, Diana Turbay, leads to her accidental shooting. She dies when a bullet hits her in the back and fatally damages her liver and left kidney. The tragic story of her kidnapping will later feature in a non-fiction book – *Noticia de un Secuestro*, 'News of a Kidnapping' – penned by Colombia's greatest novelist, the Nobel Prize winner Gabriel García Márquez, known affectionately across Colombia as Gabo or Gabito. Meanwhile, despite their common aim of ending extradition, the Medellín and Cali cartels are still enemies – to the extent that Pablo continues to fear for the safety of his family, not least when he suspects Cali might be plotting to abduct his teenage son at a motorbike race. He sends the kids on a 'holiday' to the USA to keep them out of harm's way. It is just another bizarre chapter in the childhoods of Juan Pablo and Manuela Escobar.

Eventually it is a confessor and intermediary of sorts, Father García Herreros, who helps Pablo navigate the next stage in negotiations. The priest convinces El Patrón to release some of his key hostages. And on 20 May 1991 Maruja Pachón, the sister-in-law of Luis Carlos Galán, is set free. Her story too will form a key part of Gabito's book. Then, a month later, comes a day most in Colombia never imagined would arrive . . .

On 19 June Pablo wakes early at a farm in Envigado. He dresses as casually as ever – in blue jeans, dark socks, a white shirt and his ever-present trainers. At midday a crucial vote is held by the Constituent Assembly in Bogotá. In a preliminary ballot the government is defeated 51 to 13 in the vote over extradition. The law will be changed. Pablo has what he needs. In fact, he probably already knew this would be the outcome – as he has arranged his surrender for this very day. He has been preparing for this moment for some time, and every term has been carefully negotiated. The crux of the deal is that he will admit to the charges brought against him in return for a lenient sentence of only a handful of years to be served in a Colombian prison, and with no chance of extradition – and that his incarceration will take place at a new facility that he himself has designed: *La Catedral.*

With the vote decided, Pablo steps out onto a football pitch – naturally – attached to his hideout. He has given the negotiating team the details and they arrive to collect him, whisking him away in a helicopter. The skies are empty, a total airspace ban is in effect over all of Medellín to guarantee the safety of this momentous flight. The whole of Colombia holds its breath.

Pablo, accompanied by Father García, is flown up into the hills above Envigado, to his new home, a former drug addicts' rehabilitation centre that he has had converted into a secure prison facility. When he gets out of the chopper, which lands on a football pitch constructed within the prison at Pablo's request, he hands over his pearl-handled 9mm SIG Sauer pistol to the warden in a symbolic gesture of surrender.

Pablo being Pablo, he of course has some words to share with the nation, on this historic day:

'I have decided to hand myself in. With my surrender, I would like to recognize the members of the Constitutional Assembly for their noble contribution to national peace . . . as I surrender to the authorities, I'd like to pay homage to my parents, to my irreplaceable wife, to my 14-year-old pacifist son, to my toothless 7-year-old dancer, and to my whole family whom I love so much.'

As Pablo settles into life at La Catedral the Search Bloc is stood down, its leader Colonel Martínez sent to Spain on a diplomatic posting, and the Colombian political machine begins to enshrine in law the new constitution, which precludes extradition to the USA. Pablo is no longer being hunted by the authorities and, protected from his enemies in Cali by the security at La Catedral, he – along with the key members of his cartel who joined him in surrendering, Popeye principal among them – is able to enjoy his favourite pastime: football. Pablo is not only able to enjoy a kickabout on the pitch he has had built at his request, he is also able to follow the fortunes of Los Cafeteros on the radio and even on the giant televisions he has smuggled into his increasingly luxurious prison. And, 4,000 miles south of Medellín, the Colombian squad are about to embark on a new chapter in their story.

*

On 7 July Colombia open their 1991 Copa América campaign against Ecuador in Valparaíso, Chile. With only the top two teams in their five-team Group B qualifying for the four-team series of final matches, Los Cafeteros know they need to start strongly to escape from a group also containing Brazil, Uruguay and Bolivia. And, although the squad is still intact and based on the talent of El Pibe in midfield and the nucleus of Atlético Nacional players including Higuita and Andrés Escobar, the side has a new manager in Luis Augusto García. Pacho Maturana has in fact not only left his post as national team manager, but has also taken a new job away from Pablo and Nacional entirely – as the coach of Real Valladolid in Spain. His replacement at Nacional is his former assistant Hernán Darío Gómez – who had been approached to take on the same dual role and lead Colombia too, but had turned the opportunity down.

Colombia start brightly, avoid conceding a shock goal on the break, and then take the lead after 25 minutes – the Ecuadorian goalkeeper spilling a routine cross and the tiny livewire Antony de Ávila, América de Cali's El Pitufo, nipping in to poke home. It's 1-0 at half time, and 1-0 at full time, with both teams creating chances but neither able to further trouble the scorers. It's far from champagne football, but it's a winning start for Colombia and their new coach.

Next comes a disappointing 0-0 draw against Bolivia, perhaps the weakest team in the group, in Viña del Mar. With two games left, the Colombians know they will need to take something from matches against Uruguay and Brazil to have a chance of making the final. It's only two days after the stalemate with Bolivia when Los Cafeteros take to the field again to face three-time World Cup winners Brazil. But while Brazil have the air of a side in transition, lacking superstars and with a new manager of their own, Colombia field a starting XI that is reassuringly used to playing together: Higuita, Escobar, Perea, Herrera, Osorio, Álvarez, Rincón, Redín, Valderrama, Iguarán and de Ávila. In the crunch tie, it is the talismanic captain Valderrama who is the difference, El Pibe's two assists, one in each half for the twin strikers de Ávila and Iguarán, helping Los Cafeteros to a famous 2-0 victory over their far more illustrious neighbours. First, on 35 minutes, his cross from the left finds de Ávila who steers home from six yards. Throughout the first half, Valderrama is everywhere, passing, probing, tackling, crossing. He starts the second half in the same fashion, at the heart of everything. On 66 minutes he dives in to win the ball 30 yards from the Brazil goal. His prod forward is returned to him via a backheel and he instantly moves the ball onto his left to find Iguarán in space. The veteran striker pulls back his right boot and curls an unstoppable shot into the top corner of Cláudio Taffarel's goal. Colombia hold on, El Pibe continuing to cast a spell over the pitch, and secure a famous victory.

Two days later the side slump to a disappointing 1-0 defeat at the hands of Uruguay. But it is academic. For Uruguay it's too little too late, as they finish third in Group B and are eliminated along with Ecuador and Bolivia. Colombia finish top, ahead of Brazil on goal difference, and they both enter the four-way final, to face the top two teams from Group A – Chile and the only team with a 100 per cent record in the tournament, Argentina.

In the first game of the final round Argentina defeat Brazil 3-2 at the Estadio Nacional in Santiago. They are inspired by their new striking hero Gabriel Batistuta, called up to replace Diego Maradona who is suspended from all football after testing positive for cocaine. On the same day, in the same stadium, Chile and Colombia face off. With home advantage, Chile start dangerously, striker Iván Zamorano a constant threat. Then Colombia launch a fast break and Freddy Rincón's cross finds Arnoldo Iguarán six yards out with the goal gaping, but his shot is scuffed straight at the Chilean keeper. And Los Cafeteros look like they will be made to pay for their profligacy not long after, when a rash lunge inside the 18-yard box from a Colombian defender draws the referee's whistle. Penalty to Chile. The home crowd of 44,000 wait expectantly. Zamorano strides up and strikes the ball low and hard towards the bottom corner – only to see Higuita dive and tip it around the post. It's a world-class penalty save from a true expert in the art, and it keeps the tie level. And before the half is over Colombia take the lead. A free kick from out near the left corner flag is curled in and Iguarán bulldozes his way through three Chilean defenders to leap and plant his header into the corner of the goal, his earlier miss atoned for. It's 1-0 at half time, and as the second half progresses it looks like Colombia might hold on for a famous win. Then, on 74 minutes, the pressure exerted by the home side finally tells. Zamorano peels off the back of his defender, finding a yard of space between centre back and full back, and controls a curling cross perfectly on his chest. The ball drops into his stride just inside the box and his next touch is a languid swing of his left boot that wrong-foots the diving Higuita and finds the net. Chile have the momentum, but their late flurry fails to produce a winner, and the teams must be content with a share of the spoils.

Two days later Chile are able to hold Batistuta and Argentina at bay and secure a point courtesy of a 0-0 draw. Colombia have a chance to climb the table, if they can repeat their famous win against Brazil. Just six days after that 2-0 victory, Los Cafeteros take them on once again. It's a wet, muddy, almost waterlogged pitch, every kick throwing up a spray of water. And, while their opposition start brightly, Colombia seem bogged down and are thankful to Higuita for keeping the scores level. At the other end de Ávila goes down in the box, but no penalty is given.

Then, on 29 minutes Brazil take the lead. A cross from the left, a powerful header from Renato, and Higuita is beaten. An Exocet of a 35-yard free kick hammers against the Brazilian crossbar, but no matter what they try Colombia cannot find a goal to get back into the game as the playing conditions deteriorate dramatically. Then a crucial decision by the referee swings the tie further in Brazil's favour. In the same penalty area where he had waved away Colombian penalty appeals in the first half, he points to the spot after what looks like an acrobatic dive by a Brazilian attacker. The perceived injustice is compounded when Higuita dives to his left only to see Branco slam his penalty straight down the middle to make it 2-0. A late flourish from the Colombians comes to nothing, and Brazil hold on to avenge their earlier defeat.

With no travelling needed for the four finalists, the games at the Estadio Nacional come thick and fast, and it's just two days later, on

21 July, when Colombia must dust themselves off and face 12-time Copa América champions Argentina in their final game in Santiago. With Brazil running out 2-0 victors over Chile, victory for Colombia could see them finish second behind Falcão's *Seleção Canarinha*. But Argentina know a win would see them leapfrog Brazil to the top of the league, and secure them the Copa.

The captains, Valderrama and Oscar Ruggeri, trade pennants and the referee tosses his coin. With ends chosen, the game kicks off on an overused and muddy Estadio Nacional pitch that is in a pitiful state. With just ten minutes gone, a ball in behind the Colombian defence and into a rare patch of green grass out on Argentina's right flank sets an attacker away, and his cross, deep to the far post, is met by the head of Diego Simeone six yards out. The sheer power of the header prevents Higuita from doing any more than palming the ball into the net. Argentina look like they're on their way to a first Copa since 1959, and all without their talismanic, troubled superstar Diego Armando Maradona. Colombia now have a mountain to climb to match their best ever finish in the tournament.

And that peak looks insurmountable when, just eight minutes later, a delightful lofted through ball from Leo Rodríguez clears the last Colombian defender and is taken in his stride by the irrepressible Batistuta, who lashes it home to double the Argentina lead. Colombia are rocking, and do well not to concede again before half time. And the second half brings more of the same, the Argentinians pressing for a third to kill off the game and guarantee the trophy. But, despite their apparent superiority, that decisive moment fails to materialize. Then, with 20 minutes still to go, Antony de Ávila rounds off a fine Colombian move with a finish high into the net from an acute angle for his third tournament goal to make the score 2-1. As the players wrestle to retrieve the ball from an Argentinian defender inside the goal, desperate to restart the game as quickly as possible in search of an equalizer, Colombia's now famous Birdman waves his wings in the crowd, urging his side on one last time. Los Cafeteros find a new gear, and pile forward, but cannot find a way past Sergio Goycochea in the Argentinian net. When the whistle finally goes, Argentina have won not just the match but the entire Copa América, their triumph in Chile coming thanks to the goals of tournament top scorer Batistuta and despite the absence of Diego Maradona.

Back in Colombia, in his La Catedral prison high in the hills overlooking his city of Medellín, Pablo may be briefly disappointed, but he is too busy enjoying his new gilded cage to dwell on the defeat for too long. He has plenty of fun planned, not least a visit from Maradona himself . . .

*

La Catedral is a prison in name only. Built on Pablo's choice of plot, and to his specifications, it is also staffed by guards who he has hired and who he himself pays. He had forbidden the authorities from cutting down even a single tree from the forest behind the facility, and no government forces or police are even allowed within a 12-mile radius without his permission. And, while the original specifications of the premises were basic, since his incarceration Pablo has wasted no time getting up to his old smuggler's tricks. He sneaks a vast array of luxury items past the distant checkpoints and the scrum of the press pack and into the precinct, hidden in the back of the delivery trucks that visit with ever-increasing frequency – entirely unbeknown to the outside world, the press, the public, the police, and the politicians in Colombia and indeed the USA.

Pablo's gilded cage soon earns the name 'Hotel Escobar', and with good reason. It has everything from giant TVs for watching the football to a discotheque, a football pitch with floodlights, and even a playhouse for the visits of daughter Manuela. The buildings are riddled with caletas – Pablo's favourite hollowed out hiding places – stuffed with cash, drugs and guns. The electrified fence is controlled by a master kill switch that the inmates can easily access, and is more to keep out unwanted visitors – like cops or the Cali Cartel – than it is needed to keep Pablo and his cronies in. In fact, Pablo never has to wear prison uniform, and he and his men are frequently able to escape into town in the secret compartment of the trucks which bring in their illicit luxury goods, and likewise regularly smuggle people – from narcos to prostitutes, models to footballers – inside La Catedral for an audience with El Patrón. Pablo hosts over three hundred unauthorized visitors in just the first three months of his incarceration.

Pablo is able to run his criminal enterprise seamlessly from within the four walls of his nominal prison using fax machines, radio transmitters and telephones. Finally free from the constant pressure of the authorities' hunt for him, he relaxes at last – learning Mandarin, entertaining a string of mistresses and occasionally spending time with his family when they visit. But his favourite pastime, as ever, is football. And, this being Pablo Escobar, the games at La Catedral are no simple inmate kickabouts . . .

On 24 September, the celebration day of the Virgen de las Mercedes, the patron saint of prisoners, Pablo's friend René Higuita and his Nacional teammates are smuggled into La Catedral, where they can see their flag flying proudly on a pole just outside the perimeter. Pablo briefs the visiting players – games on the prison pitch last three to four hours with no breaks, and only two substitutions are allowed. In the event of a tie, the game will go to penalties. The Nacional players line up in their full club kit, the prisoners wearing the colours of the winners of the 1990 World Cup in Italy, West Germany. Pablo is marked closely, and grows increasingly upset at both the close attention he is getting and the fact that Nacional quickly take a commanding 3-0 lead. But none of the visiting pros are stupid enough to push their luck. Eventually the topsy-turvy game ends a respectable and convenient 5-5, which means penalties. The shoot-out is decided thanks to a rare miss from penalty specialist René Higuita and a successful left-footed finish from 12 yards from El Patrón himself, almost as if it was scripted.

Every time Tata visits with the kids it seems Pablo is playing football. Deportivo Independiente Medellín soon follow their cross-town rivals up the mountain. They too are unable to best the prison side captained by their infamous benefactor, as are a further local Envigado team. On the day of each of these games the flag of the visiting side is hoisted outside the prison. But after dark Pablo sneaks out to replace it with that of the first to visit, and his first footballing love, Atlético Nacional.

The regular games on the bumpy La Catedral pitch are highlights of El Patrón's time behind bars. Grainy video archive shows a stocky Pablo dribbling down the right wing alongside the chain-link fence. He cuts back and inside on his left foot, in what looks like a practised and trademark move, trying to evade the attentions of his marker. In the footage, the on-screen text describes it as a match between *Los Barrigas* ('The Bellies') and *Los Picapleitos* ('The Troublemakers'). Whatever it is, Pablo is relishing the game.

And it's not just Colombian footballers, players from his club sides or hometown, that Pablo is able to smuggle into La Catedral. There is one player, perhaps the single greatest footballer of the age, who would be the ultimate coup for Pablo: Diego Armando Maradona.

Maradona is more than just a footballer to Pablo, he is a kindred spirit, or so he imagines. Both men, one Colombian one Argentinian, share the same 5ft 5in stocky frame and are left-footed. Both were born into large families. Diego's father was a manual worker, although his family were significantly poorer than Pablo's and he grew up in Villa Fiorito, one of the poorest slums in Buenos Aires. Maradona's signing by Napoli from European giants Barcelona was for a long time suspected by many to have been funded by organized crime, by *Camorra* money, and his time in Naples was characterized by his close friendship with the Giuliano crime family. Pablo was the world's biggest narco – and Maradona was increasingly closely tied to the Italian mafia. Maradona's Naples and Escobar's Medellín could almost be twin cities, and while Pablo had helped bring the Copa Libertadores to his hometown in 1989, Diego, fresh from winning the World Cup for Argentina in 1986, had made himself a god in Naples by winning the city its first ever *Scudetto*, the 1987 Serie A league title. Both are beloved by huge swathes of the poor and the working class, both have walls across their cities adorned with murals depicting them as saints. Both Pablo and Diego are ladies' men, and now both – the footballer and the narcoterrorist – are linked by cocaine.

Maradona helped Napoli to win the 1989 UEFA Cup but, perhaps keen to escape from his toxic friendship with the Giulianos, he was desperate to leave the club and the city. His transfer request was refused, and he was made to stay and play on. He did his part, winning a second Scudetto for the club in 1990. But his life was increasingly dominated by partying, by cocaine and by the control over him that his addiction gave to Carmine Giuliano.

In January 1991, while Pablo is secretly negotiating with the Colombian government and preparing for his eventual surrender, Maradona is recorded by Italian police wire taps discussing girls with members of the Camorra. Soon they are actively investigating the hero of Naples – and eventually, when they are able to prove he offered cocaine to several prostitutes, succeed in charging him with 'Possession of Drugs for the Purpose of Trafficking'. A plea bargain helps him get a fourteen-month suspended sentence and a five million lira fine instead of a possible twenty years in prison – but he is now a convicted drug trafficker, and his fame has trained an unwanted spotlight on the mafia's activities.

The final straw comes when he fails a drugs test. His positive test after a 17 March 1991 game against Bari leads to a 15-month ban on playing for his club, from April 1991 to June 1992. FIFA immediately follows suit and bans him from representing his country – preventing him from featuring in the Copa América which Argentina will go on to win thanks to the goals of his replacement, Gabriel Batistuta.

Diego is lost. He packs up his bags and leaves Naples. Abandoned by his club, cast out by the game he loves, he heads home. Weeks later he is out with friends in Buenos Aires when he is arrested. Police find him in possession of cocaine and determine he is under the influence of the drug. He is given a 14-month suspended sentence. At an all-time low, he is approached by an intermediary. The go-between tells him only that a very important person in Colombia wants to pay him 'an enormous fee' to play a friendly alongside the likes of René Higuita.

And so it is that the world's most infamous footballer is taken to the hills of Antioquia to meet the world's most infamous drug trafficker. A bewildered Maradona arrives at La Catedral, and is shocked to realize it is a prison, surrounded by what seem like thousands of guards. He's nervous, unsure of what on earth is going on, perhaps he is being abducted or arrested, or worse? But inside, the facility is more like a luxury hotel than a high security prison. He is taken to a room in the main building that serves as a kind of home office, and there his guard introduces him to the man known only as El Patrón. Diego, who neither reads the newspapers nor watches the television, has no idea to whom he is talking. The man is perhaps ten or more years older than Diego, but he tells the disgraced footballer how much he loves and admires his game. He is a fan. And more than that, he explains how much he identifies with him – that they had both triumphed over adversity and poverty.

It is surely the strangest exhibition match Diego has ever played in, but he and his fellow players – pro footballers and narcos alike – all seem to enjoy the game. Diego is to be Pablo's guest for the night, and what ensues is one of the most lavish of all the parties that La Catedral will host during Pablo's time there. Even Diego, no stranger to the attentions of the fairer sex, is bowled over by the parade of beautiful women who appear, as if by magic, to join the festivities. The next day he is handed his 'match fee' in cash and is bid adios by the world's richest criminal, Pablo Escobar.

Alongside the footballers, and the girls, Pablo does also arrange occasional visits from his family. In December 1991 he welcomes them to his palatial prison to celebrate Christmas together. But incarceration seems to be taking its toll on him – his almost festive green sweatshirt struggles to hide his expanding waistline, his hair is shaggy and greying, and he looks old, and tired. He's not looking much better when they return in May to celebrate Manuela's birthday with cake and presents.

Chapter Sixteen

The Caged Bird Sings (1992)

The football at La Catedral seemingly never stops. Not content with bringing in players from Nacional, or DIM, Pablo decides he wants the entire Colombia national team to visit him. While for some, like friend René Higuita, it's not so shocking, others – Andrés Escobar among them – struggle to reconcile themselves with visiting the self-confessed narco in his luxury prison. In the end, they all go, hiding under blankets to avoid being identified not just by the police at the outer checkpoint but by the inevitable scrum of photographers.

Higuita's role seemingly goes even further. He is perhaps the most regular footballing visitor to La Catedral, but his function is not purely sporting. Pablo knows he is safe from the authorities – but he is still at risk from the Cali Cartel, and their ongoing feud is still hurting the business he is conducting unimpeded from within the prison. He enlists Higuita as an intermediary who, together with Father García, makes overtures to the Rodríguez Orejuela brothers, but no peace deal can be struck. In fact, Pablo gets wind of a rumoured plot – that they are planning to fly a plane over La Catedral and drop a bomb on the prison. He takes to sleeping out in the recently built jungle camp, screened by the trees behind the main buildings. But in the end it is Higuita, and two more of Pablo's own, who inadvertently hasten the end of Pablo's time in prison.

Colombia's famous keeper is well-used to the rigmarole of visiting El Patrón, to being driven through the long, winding, bumpy, dusty pothole-filled roads up to the prison by narcos sporting mirrored sunglasses and toting machine guns; to presenting his documentation at the checkpoint barrier. But by now La Catedral has become something of a media circus. As he walks down the track after a visit the reporters instantly recognize the star footballer with his shiny, curly black locks, trademark moustache and black leather jacket. He is swamped by reporters who thrust microphones under his nose and TV crews who film his every step. With military police watching on, a bespectacled reporter claps him on the back and asks him a casual question: 'Is Pablo Escobar your friend?' For Higuita, always honest to a fault, there is only one answer – he has known El Patrón for years, since Pablo campaigned in Envigado. He gives his reply, smiles awkwardly and ducks into the waiting white Suzuki jeep. He is whisked away from the scrum, but the damage is done. In moments, the word is out – and the truth about Pablo's life in, and control of, La Catedral becomes unignorable, becomes public knowledge, and becomes a national – and even international – embarrassment for the authorities. And, if that wasn't bad enough, one last event will finally spur them into action . . .

*

In July 1992, just over a year after his surrender, Pablo learns of a stash of buried cash that has been discovered by some of his men. The cartel makes so much money it is almost impossible to store or launder all of it, so hiding huge caches of US dollars in hollow walls, or buried beneath the ground as this one was, is common practice. But this money apparently belongs to Pablo's trusted lieutenants Kiko Moncada and Fernando Galeano – and they have seemingly never declared it to Pablo. All of his men must pay him a percentage of the money they make while he is 'inside' – a tithe owed in gratitude for his selfless act of sacrifice in giving up his freedom for the greater good of their shared criminal enterprise. But if this is their money, they have never given Pablo his cut. Convinced they have shorted him, a furious Pablo summons the pair to La Catedral. The luckless pair, guilty or otherwise, are unable to placate El Patrón and convince him of their innocence. They are soon dead, killed by whom we may never know for sure – some say it was a rare case of Pablo himself pulling the trigger, others point the finger at his trusted sicarios Popeye and Otto. But while the identity of the killers is not certain, one thing is – the news gets out, and now the authorities really must act. Pablo isn't just partying in La Catedral, or playing football with superstars, or even quietly running his multi-billion-dollar criminal empire – he's openly murdering people. An embarrassed Colombian government know their convenient pact with the devil has now become a political hot potato that could bring down the whole regime. Something needs to be done, and fast.

Pablo receives the news he has been dreading – his time at La Catedral is about to be cut short. Government forces are en route to the mountain to 'relocate' him. One version is that he is to be moved to a high security prison where the guards aren't all on his payroll and where the authorities can actually at least attempt to control him. But Pablo is certain his enemies instead plan to have him killed or – perhaps worse, in his eyes – extradite him to the United States. After just under 400 days behind the high, electrified fence of his self-built prison, he hurries to plan his urgent escape.

Pablo's network is not wrong, and his fears are not unfounded. On 21 July 1992 Pablo notices unusual troop movements around the perimeter. Assistant Minister of Justice Eduardo Mendoza and Director of Prisons Colonel Hernando Navas have been dispatched to La Catedral to search the premises and prepare the prisoners for their transfer. But the pair, keen not to escalate a tense situation, arrive at the compound itself with just a handful of guards, leaving the bulk of their forces behind. Pablo, believing he might be killed within the prison, makes a bold move. He takes the men prisoner. But his attempts to contact President Gaviria fail, and he is unable to negotiate. The troops mass on the slopes below as the tension within and without ratchets up, but night falls without further aggression from either side.

It is 1:30am when Juan Pablo Escobar, unable to sleep, gazes up at the lights studding the inky black hillside above Medellín. They are the lights of his father's prison, of La Catedral. And then, they are gone. Up on the mountain, Pablo and his inner circle – brother Roberto and six of his most loyal men – are already fleeing. They have tripped the facility generator's 'kill switch', grabbed what weapons and supplies they can hastily extract from the caletas within the prison and, under cover of now near-total darkness, are making a run for it, through the back of the compound and into the trees behind.

Pablo was known for walking around with the laces of his trainers or football boots untied, and those closest to him frequently joked that the day he did up his shoes properly would be the day they were all in real trouble. As they had prepared to flee, toting guns and with wads of cash stuffed in their pockets, he had picked the fittest, fastest men to go with him and the rest to stay; then, wearing army camouflage gear, he had bent down . . . and tied his laces.

When the troops down in the valley finally launch their pre-dawn offensive they are met by gunfire from the confused prison guards and the handful of prisoners who have stayed behind to cover El Patrón's midnight flit. When they finally take control of the premises Pablo is nowhere to be seen. A gaping hole in the wall of one room, partially obstructed by a fancy electronic treadmill, hints at his possible escape route.

Then a call comes into a radio station. The young man on the line claims to be Roberto Escobar's son, and says Pablo is hiding in a tunnel under La Catedral, that he has guns and ammo, and enough food for a month, but all he really wants is to surrender under the same terms. If the authorities will guarantee his safety, and promise not to extradite him, he'll go willingly once more – they just have to offer him a fair trial, and a jail overseen by the United Nations. Up on the hillside the soldiers set about trying to find the tunnel. But Pablo is by now scrambling down the muddy slopes in the dark, leaving the prison behind him. He almost gets lost, but eventually finds his way to a village in the valley below, where a family still loyal to El Patrón give him refuge.

After 396 days, Pablo is back on the run. President Gaviria is forced to give an excruciatingly embarrassing press conference in which he admits the world's most powerful criminal has escaped.

PART THREE

CHRONICLE OF A DEATH FORETOLD

(1992–2023)

Chapter Seventeen

100 Years of Solitude
(1992–1993)

Pablo's escape is rushed and desperate. He is back on the run, and weaker than ever, hunted at every turn by a plethora of enemies. The Colombian government, police and army; the rival Cali Cartel, and their deadly kill squad Los Pepes – its name derived from 'Los Perseguidos por Pablo Escobar', those persecuted by Pablo Escobar, and its ranks swollen by, among others, the friends and families of the slain Kiko Moncada and Fernando Galeano – and, with news of Pablo's flight soon reaching Washington DC, the rejuvenated resources of the United States of America.

In fact, as soon as they hear that El Patrón has flown the coop, the DEA agents in Colombia secretly rejoice – they know they'll now get a second chance to nail him themselves. They're not wrong. Back in Washington, George HW Bush, flanked by a pair of flags, looks directly into the camera and addresses the world. Dressed in a dark suit, white shirt and red tie with white spots, a white handkerchief poking out of his top pocket, he sits in the Oval Office of the White House, his hands clasped in front of him and resting on his desk. His words speak directly to the millions in the US and across the world, but in particular to those in Colombia, in Bogotá and Medellín, and to one man specifically, the focus of the hunt, Pablo Emilio Escobar Gaviria: 'We have a responsibility not to leave our brave friends in Colombia to fight alone. We will for the first time, make available the appropriate resources of America's armed forces. And our message to the drug cartels is this: the rules have changed. For the drug kingpins? The death penalty.'

With President Bush not only upping the reward for information leading to Pablo's capture from $1 million to a whopping $2.7 million – but also putting targets on the backs of all the cartel heads, including those down in Cali – the spotlight is back on Colombia in the war on drugs. But, just as Pablo was caught out by the government's sudden change in stance, so too are the various entities who now scramble to re-capture him. The hunt is frantic, but chaotic. With the astronomical reward money now on offer, international bounty hunters descend on Medellín to join the quest.

Pablo opts to hide in the sprawling concrete metropolis of his beloved Medellín rather than camping out in the inhospitable Antioquenian wilderness. He moves from safe house to safe house, travelling using his own personal fleet of taxis. These cars, equipped with powerful radio antennas, become his mobile bases of operations – allowing him to make calls and conduct his business while on the move, and thus evade the authorities' efforts to use triangulation techniques to pinpoint his location. This has become a major concern for Pablo ever since the US brought over to Colombia two specially adapted civilian light aircraft kitted out with state-of-the-art radio direction finding equipment. Codename Centra Spike, this new DEA asset is operated by a top-secret US army intelligence unit, who pilot the planes over Medellín.

Pablo is almost caught less than a month after his escape – but he just about manages to evade the clutches of Los Pepes when they descend on one of his hideouts in Belén Aguas Frías in Medellín. However, with those closest to him being found and killed, or handing themselves in to try and save their lives, what was once a huge army of sicarios and loyal foot soldiers has dwindled to just a handful of loyal men. Likewise, Pablo's finances and resources have taken a huge hit. And then Pablo's nemesis Colonel Hugo Martínez is brought back to head up the reinstated Bloque de Búsqueda. Centra Spike takes to the skies once more, and the DEA share their data with Martínez and the Search Bloc in a joint effort to track down Pablo. The tables have turned in a big way.

In August 1992 Pablo moves to a new safe house. It is in the Poblado quarter of Medellín, close to the escape route afforded by the Las Palmas highway, and from its elevated position it commands a stunning, and tactically advantageous, panoramic view of the city below. In a rare nod to domesticity, Pablo takes the risk of hiring a handyman to paint the walls of his new hideout in his favourite colour, light blue. It takes the man two weeks, and for the entire time Pablo remains in hiding in a single room in the property. The house is given its codename: *Casa Azul*, the 'Blue House'. Pablo is forced to rely on a married couple – Gladys and her husband, nicknamed *El Gordo*, 'the fat one' – to manage the house for him.

Two months later the situation is dire. Pablo, close to giving up altogether, decides on a new plan of action. His brother Roberto will give himself up, and will then negotiate the terms of Pablo's own surrender. It's a desperate move. On 7 October 1992, Roberto Escobar – along with two of Pablo's top sicarios, Popeye and Otto – does indeed hand himself in. But, when he then finds the authorities have no interest in discussing any deal whatsoever for him or his brother, it's clear the plan has backfired.

Before the end of October one of the last of Pablo's top brass from the Medellín Cartel still alive and at large, Brances Muñoz Mosquera – nicknamed Tyson because of his resemblance to the American boxer Mike Tyson – dies in a gunfight with Colombian police who had tracked him to a property where he was spending the night with his girlfriend. The death of Tyson leaves Jhonny Edison Rivera Acosta, aka El Palomo (but no relation to the footballer with the same moniker, Albeiro Usuriaga), as the only surviving member of the group that ensured Don Pablo's escape from La Catedral and now Pablo's right-hand man and de facto head of security.

It is just after midday on Sunday 22 November. Five men sit at a table in a restaurant in a park in the city of Itagüí. Half an hour later they are joined by a man in a red sweatshirt, who carries a newspaper under his arm. They are police detectives, and this man is a vital and invaluable informant – who delivers to them a package of intelligence that details the movements of their next target: El Palomo. A team of 150 is mobilized, and the operation to take down Pablo's right hand begins in earnest.

Just a day later, a small car containing three men and a woman races past a Search Bloc team at an intersection outside Itagüí, nearly knocking down the patrol. When the description of the driver of the vehicle is called in it matches the description of El Palomo. Patrols intensify and focus on Itagüí. Forty-eight hours later they get their next break – as El Palomo and his companions are spotted at a clothing warehouse in a shopping centre. The authorities are able to keep their distance and mount a surveillance operation. They track the group back to their hideout, watch them overnight, log the number of bodyguards present and set up a perimeter of plain clothes officers to ensure the gang don't slip away.

At midnight on Thursday 26 November a tank rolls along a seemingly empty street. It turns, lines up with the front door, and ploughs straight into a residential building. The Search Bloc swarm in in its wake. A firefight rages, finally ending with the death of El Palomo and one of his bodyguards. Their female companion is captured alive, and is revealed to be the sister of Jorge 'Tato' Avendaño – one of the Medellín Cartel bosses who surrendered in 1991. And so, as 1992 draws to a close with Tyson and El Palomo now both dead, the last of the Catedral gang gone, Pablo has never been so alone.

His loyal sicario Angelito now his only companion, Pablo is even forced to take each night's final guard duty shift at the Casa Azul himself. Despite everything, he still sneaks out of the house to watch Atlético Nacional play whenever he can – often wearing his favourite disguise of a wig, beard and glasses.

Just before the end of the year he sends for his family, and they join him at the Casa Azul. On 1 December they celebrate his 43rd birthday with a cake and a modest meal. Six days later they celebrate *Día de las Velitas*, the 'Day of the Little Candles', the eve of the Immaculate Conception and the unofficial beginning of the Christmas period, as a family – and the very next day Pablo leaves them to disappear further into the underbelly of Medellín, and to prepare one last roll of the dice.

*

It is 3:40am on 19 December 1992. The glittery twinklings of Christmas decorations adorn the nearby properties and local businesses as a caravan of ten vehicles drives up to a house on a corner plot in the residential area of Las Acacias in Medellín. The cars park strategically, on each corner of the block. As dawn approaches men from the cars get out and hurry over to the house and place 90lb of dynamite on the property's outer wall, outside the bedroom where the head of intelligence of the city's police, Captain Fernando Posada Hoyos, is sleeping. They race away to a safe distance and wait.

When the bomb goes off, 40 men – a hastily gathered troop of young foot soldiers and hired guns led by Pablo himself – descend on the smoking ruins of the home, automatic weapons at the ready. *El Capitán's* bedroom is completely destroyed, but the sicarios search the rubble, find the young lawman's body and finish him off with shots from their AR-15 rifles. Moments later, they come under fire from the two police officers, Posada's permanent bodyguards, who were sleeping on the other side of the house and have miraculously survived the detonation. Fleeing in their cavalcade of stolen cars, Pablo and his men encounter a police patrol that has heard the blast and is en route to the scene. A second gunfight ensues but, with more officers injured, the narcos are able to escape, and race off into the night.

Captain Posada, the man Pablo blames for several recent operations against him and the cartel, including the deaths of Tyson and El Palomo, is finally dead. He had survived a car bomb attack on him at the Olaya Herrera airport less than a week earlier, but this time El Patrón has left nothing to chance.

Just four days later Tata, Juan Pablo and Manuela are brought, blindfolded as they now always are when taken to visit, to a remote mud brick house in Belén Aguas Frías. Here they spend a cold, scary

Christmas and New Year with a Pablo who is slowly unravelling before their eyes. It is the last New Year's Eve they will spend together.

*

In January 1993 things are dire for Pablo. The biggest threat is increasingly from Los Pepes – who are able to kidnap and murder anyone even suspected of being associated with Pablo and the Medellín Cartel with apparent impunity. The paramilitary organization was initially founded by the Castaño brothers and Pablo's fellow drug trafficker 'Don Berna', as an army dedicated to fighting the guerrilla groups who were kidnapping their friends and families and holding them to ransom. But, with support from the Cali Cartel, and the apparent tacit approval of the Colombian authorities, Los Pepes pivot and take on a singular mission – to destroy Pablo Escobar. To this end, no methods are too brutal.

Fidel Castaño is himself a drug trafficker, and a former ally and close friend of Pablo's. His in-depth knowledge of the Medellín Cartel, and the freedom to operate wholly outside the law, gives Los Pepes a huge advantage in the war against Pablo. Like Pablo, Los Pepes will use any means necessary to get what they want: kidnappings, assassinations, bombings. They give those associated with Pablo a simple choice, itself a haunting echo of El Patrón's infamous plata o plomo offer – suspects could inform on Pablo and the cartel, or they could die. And die many did – their bodies left on display in the streets, or dumped in ditches, face down, ankles tied with their own belts, with wooden signs around their necks, the words scrawled in black marker pen reading: *Por ser amigos de Pablo Escobar* ('For being friends with Pablo Escobar').

On 2 February, a house in the El Diamante neighbourhood burns down. It is no accident, nor is it a random act of arson, for this is the home of Tata's sister. The message is clear: Los Pepes are coming after Pablo's nearest and dearest.

Increasingly desperate, Pablo summons his family once more. He has a new plan. He will negotiate his surrender, but first he wants them safely out of harm's way. Los Pepes are too big a threat. Pablo has procured a property in Miami, Florida, an apartment – a safe haven. Tata, Juan Pablo and Manuela must leave Colombia.

*

First, Juan Pablo, still only 15 years old, goes alone to the US Embassy to beg for visas to enable him to take his family out of the country to safety in the USA. His request is denied. But the Escobars are nothing if not resilient. They decide to push ahead with their plan regardless.

On 19 February, a teenage Juan Pablo hustles his mother and younger sister, and his girlfriend Ángeles, out into a waiting car. Along with their luggage, they are driven to Medellín's Rionegro airport. In order to evade Los Pepes, they arrive a full seven hours before their flight to Miami is due to depart. But something is not right. The airport is busy, and every queue seems to take an age. They are delayed at every turn, at every checkpoint and desk. Juan Pablo's pleas fall on deaf ears. The hours tick by and still they are not allowed onto the plane. No sooner have they missed the cut-off time for boarding, and been asked to leave the airport – by now their presence has been noted and is starting to draw a crowd – than Juan Pablo spots a truck waiting outside and a gang of men in balaclavas. Los Pepes have found them.

Knowing that leaving the terminal building will mean falling into the clutches of his father's deadliest enemies, a desperate Juan Pablo enlists the help of a friendly stranger in chartering a helicopter. The family run across the airport tarmac, doing their best to hide their faces behind bags or jackets, and jump into the waiting chopper. As they take off, a second helicopter takes to the sky to follow them, filled with the press corps who have got wind of events. Moments later another, third helicopter takes to the skies above Medellín. Juan Pablo strains to see if he can make out any members of Los Pepes within.

After a frantic flight, the family are able to land and make it safely back to central Medellín, but Pablo's plan has failed. He decides to change his approach. If he can't send them far away, then he will keep his loved ones as close as possible. From now on they will have to live as he does – constantly travelling between half a dozen different safe houses. And, with his resources stretched and many of his properties seized or under surveillance, these are not luxurious city apartments or sprawling farms, but instead rustic farmhouses and shacks in the wilderness, places with no kitchen, no lights, no electricity.

Having missed out on snatching Pablo's family at the airport, Los Pepes renew their offensive. On 2 March they assassinate the manager of Hacienda Nápoles, Hernán Darío 'HH' Henao. A day later they kill Pablo's lawyer Raúl Zapata Vergara. They burn down family properties, set off car bombs outside buildings where friends or family are living, and threaten and kill as many of those closest to Pablo's operation and his family as they can. And the police too are turning the screw. In May, Pablo's nephew Nicolás – the son of his brother Roberto – is captured and interrogated. He refuses to give up his uncle though, and as soon as he is released he succeeds where Juan Pablo had failed and helps his own remaining family to escape from the country.

But while Pablo is still managing to avoid prison, one of his friends is about to spectacularly, and surprisingly, fall foul of the law . . .

Chapter Eighteen

News of a Kidnapping (1993)

One day in May, René Higuita is summoned to the office of the president of his club side Atlético Nacional. The goalkeeper and charismatic star of Colombian football has no idea what he might have done this time. But nothing could have prepared him for the conversation that follows, nor for the eventual fallout from his actions.

The story he is told is this. On the morning of 30 April a young girl, the 13-year-old daughter of a wealthy man, a fan and close friend of Atlético Nacional, was being driven to school. Two motorbikes appeared as if from nowhere, drove past the car, and pulled across the road, blocking its path. The men on the bikes approached the now stationary vehicle, forcibly ejected the driver, got in themselves, and drove the car off. The girl is told to get down in the footwell of the back seats and stay down. She has been kidnapped, and the men are holding her for ransom.

So far, the girl's father has obeyed the demand of her captors not to involve the police – and now a trusted intermediary has been requested to oversee the payment of the ransom. That go-between is to be none other than celebrity footballer René 'El Loco' Higuita. When asked if he will do this favour, if he will help get back the daughter of this friend of Nacional, a 13-year-old girl named Marcela, Higuita doesn't hesitate.

On 28 May, a month after the teenage girl was taken, Higuita receives a call from her father. He goes to the man's home, where he is played a cassette recording he has made of the most recent phone conversation with the criminals. The voices he hears speak his name, they request that from now on all calls will be directly with Higuita himself. They reiterate that no cops must be involved. The father hands over an envelope with the ransom cash, thanks him, and sends Higuita on his way.

Back at home, it's not long before several men arrive. They ask for the money, but when he hands it over they fail to produce the girl. When Higuita presses them, they insist he must trust them. One of them stays behind with the keeper, while the others leave. Hours pass. Day turns to night, turns to day. Finally, a call comes in; it's go time.

On 29 May, René Higuita and his new shadow drive to a pre-determined spot at Medellín's UPB University. They park up and wait. Soon Higuita's trademark hair gives away his presence and the car is surrounded by fans and autograph hunters. In a bid to get them to leave them alone, and ever the showman, El Loco gets out of the vehicle and sets about signing anything thrust in front of him. He's so distracted by the throng of enthusiastic young fans that he fails to notice a second car arrive and pull over to the kerb. He's still busy giving out autographs when a girl calls to him. She's jumped the queue, and he asks her to wait her turn. When she says 'René, I'm Marcela!' he practically drops his pen. He turns to her, scoops her up and runs to his car, the autograph hunters instantly forgotten. His shadow having seemingly vanished, he floors it. He drives like a man possessed, running every red light that threatens to halt his flight and driving up onto the pavement whenever traffic blocks his way. Eventually, he makes it safely to his destination – and is able to hand Marcela over to her grateful and overjoyed family.

On 4 June the family host a huge party to celebrate the safe return of their daughter. Higuita pops by to wish them well, and they insist on giving him something as a thank you, a token of their gratitude. He tries to say no, that he needs no reward for doing a good deed, but they insist. They hand him an envelope. Inside is $50,000. They are a wealthy family, and they are not taking no for an answer. Higuita thanks them, and accepts their gift. But within hours he is under arrest.

Article 40 in the Colombian Criminal Code, the *Código Penal*, states that anyone who benefits financially from the crime of kidnapping can be imprisoned. Failure to report knowledge of a kidnapping is also in itself a crime. The authorities know they've got El Loco over a barrel. And it quickly becomes clear to him exactly why they've pounced on him so enthusiastically . . .

When he is questioned, all the cops ask him about is his friendship with their public enemy number one and the world's most famous fugitive: Pablo Escobar. They tell Higuita to give them Pablo and he won't have to go to jail, implying that if he gives up his friend then all this will go away. When he refuses point blank, they swear at him and tell him he'll rot in a prison cell. El Loco is placed in handcuffs, taken by helicopter to Bogotá and then escorted by a massive cavalcade to prison. The authorities and many of the news reports make out that he was one of the kidnappers, and imply that he was involved in drug trafficking too. Some, at least, offer an alternative theory: 'René Higuita, goalkeeper for the Colombian National Team, was arrested today for mediating a kidnap negotiation. However, many believe

Higuita's visit to Pablo Escobar in prison was the true motive for his arrest.'

Refusing to help the authorities to capture El Patrón earns Higuita a seven-month stay in prison, and will cost him dearly . . .

*

Just two days before René Higuita is arrested for his part in the paying of a ransom, Tata's eldest brother Carlos is on his way back to Medellín from Cartagena. No sooner has he set foot back in the city than he is kidnapped by Los Pepes – and murdered. Slowly but surely those closest to the Escobars are being picked off, one by one. In August 1993 Pablo once more summons his family to the Casa Azul – but this time they are to stay with him.

Tata arrives with Juan Pablo, Manuela and Ángeles – Juan Pablo's girlfriend has turned down the opportunity to abandon her beau and is staying close to the bosom of the family. They pass through the green security gate and, as they enter through the second gate, dark blue and topped with barbed wire, they are greeted by a familiar chorus – the barking of the German shepherd guard dog and the honking of a mean white goose named Palomo that El Gordo had bought from a Medellín market for 30,000 pesos.

The family settles into a routine. Pablo stays up late, standing guard and cogitating over his plans to keep his loved ones safe. When, come mid-morning, he finally rises, Tata cooks him brunch. They try to make it healthy, he has put on more than a few pounds since his rushed escape from La Catedral. As he eats, Pablo watches the news on television and avidly scans the newspapers, desperate to absorb every morsel of news about the hunt for Colombia's most wanted man. When his hair gets too long and shaggy, Tata trims it herself. When Juan Pablo gets stir crazy his dad takes him out into the property's private drive where they play football together, kicking a ball around on the concrete and forgetting their situation for a few precious moments. When Manuela is feeling down, Pablo shares his Coca-Cola with her and cooks them fried sausage with rice. But Pablo knows this simulacrum of domesticity cannot last. Without the men, the money, or the freedom to carry out further terrorist attacks he has lost his leverage over the government. His best and only hope is to cut a deal for his own surrender that might somehow protect his family. His best bet is convincing the Attorney General, Gustavo de Greiff, to help his family secure refugee status abroad. If de Greiff can deliver that, he will happily hand himself in once more. But, despite the best efforts of his lawyer, who Pablo communicates with via a series of messengers and using the kinds of covert means of communications more common in the spy trade, his entreaties to the offices of the AG and of President Gaviria himself have fallen on deaf ears. Tata is growing increasingly suspicious, the stalling on the part of the authorities hints at a darker agenda – that they would rather give Los Pepes, or Search Bloc, time to track down and kill Pablo instead of bringing him in and having to guarantee his safety.

She has noticed a change in Pablo too. One minute he is telling her they will get new identities and start a new life abroad, the next he is outside, gazing wistfully down into the Aburrá Valley below. He takes to spending more and more time just staring out at Medellín, at Antioquia. Then one day he reveals a new scheme. He has been buying up parcels of land in the remote wilderness and now is attempting to set up an electrical grid there. His plan is to hide out, living deep in the wilds of Colombia, and from there to set up a new guerrilla organization. He intends on calling it *Antioquia Rebelde*, the 'Rebels of Antioquia'. Its aim? To fight for an independent 'Antioquia Federal', a new independent Antioquenian state, of which, of course, he would be president.

On 3 September Pablo's sicario Angelito drives Ángeles into Medellín. She is able to pick up cake from an upmarket bakery, along with six bottles of Dom Perignon and a haul of gifts from various boutiques. It may be a far cry from the excesses of the heyday of Hacienda Nápoles, but the Escobars are at least able to celebrate Tata's birthday together. It's a happy moment. Just two days later it is eclipsed by the one thing that can bring Pablo as much joy as his family: football.

*

On 5 September 1993 Pablo settles down in front of the TV at Casa Azul. Meanwhile, 150 miles away, in a room in a Bogotá jail, another TV set is turned on – this time for René Higuita. TV cameras film him as he sits to watch the tiny screen, reporters poised to transcribe his every reaction on this momentous day. The two friends, in different cities but both imprisoned in one sense or another, are preparing to watch one of the most crucial games in the history of Colombian football. Legend has it that even the narcos and paramilitaries downed their weapons, their bloody conflict temporarily forgotten, in order to watch the match – like a game of no man's land football during a Christmas truce in the Great War.

It is the last game of South American qualifiers for the 1994 World Cup. Los Cafeteros are in Buenos Aires to take on the mighty Argentina in their capital city. And everything is on the line. Colombia sit atop Group A, and a win or a draw will see them qualify for their second successive World Cup. For Argentina, only a win will be enough for them to leapfrog Los Cafeteros and secure the single automatic qualification spot for USA '94. Whichever side loses will have to win an intercontinental qualifier to avoid missing out.

While El Patrón and El Loco watch on TV from afar, one man is in the stadium but unable to take to the pitch – Diego Maradona. Like the majority of the baying crowd of 75,000, he proudly sports his white and light-blue striped Argentina football shirt and settles into his seat hoping for, and most likely expecting, a home win. After all *Los Albicelestes* ('The White and Sky Blues') have never lost a World Cup qualifier in Argentina, and haven't lost a single match on home soil in six years. They have won the World Cup twice, and have also recently won the 1991 and 1993 Copa América tournaments and the 1992 King Fahd Cup (later renamed the FIFA Confederations Cup).

But Colombia have hope of their own. The nucleus of the side is intact – in fact even coach Maturana is back, taking charge once more after season-long stints at Real Valladolid and even Pablo's hated América de Cali with whom he has just won the Colombian domestic league. And Los Cafeteros have already beaten Argentina in this year's qualifying, securing a vital 2-1 home win in the oppressive Caribbean heat of Barranquilla and ending Argentina's 33-game unbeaten run that stretched back all the way to the 1990 World Cup final.

The Colombian team have been left in no doubt as to the magnitude of the task before them, however. Harassed by fans from the moment they touched down in Buenos Aires, not given a moment's peace in their hotel or en route to the stadium where crowds shout 'drug dealers!' at them incessantly, when they walk out onto the 'El Monumental' pitch that evening the ticker tape and vitriol pour down on them in equal measure.

The Argentinian side, led once again by skipper and centre back

Oscar Ruggeri, and including goalkeeper Sergio Goycochea alongside the likes of Diego Simeone, Fernando Redondo and Gabriel Batistuta, start aggressively. Batistuta spurns an early chance, poking wide from eight yards out with the goal at his mercy, but then the game descends into something of a midfield war of attrition. Free kick after free kick is awarded and neither side can gain a toehold in the stop-start game. Then, just minutes before half time, a rare moment of quality. Captain and playmaker Carlos Valderrama collects the ball from an Argentinian headed clearance, and a hip feint wrong-foots the entire defence. He slides his pass through to Freddy Rincón who, at full tilt, knocks it past Goycochea and rolls the ball beyond the defender's despairing last-gasp slide, through the fluttering strands of discarded ticker tape that litter the penalty area, and into the Argentina net. As Rincón wheels away to celebrate, Valderrama leaping onto his back in joyful defiance, the cameras pick out a rueful Diego Maradona in the stands. On the home bench, Argentinian coach Alfio Basile smokes yet another cigarette to the nub. The half ends 1-0. What comes next has become football folklore.

First, on 49 minutes, Freddy Rincón, just outside the centre circle, gets his head up and pings an arcing long pass into the inside left channel where Faustino Asprilla has peeled away into space. The new striking hero of Colombian football, 'Tino', who had only a year earlier left Pablo's Atlético Nacional to play for Parma in Italy's Serie A in a $10 million deal, brings the ball down perfectly, fakes to go down the outside of the covering defender and cuts back in onto his right foot. Darting inside his man he falls, but somehow sticks out a long, telescopic leg and hooks his shot between the legs of goalkeeper Goycochea. The striker, nicknamed *El Pulpo* – 'The Octopus' – for his elastic limbs, runs to the small contingent of Colombian fans and performs his trademark flamboyant celebration, a handspring cartwheel. It's 2-0 to Colombia.

Stung into action, for nearly half an hour Argentina pour forward. But, in the Colombian net, they are met by a series of saves by Higuita's inspired stand-in, Óscar Córdoba. Two saves in particular, from Batistuta, have the Argentinian shaking his head in disbelief. Basile makes two changes, but still his side can't find a goal and a way back into the game.

On 72 minutes it's two for Rincón and three for Los Cafeteros, as the forward arrives at the back post to strike an untidy, bouncing volley into the net. It's not the most beautiful goal of the night (that will come next) but it's priceless for Colombia. Maradona slumps in his seat, his head in his hands. Two minutes later, with the home crowd still trying to make sense of what they are witnessing, comes a moment that will become frozen in time, like a beautiful butterfly pinned to a collector's board, or an exotic bug trapped in amber resin, for all fans of Colombian football.

Faustino Asprilla intercepts a loose opposition pass and dribbles to just inside the left corner of the Argentinian penalty area. Goycochea runs out to narrow the angle but, as he reaches that no man's land halfway between his goal line and the onrushing striker, El Pulpo opens up his body. Time seems to stand still as he nonchalantly caresses the ball up over the keeper. The delicate chip drops just under the bar. It is a moment of footballing genius, of sheer audacity and perfection of execution that takes place in a split second but seems to last forever. Asprilla's celebratory forward roll ends with him being mobbed by his jubilant teammates. All the Argentinian bench can do is sit and smoke, and ponder what might have been.

And yet, Los Cafeteros are not done. The final nail in the coffin, the humiliating fifth goal, comes ten minutes later. Valderrama releases the rampant Asprilla with an outside-of-the-boot pass down the wing. The striker delays, then breaks the offside trap with a cleverly disguised through ball into the stride of the onrushing Adolfo Valencia who, fittingly given his nickname of *El Tren*, arrives like an express train to tickle the ball past the advancing Goycochea. For Argentina, utter dejection. Humiliation. Disbelief. For Colombia, unbridled joy. The Colombian performance is so stunning that it inspires an almost unprecedented act – their rival fans in the packed stadium give them a standing ovation. The jeers have turned to cheers, and La Selección are able to celebrate as a team on the pitch.

In the Casa Azul in Medellín, Pablo is as overjoyed as Tata can ever remember seeing him. He has been spellbound by the game, miraculously able to forget his travails for 90 minutes as he witnesses the miracle in El Monumental. He whoops with joy at every goal, and his good mood will last for days afterwards. She does not know it at the time, but this is the last time Tata will see her husband happy.

Meanwhile, in the corridors of the stadium in Buenos Aires, when any of the Colombian players are stopped by a reporter and asked to comment, they all share the same refrain – one that they have oft repeated throughout their qualifying campaign – that this is for their families, and for their brother-in-arms Higuita. In the changing room after the game the players hug, Valderrama's blond curls bouncing above the tight huddle. And then the chant begins: 'René! René! Higuita! Higuita!' But, in his Bogotá jail cell, the victory appears bittersweet for a subdued, impassive El Loco.

One of the most invested fans watching in the stadium is none other than the President of Colombia. He has been busy hitching his horse to the Los Cafeteros bandwagon – ensuring he is positioned as a fan of the team and of football. In many ways it is straight out of Pablo's playbook. He has attended almost all of Colombia's qualifying games. Where El Patrón had invited the players to Hacienda Nápoles and La Catedral, the President has been calling them on a satellite phone from the grounds of his official residence to congratulate them after their victories, dressed in a suit for the cameras and thanking the likes of Faustino Asprilla for his goals and the team's triumphs on behalf of a grateful nation. After the game in Buenos Aires an ecstatic President Gaviria, dressed down in a jumper, heralds Colombia as 'the best team on this continent'.

Throughout their qualifying campaign, the Colombians had played their home games to packed stadia. Their fans, from all walks of life, all professions, rich, poor, middle class, had united in a way neither the cartels nor the government could unite a people. Inside the stadium everyone was the same. The side were a symbol of the power of football, and when the team won the whole country won. This was not Pablo's squad, nor was it the side of President Gaviria, this team was Colombia.

Back in Colombia everyone – from guerrillas to paramilitaries, from narcos to cops, politicians to street cleaners – celebrates long and hard. Colombia is going to the World Cup. The team are greeted as conquering heroes as they step off the Avianca plane back from Argentina, Colombian flags waving on the tarmac, fans mobbing them all the way to the team bus. In Bogotá, Medellín and beyond there are parties in the streets, as fans ride the roofs of minibuses, waving flags.

But, as Pablo's previously iron grip on Medellín loosens, he struggles to protect even the superstar footballers who play for his team and who have become national heroes after their heroics in

Buenos Aires. Just three days after the miraculous 5-0 victory, gun-toting motorcyclists in Medellín flag down a car in broad daylight and a young boy is removed from the vehicle and spirited away. He is Fernando 'Chontico' Herrera Castillo, the two-year-old son of Atlético Nacional and Colombia star full back 'Chonto' Herrera who has only just returned from playing for Los Cafeteros in the thrilling victory in Argentina. 'Junior', as he is known to his family, was being driven back home from nursery when the kidnappers struck.

Soon Chonto hears his wife screaming to him, 'Chonto! They kidnapped our boy!' The kidnappers who have snatched Junior demand a ransom of 150 million pesos – nearly $200,000. He is held for three days – before Colombia's elite anti-kidnapping force swoop and free him, unharmed. Two people are arrested – seemingly just regular street hoods looking for a fast buck. Junior is returned safe and sound to his parents, the ever-present cameras there to show Chonto, with his close-cropped dark hair, hugging his son tight, kissing him as the boy looks on bemused in a pristine white T-shirt and the crowd of reporters, police, medical staff and well-wishers jostle.

When Chonto and the rest of the besuited Colombia team are paraded before an Estadio El Campín packed to the rafters with fans, and with national TV broadcasting live, the chant of '*Libertad! Libertad!*' – 'Freedom! Freedom!' – rings out. The people want their idol René 'El Loco' Higuita released. But it will take the death that the entire country, the entire world, has been waiting for, for that to be allowed to happen . . .

Chapter Nineteen

Endgame (1993)

It is 18 September, 13 days after Colombia trounced Argentina in Buenos Aires. The brief halo effect of that victory has long since dissipated. Pablo is at his wits' end. A letter arrives, and Pablo takes it to his office to read it in private. When he emerges, he takes Tata aside and reveals that his negotiations have finally borne fruit. She and the kids are to be moved into protective custody – they will be leaving for the Altos del Campestre building, where the authorities are setting up additional security measures, that same day. Tata is nervous, but her husband insists. They will be safe, and he will reunite with her no matter what.

It is 11pm by the time they are packed up and ready to leave. As Pablo hugs his daughter Manuela, his eyes fill with tears. It is the only time Tata has ever seen her husband cry. Juan Pablo drives his mother, sister and girlfriend in one car, his father follows them in a second vehicle, his sicario Angelito riding alongside him. As they come to a junction just before Altos, Pablo waves to his family and toots his horn, before driving off. It is the last time they will see him alive. Juan Pablo drives on the short distance to the apartment block and the start of their new life. For two days after the departure of his family Pablo refuses to eat or shave. At night he stands outside, looks out at the stars over Medellín and pulls absent-mindedly on his beard.

Then, with his family at least temporarily out of harm's way, and with his war chest now almost empty, Pablo comes up with yet another crazy plan. He is going to carry out 100 quick kidnappings in Llanogrande, a short drive south east of Medellín, charge 500 million pesos for each person's release and use the cash to flee to Bogotá and hide out there. He plans the operation for 31 December. But first he needs the ever-loyal Angelito to recruit a hundred young men to carry out the plan simultaneously.

This insane night of the 100 kidnappings never comes to pass, however. On 6 October Angelito is delivering money to his brother when the pair are ambushed by the Search Bloc and killed in the ensuing gunfight. At the Altos building one of the security detail supplied by the Attorney General's office – a young man who had become friendly with the Escobar family and had even played football with Juan Pablo down in the building's cavernous basement – gives them the news. At the Casa Azul, Pablo begins to lose all hope, and takes to donning a disguise and going for walks in downtown Medellín with El Gordo.

Eventually his time at 'the Blue House' comes to an end. First, helicopters appear and circle above the building. El Gordo and Gladys go outside and begin to work in the garden, desperately trying to act casual while Pablo hides inside in a closet. Eventually the choppers fly off. Pablo waits. No one from Los Pepes or the Search Bloc arrives at the house. He's safe, for now, but his enemies are getting closer. Then he sends El Gordo to deliver a letter to his lawyer. Hours later the man reappears at the Casa Azul and his story has Pablo immediately packing his bags. The caretaker had stepped out of the lift on the 7th floor of the offices at Parque de Berrío, about to deliver El Patrón's missive, only to see a cluster of armed men gathered by the lawyer's office. He immediately turned on his heels and fled. He downed a couple of shots of *aguardiente*, Colombian 'firewater', at a nearby bar then hid out in a church until he was sure it was safe to return. It's the last straw. The next day Pablo leaves and heads to a new safe house to meet one of his very last remaining sicarios, Álvaro de Jesús Agudelo, known as *El Limón*: 'The Lemon'. He will never return to the Casa Azul.

But no sooner has he relocated than he has another near-miss. On 11 October Centra Spike picks up Pablo making a radio telephone call, and is able to triangulate the signal and pinpoint its origin to a remote farmhouse. Search Bloc and the DEA agents leading the hunt for Pablo fly out in a helicopter immediately – but as they circle the ranch they realize it will be impossible to land. Pablo clambers onto a horse and rides into the woods, then jumps in a boat that takes him along the river to where a Land Rover is waiting. Before those hunting him can regroup, he is gone. But they have gained one vital piece of intelligence. It is not the first time they have spotted him calling this specific number, and they soon become convinced it is his Achilles' heel – his family. The day after Pablo's madcap escape, he almost has no family left to worry about, however . . .

*

It is shortly after midnight on 12 October, just hours after Pablo's most recent near-capture. Tata, Juan Pablo, Manuela and Ángeles are asleep in their apartment in the Altos building. There is a lull in the gunfire that has plagued them incessantly for the weeks they have been in protective custody. The building has become such a focal point for Los Pepes and the war on Pablo, despite the small army of agents from the AG's CTI (the *Cuerpo Técnico de Investigación*) and the sandbags and security checkpoint they have set up at street level, that almost all of the residents of the building have left. The family have already survived one major assault: the warning siren triggered just moments before a burst of gunfire and then a loud thud against the wall of the building. Two cars had pulled up, three men had got out, and while two opened fire a third had launched a rifle grenade at Altos. It had hit the outer wall just above the Escobars' apartment, but had failed to detonate.

As midnight bleeds into 1am, a red pick-up truck, parked just outside the building perimeter, explodes. Its payload of 175lb of dynamite blows out every window in the Altos, and those of the buildings surrounding it. The debris from the truck rains down on the forecourt, a smoking tyre rolling along the asphalt. The Escobars survive unhurt, but they – and Pablo – can all too clearly see that their situation is becoming untenable.

Colombia's Attorney General, Gustavo de Greiff, knows that finally he holds all the cards. He seems in no rush to help find Tata and the kids a safe haven abroad, and Pablo's bargaining position is the weakest it has ever been. As the family wait for the authorities to help them escape, Los Pepes tighten the noose.

First, in early November, the family's personal bodyguard – Juan Carlos Puerta, aka 'Nariz' ('the Nose') – disappears after leaving them to visit his son – and Tata fears the worst, that he has been captured by the Cali Cartel's kill squad. Over the next few days three more vital links between the Escobars and the outside world – including with Pablo – are 'disappeared'. First is the building manager of the Altos – Alicia Vásquez – who the family have increasingly relied on to help with getting them vital supplies. Next, two teenagers arrive at Tata's door. They are the children of her former high school teacher Alba Lía Londoño. Tata had prevailed on Alba to help her with materials for home-schooling the kids, and now she too has vanished. The last to disappear is Manuela's nanny, Nubia Jiménez, another of those close to the family who had been used to deliver messages between them and Pablo. With these kidnappings it is clear that Los Pepes are severing the lines of communication between Pablo and his family. Tata is worried that a frightened or angry Pablo might show himself – and walk right into their trap. Meanwhile the AG's office have adopted a hard line: they are demanding Pablo hand himself in *before* they will repatriate the family. And so, Tata decides to take matters into her own hands. Hoping to follow in the footsteps of Roberto's son Nicolás, who had eventually found refuge in Germany, she buys plane tickets to Frankfurt. She has had enough of waiting for the AG's office to help them, and of skulking like prisoners in the Altos while Los Pepes torment them. They will leave Colombia before the end of the month.

As the family prepare for their departure, Tata contacts the AG's office to ask for protection on their journey. She's desperately aware that they will be out in the open, especially on this short but dangerous first leg of the journey as they travel by car across Medellín from the Altos to José María Córdova airport in Rionegro, nearly 20 miles east of the city, in order to get a flight to Bogotá and then finally on to Germany. As the Escobars pack their bags, a pair of journalists – Óscar Ritoré and Manuel Alberto Monsalve – get a tip-off. They book two of the last available seats on the Lufthansa flight from Bogotá to Frankfurt and get ready to head to the airport themselves.

At 1pm on 28 November 1993 armed helicopters are circling the Altos building as a caravan of ten SUVs pulls away. The Escobars are in motion. They are able to get to the airport in Medellín and fly to Bogotá without too much incident, but when they arrive at the capital city's El Dorado airport it is pandemonium.

The press are swarming the building, desperate for that perfect shot of the little-seen family of their country's most infamous fugitive. Tata tries to hide her face behind a loose item of clothing, and encourages her daughter Manuela to do the same. In contrast the surprisingly tall, broad figure of the teenage Juan Pablo, looking old beyond his years and dressed more like an aspiring rapper than a fugitive, merely pulls the peak of his baseball cap down lower over his eyes. They fight their way through the press pack and throngs of onlookers that follow them even into the VIP lounge, before eventually they are able to make their way through security.

Following in their wake is DEA agent Ken McGee. His office had also received intel on the Escobar family's departure – but had only been told their likely destination was either Frankfurt or London. He has tickets to both in his pocket. It's only when he sees the family head to the Lufthansa departure gate that he finally knows where they, and he, are going.

The Escobars, Ken McGee and the journalists Ritoré and Monsalve, finally board the jumbo jet. It's a commercial flight, and it's packed. Tata, Juan Pablo, Manuela and Ángeles have a row to themselves and McGee is able to observe them, and take covert photos on board. Manuela has a scarf wrapped around her head to protect her ears from the noise – her hearing damaged in the blast that had rocked the Altos only a few weeks earlier.

When the flight takes off, and the fasten seatbelt sign is finally switched off, Óscar Ritoré spots his chance. He hands Juan Pablo his business card, explains that he is a reporter, and offers to tell the family's side of the story if they will share it with him. In the end, Juan Pablo refuses an interview on the plane, but the reporter and his card will not be forgotten. The rest of the 5,000-mile flight passes without incident, at least until the plane touches down on German soil . . .

While the plane has been in the air, the DEA's Bogotá office have been on the phone to the German authorities. As soon as the Lufthansa jet's wheels hit the tarmac it comes to a very abrupt stop in the middle of the runway, the passenger terminal visible in the distance. From which is issuing a procession of vehicles – police cars, tanks, a fire engine, a set of mobile stairs.

The doors to the plane are opened by the cabin team, and the German police outside call out for the Escobar family to exit immediately. They are helped to the door and, as they descend the rickety metal staircase, Óscar Ritoré turns on his video camera and captures the moment they are met by police and escorted into separate vehicles. With the controversial passengers disembarked, the plane – with McGee, Ritoré and co all still on board – taxis over to the terminal.

The Escobars are met by agents from Interpol, and are whisked away to interview rooms within the airport. They don't pass through immigration or passport control, and are in limbo – they are neither allowed to formally enter Germany nor to take a flight to a further destination. Outside, the press pack have once again gathered, poised to pounce on any titbit of news. Ken McGee is afforded a look at the family's passports, and photographs every page, looking for clues in where they have been that might somehow help the DEA track down Pablo. As the hours pass, Tata and Juan Pablo plead their innocence.

They try to explain their situation, that they are requesting asylum in Germany and that if they are sent back to Colombia Pablo's enemies will surely have them killed. But their entreaties fall on deaf ears. Eventually they are escorted onto the next available flight back to Bogotá. After fewer than 24 hours in Germany, the escape plan has failed, and they are on their way back to Colombia and Los Pepes. They are accompanied on the plane by Ken McGee, still undercover, and now too by several German officials who join the flight to make sure these most toxic of visitors do indeed leave. The flight back to Colombia feels like a death sentence.

As in Frankfurt, when the plane touches down at El Dorado it stops in the middle of the runway. Colombian police approach and inform the Escobars that they have two choices: they can alight now and go with them, staying in Bogotá and once more entering into their formal protection, or they can carry on with the plane to the terminal and fly back to Medellín and take their chances. As the returning fugitives leave to go with the police, Ken McGee searches their seat pockets but finds little besides an empty envelope that might once have contained their travelling cash in US dollars and a note, handwritten and in English, that explains that they need help – presumably to be handed to a friendly face if they had ever been able to leave the airport.

The Escobars are taken to a new location for their protection: the Residencias Tequendama. This hotel and apartment complex is owned by the Colombian Armed Forces Retirement Fund, and is the only place the government claim they can guarantee their safety. But it has been deliberately chosen, and the family are given no choice, because as soon as they had had it confirmed that the Escobars were being deported from Germany the Colombian police had rigged the entire 29th floor of the building, where the family are to be housed, with wireless microphones. They are more certain than ever that Pablo will continue to try to communicate with his family and that this will give them the chance to finally apprehend him. The hotel is bugged, the bait is laid, and the trap to catch Pablo is set.

Far below, at ground level, 150 military policemen and plain clothes police and security officers keep an eye on all comings and goings, look underneath every car with angled bomb mirrors, and observe the surrounding buildings for snipers. The authorities need to keep the Escobars alive if they are to track and trap Pablo. They now fear that if Los Pepes manage to kill Tata and the kids, Pablo, with nothing left to lose, will unleash a new and deadly wave of desperate war.

Juan Pablo knows he must find a way to let his father know that they are okay, that they are, for now at least, safe. With no private means of external communication, cut off in a way they never were at the Altos, he comes up with a novel plan. Remembering the journalist from the plane, and his business card, he makes a call. It is no surprise that Óscar Ritoré drops everything to hurry to the hotel complex. The video footage from his time with the Escobars at the Tequendama is surreal and heartbreaking.

A nine-year-old Manuela sits on the apartment sofa, a big, fluffy, cuddly toy bunny beside her, and sings a song for the camera. She dedicates it to her dad. Her innocence lends her a calmness that borders on bravery if not happiness. In contrast, her mother looks pained, and Juan Pablo is clearly also feeling the strain. He speaks to the audience in a low, faltering, almost mumbling voice: 'We want to leave the country. We want to ask somebody to help us. I want to call on all violent people in Colombia to stop being violent and to find peace for this country.' After Ritoré leaves the apartment, curtains remain drawn, and eventually Juan Pablo heads up to the rooftop helipad to get some air.

Los Pepes issue Pablo a final ultimatum: 'If you don't hand yourself over by midnight on 31 December, then on New Year's Day we will start killing your family members. Your choice.' The pressure is on the Search Bloc team to find Pablo, and fast.

Chapter Twenty

The King is Dead (1993)

On 1 December 1993, Pablo Escobar turns 44 years old. He is hiding out with El Limón in an apartment in Los Olivos, a part of Medellín not far from the Atanasio Girardot, the home of his beloved Nacional (and indeed of their city rivals DIM). Despite everything, El Patrón has not been able to deny his love of football, and has even donned his disguise and sneaked out to go to one last game during November. But today he has no such joy. There is no cake, no champagne, no visit from his wife and children. He goes to bed alone.

It is the morning of 2 December 1993 when Victoria answers the door at the apartment at the top of the Tequendama to find three generals – one each from the army, navy and police – on her doorstep. Inviting them in, she barely registers the phone ringing. Juan Pablo answers the call. He alone hears the Tequendama receptionist as she tells him: 'Pablo Escobar is on the line, he'd like to speak to you.' He takes the call, but as soon as he realizes it is indeed his father he's desperate to get him off the line as quickly as possible – it is Pablo himself who has taught him that 'the phone is death'. Pablo placates his son, he's calling from a radiophone in one of his cabs and is on the move. As Juan Pablo pretends to be speaking to his grandmother, his father reiterates his plan to get AG de Greiff to send the family abroad. The young man ends the call but, before the generals leave, the phone rings again, and again it is Pablo. He demands to speak to his wife. Juan Pablo hands over the phone, saying it's his grandmother calling, and ushers the high-ranking visitors out before rushing back to make sure his mother hangs up the call.

But over the next few hours the calls continue, and each one seems to be dragged out a little longer despite Juan Pablo's best efforts. On the fifth call Pablo discusses an interview they are arranging with a German magazine which he hopes will help the family's case for asylum. He asks Juan Pablo to read out the questions so he can prepare his answers, and has El Limón, who is with him, transcribe them. Halfway through the list of questions, his father tells Juan Pablo 'I'll call you right back', then ends the call himself for the first time. Twenty minutes later the phone rings again as Pablo makes good on his promise. Little does Juan Pablo know that by now his father and El Limón have returned to the safe house in Los Olivos. Moments later Pablo abruptly ends the call without any warning or explanation. The phone does not ring again.

A DEA informant in the Tequendama has overheard Juan Pablo speaking to someone on a radiophone and, spotting the frequency and memorizing it, has called it in to Javier Peña – one of the key agents in the hunt for Pablo. Peña is able to relay the information to the Centra Spike pilot, who is in turn able to narrow down the signal.

On the ground a young lieutenant in the Search Bloc is racing to the area radioed in by Centra Spike in order to pinpoint the call's origin. He is Hugo Martínez Jr – the son of the inspirational leader of the Search Bloc. Using the radio triangulation techniques he has perfected over months of hunting for Pablo, he drives around the sector until he is finally able to identify a three-storey house in a quiet residential street in Los Olivos as the likely source of the signal. When he looks up and sees a dark-haired, bearded man at the second-storey window he knows he's hit the mother lode. He recognizes Pablo Escobar – the most wanted man in the world – instantly. He calls the sighting in to his father, and requests back up. But then, fearing the chance will slip away – El Patrón has slithered through their clutches more times than they can count – he takes an executive decision. With the support of just two fellow plain-clothes Search Bloc officers, he goes in.

Almost immediately they encounter El Limón and are pinned down by gunfire from the upper floors of the property. Only when the two narcos run low on ammunition do they retreat, giving young Martínez and his colleagues the chance to move up the stairs. As Pablo and his sicario attempt to climb out of a window and onto the neighbouring roof El Limón is hit and goes down. Then, as El Patrón, the world's most infamous narcoterrorist, makes a mad dash across the terracotta tiles of the Medellín rooftop, his beloved Atanasio Girardot almost visible in the distance, he too is hit. A bullet to the back of the leg makes him stumble, a second strikes him in the buttock as he falls, a third – the fatal kill shot – enters his skull beside the right ear. Or at least that's one version of events. Like almost any part of the Pablo Escobar story, there are several competing accounts. Was he shot, or did he put his gun to his head and pull the trigger himself? Rather a grave in Colombia, after all . . .

Whatever the truth of those final seconds, when the first of the Search Bloc officers reaches Pablo's body the message he gives on the radio changes the reality of an entire nation: *¡Viva Colombia!*

¡Matamos a Pablo Escobar!' 'Long live Colombia! Pablo Escobar is dead!'

In the Tequendama, Manuela is singing in the shower as Juan Pablo and his mother see the news breaking on television. At first they're not sure, Pablo's death has been reported erroneously before and somehow they can't bring themselves to believe that this time it could be true. As the video footage shows a body, its shape all too familiar, they realize it has finally happened. When Manuela is finished in the shower they help her dry off, get her dressed, and tell her that her father is dead.

Then they receive a call from Gloria Congote, a Colombian journalist and reporter. She tells them that the police have confirmed that it's Pablo, and that he's dead. As the experienced newshound prods him, Juan Pablo – a 16-year-old boy who has just learned that his father has been shot dead – is goaded into enunciating his anger: 'The ones who killed him . . . I will kill them. I myself will kill those bastards.' His words are broadcast across the country. No sooner is he off the call than he realizes his terrible mistake. He immediately calls a rival news outlet to recant his words: 'I want to clarify that I won't avenge my father's death, because now I am only concerned with the future of my suffering family. As Colombians, we want to live and for peace to prevail in this country.'

He then calls Gloria back to ask her to record a brief statement retracting what he had said. It is too late, that horse has bolted. Despite his best efforts to pour water on his instinctive, emotional and inflammatory words, it will take a quarter century of exile before Juan Pablo Escobar is able to safely return to Colombia under his own name and make peace.

At the DEA's office in Bogotá, 150 miles away, Special Agent in

Charge Joe Toft gets the news of Pablo's demise. His agent, and Javier Peña's partner on the coal face of the US hunt for Pablo, Steve Murphy, is immediately dispatched to the scene to confirm the kill. And confirm it he does: the photos show a blond, bespectacled Murphy squatting beside Pablo's body, looking more like an analyst than an all-action DEA field agent with his red V-neck T-shirt tucked into his blue jeans as he grabs El Patrón's sleeve and gives a moustachioed smile to the camera. Pablo, lying lifeless on the warm terracotta roof, looks like a man who has been on the run for too long. Barefoot; unshaven; long, lank, greasy hair haloed around his head; his pale blue jeans rolled up above his ankles, his long-sleeve blue top riding up to show a glimpse of a bare, pale, hairy stomach; his sleeves rolled up, his forearms smeared with blood. It is, in every way, an untidy end for the era's most infamous criminal.

Joe Toft heads straight over to the US Embassy, the biggest outside America, to tell the ambassador himself. As the Americans celebrate, the news shows Pablo's body being removed from the roof in Los Olivos. Helicopters buzz overhead, the street is filled with troops and onlookers – among them Pablo's bereft mother and sister who have themselves rushed to the scene. A man in a suit and tie helps pass the body down on a stretcher. The corpse is accepted by a man in a white coat and a trio of soldiers. Pablo's face is wiped clean of some of the blood with a multicoloured rag that might be a T-shirt, or a shell suit jacket. His eyes closed, from afar El Patrón looks like he might be at peace, at last.

President Gaviria gives a TV address, live to the nation. He stands at a lectern, reading from a sheaf of paper, chandeliers glowing in the background, guards standing smartly to attention, their golden helmets gleaming. 'I just received confirmation from the Minister of

Defence of the death of the narcoterrorist Pablo Escobar.' In his prison cell, Popeye cries the tears of a man who feels like a coward for not dying bravely beside his leader.

*

Pablo's body is quickly released, the autopsy completed as a matter of urgency, and lies in state overnight in a Medellín chapel. On 3 December comes the last polarizing act in the life, and death, of Pablo Emilio Escobar Gaviria: his funeral. While the rich and powerful celebrate the demise of the man who has brought untold death and destruction to a nation, the poor of Medellín swarm across a hillside in the southwest of the city.

Against Juan Pablo's advice, Tata has insisted she attend the funeral. After a short flight from Bogotá, the family are met as they disembark the small plane and are helped into official vehicles which spirit them away in a convoy to the Jardines Montesacro cemetery. As they drive up, they can see thousands of people lining the road, queuing for miles alongside the high, chain-link fence. At the entrance military police in their armbands frisk each and every visitor. It's a painstakingly slow process, and the crowds build, the bottleneck increasing. The queue swells, the mourners chanting: 'We want to see Pablo! We want to see Pablo!' Soon order evaporates. The crowd breaks, and pushes through the security cordon. Men and women are running up the steep, slippery grass hillside of the cemetery grounds. In the chaos, the security detail attempts to close ranks around the Escobar family, their safety suddenly a very real concern. To stem the tide, the gates to the cemetery are closed, but this only enrages the thousands locked out. Those who have made it within, climb up on the roofs of the buildings, smash windows, chant and sing. It's part-festival, part-riot. Tata is escorted up towards the chapel but Juan Pablo has been held back, and only learns that she has made it safely inside when he hears it on the radio commentary of events as he shelters in an armoured car. She is mobbed as soldiers help her take the last few steps inside to the relative calm of the cool, dark building.

The mournful, celebratory, overwhelming spectacle reaches a crescendo as the long, slim silver casket bearing the mortal remains of the man who has cast a giant shadow over the city of Medellín, and the country of Colombia, for more than a decade is carried towards the chapel. The crowd swarms the casket as it pushes through them leaving human eddies in its wake. The authorities appear to have lost control. The casket tips alarmingly and seems about to fall, but is righted at the last moment. Young men in particular, in T-shirts and short-sleeved shirts, dark-haired, many sporting smart moustaches, jostle to get closer, reaching out to hug the wooden box. These are the boys from the barrios, the footballers and foot soldiers, the kids who looked up to El Patrón, who were grateful for what he had done for them, for their families, for their city. As they grasp the casket the lid is momentarily opened, to reveal a glimpse within of Pablo lying there darkly and smartly dressed, his shoulders barely fitting within the white silken interior, red and pink flowers scattered around his head, shoulders and chest. There's still a red mark on his forehead. His beard remains. Those closest are able to reach in, deposit another flower, their hands briefly stroking his face. Some even try to get scraps of his clothing, as if he is a saint; others shout 'We can feel it, Pablo is here.' Then the lid closes once more, and Pablo vanishes.

Inside, an old woman, her grey hair tied back, wails in sadness: 'Pablo, our saviour! You can't leave us! What will we do without you? You gave us our homes, a gift from your heart.'

Outside the chapel, Pablo's sister is speaking into a bank of microphones amid a noisy crowd, her eyes fixed firmly ahead. Looking right into the camera, her red lipstick and short dark hair impeccable, the twinkle of gold dangling from her ears, she utters her words: 'I ask you, Señor Presidente de la República, do you really believe the violence in Colombia will end now that my brother is dead? Don't be naïve.'

When the body of Pablo Escobar is finally committed to the soil of Medellín, his coffin is covered with a cloth of green and white – the flag of Atlético Nacional. His grave briefly bears the inscription *'Aquí Yace el Rey'*, 'Here Lies the King', before the government orders it to be removed – scrubbed clean just as he had once done to the headstones of others to turn a few pesos all those years ago.

For Medellín, for Colombia, it is the end of an awful, bloody, brutal and uncertain era. Pablo's reign of terror is finally over. The world's biggest narcoterrorist is dead. But for some his legendary status as the Robin Hood of Antioquia, the man who built homes and football pitches, and gave jobs, healthcare, help and hope to some of the most destitute, overlooked and forgotten people of Medellín, lives on. Even in death Pablo remains an impossible contradiction, an enigma the likes of which we may never see again.

Chapter Twenty-One

Nature Abhors a Vacuum (1994)

The death of the world's most infamous criminal, the narcoterrorist Pablo Escobar, has one perhaps unforeseen consequence. With the man the authorities hoped to force him to turn on now dead, on 4 January 1994 René Higuita is finally released from prison. However, he has been incarcerated for seven months, and it soon becomes apparent that he is too out of shape to rejoin the Colombia squad as they make their final, vital preparations for USA '94. No number of prison pick-up games – which he would play in at every opportunity, leaping to save in his bright green shell suit and instantly springing up to throw the ball out to a teammate – could keep him match fit enough to play in the biggest tournament in world football. Let alone when you factor in the dietary imbalance of his prison meals.

Higuita is ultimately found not guilty. In a TV interview afterwards, resplendent in a brightly coloured shell suit, he tells the female interviewer that even now, knowing the law, he would do the same thing again, to save a life, to reunite a family. He retains the love of the nation, but his friendship with Pablo has cost him not just seven months of liberty and a significant amount of pesos but his chance to play in a World Cup. It's devastating for Higuita, and Maturana and the public must now pin their hopes on the young keeper who performed heroics in El Loco's absence, not least in repeatedly thwarting Batistuta and co in Buenos Aires: Óscar Córdoba.

However, Higuita's enforced absence aside, to the casual onlooker the omens look good. Colombia have qualified for USA '94 in style, conceding only two goals, thrashing Argentina 5-0 in Buenos Aires and only losing one game in a run of twenty-six going into the World Cup finals. When Brazilian legend Pelé makes Los Cafeteros his tip for the tournament the world stands up and takes notice.

But behind the scenes, all is not as it should be. The squad is overwhelmed with sponsorship deals, advertising shoots, press calls and the entire national media circus that accompanies their success. Faustino Asprilla stars in a commercial for Pepsi. Even busier is Andrés Escobar, *el caballero de la cancha* ('the gentleman of the pitch'), the squeaky-clean pin-up of the squad for whom all the brands are clamouring. The squad are made to play pointless friendly after pointless friendly to cash in on their market value, many arranged by a key sponsor, the Colombian beer brand Bavaria. But, as the players become the new superstar celebrities who will bring success to Colombia and show the world the true, positive, joyous face of a nation for so long known only for the death and destruction wrought by Pablo Escobar, their country descends once more into chaos.

The death of Pablo does not bring an end to the drug trade, to the trafficking of Colombian cocaine to the USA and Europe, to criminality, violence and death. Instead, it creates a vacuum. The Cali Cartel act quickly to position themselves to fill the void, ready to assume the mantle as the new kings of the Colombian cocaine trade, and the illegal underworld as a whole. But this transitional period is a tortured, violent one.

Pacho Maturana and his squad prepare to depart for America not buoyed by hope but burdened by expectation and their fears for what might happen to their families in their absence from the country. They are, nevertheless, determined to show the world Colombia's true colours, and none more so than Andrés Escobar, who has devoted much of his time, energy and money to helping the homeless, orphaned and disadvantaged children of his homeland. The cultured centre back is on the cusp of signing a contract with Italian giants AC Milan, who have kept tabs on him ever since that dramatic game in Tokyo more than four years ago. But he leaves Colombia having only recently barely escaped with his life after a bomb exploded at a plaza he was on his way to visit with his girlfriend. For now at least, Medellín is just as dangerous with Pablo gone.

Shortly before leaving for the USA, Andrés is interviewed at a training session. He looks into the camera and, speaking into the microphone, utters the prophetic words: 'We're trying not to focus on the violence. The only way we'll play well in the World Cup is by focusing on the game.'

The World Cup is not just a big deal for Colombia, or for the other competing countries – it is also a huge event for host nation America, and for FIFA. When, in 1986, FIFA had chosen Mexico ahead of an impressive US bid to stage their showpiece tournament in place of Colombia – who had withdrawn their right to hold the event – it had been the death knell for the US domestic 'soccer' league, the NASL. Now FIFA are determined that the beautiful game will finally conquer this last outpost and turn the USA into a global football cash cow.

The tournament begins with an ill-fated opening ceremony in Chicago on 17 June 1994. It is hot, sunny and humid as MC Oprah Winfrey gees up the crowd – before falling off the stage. The B-52s perform, but the global audience can't help but see they are lip-syncing. Diana Ross runs up to take the ceremonial opening penalty, but screws her spot kick wide. Nevertheless, the pre-planned routine continues with the goal splitting in half from the imaginary thunderous shot, as fireworks explode. In the opening game immediately afterwards, Germany struggle to defeat a spirited Bolivian side. And yet despite everything the sell-out crowd, President Bill Clinton among them, appears to have a blast. Perhaps all will be well, after all?

*

Colombia begin their World Cup the following day. As captain Carlos Valderrama leads the team out into the bright mid-afternoon sunshine that bathes the Pasadena Rose Bowl, packed with a capacity crowd of well over 90,000 spectators, that famous win in the febrile, hostile atmosphere of El Monumental in Buenos Aires seems a lifetime ago. Their opponents for their opening game are Romania, who boast a strong side led by skipper and inspirational playmaker Gheorghe Hagi and featuring the likes of Dan Petrescu, Gica Popescu, Dorinel Munteanu, Florin Răducioiu and Ilie Dumitrescu. But Colombia, on such a tremendous run of form coming into the tournament, look the side to beat, and their starting XI is a strong one.

In goal is the new, young hope and heir to Higuita's throne, América de Cali keeper Óscar Córdoba. The defence is marshalled as ever by the calm, stately Andrés Escobar, the first Colombian ever to be offered a contract by the mighty AC Milan. Alongside him the powerful and athletic Luis Perea, with whom he has a strong understanding built over three shared seasons at Atlético Nacional in the late 1980s and for the national side ever since. The rest of the back four is made up of Escobar's Nacional teammate Chonto Herrera and a second América player, Wilson Pérez. In midfield, to allow for Maturana's open, expressive system, there are two holding players – Leonel Álvarez, who won the Copa Libertadores with Pablo's Nacional but now plays for their Cali rivals América, and Gabriel Gómez. Gómez, often referred to by his middle name Barrabás, is a Nacional legend, who in his 14 seasons as a pro in Colombia will only ever play for sides bankrolled by the Medellín Cartel: Nacional, Millonarios and DIM. He is also the younger brother of Pacho's long-time assistant coach Hernán Darío Gómez. These two enforcers, Álvarez and Barrabás, give Maturana the ability to field two very different attacking midfielders: the captain and talisman Carlos Valderrama, the twice-crowned South American player of the year whose unrivalled range of passing knits together everything Colombia do, and the pace and power of Freddy Rincón who is able to bomb forward and supplement the attack – as indeed he did to such effect so late on against West Germany a full four years earlier. In attack Pacho pairs the brute force of Adolfo 'El Tren' Valencia – who has just helped his side Bayern Munich regain the Bundesliga title in Germany, finishing joint-top scorer for Franz Beckenbauer's Bavarian side – with the unpredictable trickery of Parma and former Atlético Nacional star Faustino Asprilla, who the television commentators laud as one of the top four players in world football.

With the other two sides in what looks like an evenly balanced Group A, the home nation the United States and Switzerland, having played out a 1-1 draw at the Pontiac Silverdome just outside Detroit just a few hours earlier, Romania and Colombia know that whoever wins this game will top the table and take a huge step towards qualification for the knockout stages. The crowd is packed with Colombia fans, the stands a shimmering sea of yellow, red and blue. Over their heads soars the famous Birdman, dangling impossibly above his compatriots, suspended from the railings, his giant, colourful wings waving hypnotically. At the edge of the centre circle, Tino Asprilla makes the sign of the cross. Colombia, in their away kit – a brilliant blue that echoes the wings of the shimmering hummingbirds and bountiful butterflies of their homeland – begin the game on the front foot as Maturana, stylishly attired in a brown suit, watches on from his technical area. An early touch for Escobar calms the nerves, as he turns inside his man and out of trouble. Valderrama begins to dictate play, Valencia threatens in behind the Romanian defence with his direct running, and Los Cafeteros look dangerous. This is the Colombia the world was expecting.

But, just as Colombia are imposing themselves on the game, it is turned on its head. With their first meaningful attack, Romania score, Hagi pouncing on a rare, misplaced pass by Valderrama to set Răducioiu free, the AC Milan striker cutting inside two retreating Colombian defenders and planting a right-footed shot into the far corner of Córdoba's goal. Sixteen minutes into their World Cup campaign and Colombia are behind. In the stands a fan sporting a yellow Colombia headband swigs disconsolately from a bottle of what might be white rum, or perhaps aguardiente.

The response from Los Cafeteros is immediate. El Tren Valencia brings down a high, awkward ball on the edge of the Romanian box and fires off a right-foot volley that is clawed away by a diving Bogdan Stelea in the Romanian goal. A Colombian corner is flicked on by the long-haired Escobar and a shot from just a few yards out is somehow saved by the legs of Stelea. Another shot rains in and is saved by the Romanian keeper. Surely it's just a matter of time before Colombia get their equalizer? The commentators fear otherwise, musing as to whether this might just not be their day. And, for all the Colombian possession and pressure, Romania remain dangerous on the break – an audacious Hagi chip from fully 40 yards forcing a flying Córdoba to tip the ball away from the top corner. It's a warning that Colombia fail to heed. On 34 minutes comes one of the moments of the tournament. Hagi receives a pass from Munteanu just a few yards from the left touchline, takes a touch, and sends in an arcing shot from well outside the Colombian penalty area. Córdoba is caught out, and it sails into the top corner. It's not even half time, and Colombia find themselves inexplicably two goals down. Their World Cup dream is already threatening to turn into a nightmare.

But, just before half time, comes that most dangerous of things for any football fan – a glimmer of hope. A corner from the left is whipped in by Wilson Pérez, and there to meet it is an express train: Adolfo Valencia powering a thumping header from the corner of the six-yard box past the flailing arms of Stelea. Game on. The Colombian fans make themselves heard, the stadium erupting in a joyous cacophony. An entertaining first half ends with the score 2-1 to Romania. Colombia are not dead and buried just yet.

The second half is agony for Colombia's fans in the stadium, and those watching and listening at home in Bogotá, Medellín, Cali and across the world. Minute after minute ticks by, and no equalizer arrives. The teams trade chances in a game that becomes increasingly end to end. Asprilla is a constant thorn in the Romanian side, bamboozling their defence with his trickery and forcing Stelea into a string of saves. Then, beating two defenders in the inside left channel of the box, he falls to the turf as a desperate, lunging challenge comes in. It looks a stonewall penalty, but his imploring look to the Syrian referee is met only with the universal hand gesture for 'get up, lad'.

In response, Romanian coach Anghel Iordănescu looks to shore up his defence and see out the game, bringing on a left back in place of attacking midfielder Dumitrescu.

With a minute to go, Colombia are still pushing for the equalizer when Hagi, ever alert, knocks a cultured long pass through with his left boot. Răducioiu beats Córdoba to the ball and finishes into the unguarded net from a tight angle to finally and brutally dash Colombian hopes. It's a rude awakening for Los Cafeteros. They have dominated the game, but possession and chances mean nothing compared to goals. This is football at the highest level, and today they have been found wanting. It's a painful lesson to have to learn so publicly. The English commentary is eerily prophetic: 'and Colombia here are dead and buried'. The worst is yet to come . . .

*

At 6pm on Sunday 19 June, 15 miles outside Medellín, on the main road that links the country's second city to its capital Bogotá, Chonto Herrera's older brother Jairo Alberto is riding in a public minibus when it attempts a reckless overtaking manoeuvre on a Renault 4 and crashes spectacularly into another oncoming minibus. Jairo is killed in the accident, one of eight who perish. Nineteen are injured.

After training, Chonto returns to the team hotel to find all the players waiting for him. Pacho Maturana takes him aside and tells him his brother has been killed. When Chonto finally speaks to his father back in Colombia he wastes no time in asking him if it was indeed an accident, or if his brother was murdered. All his dad can say is that he shouldn't worry about coming home for the funeral and that the best tribute he can give his brother is to play like never before in the upcoming game.

It is the start of a long, dark night of the soul for Los Cafeteros, for Colombian football, and for Colombia in general. Back home the surviving cartel bosses have lost millions confidently backing their team. With Pablo dead, Maturana and his team have lost their patron saint, their criminal guardian angel. From thousands of miles away *una mano negra*, a 'black hand', reaches out to claim them in its grip. Los Cafeteros descend into a psychological crisis for which even they are not prepared.

That evening Andrés Escobar keeps Chonto company. The full back wants to give up, to go home, to be with his grieving family. But his teammate talks him around. Colombia is depending on them. This is their one shot at the World Cup. Little did they know the wheels are already coming off the Colombian campaign.

Pacho Maturana and his assistant Hernán Darío Gómez, known as *El Bolillo*, have received anonymous threats from back home. Given the violence still raging in Medellín, they have no doubt they are genuine. They are told they must drop Barrabás Gómez, Hernán's brother and a stalwart of Medellín's Atlético Nacional, for the next game, which is to be against the host nation. If Barrabás plays, their homes in Colombia will be bombed. The threats come to them in faxes sent to the team hotel, in calls to their rooms, even in messages displayed on their television screens.

In the words of Pacho himself: 'Someone programmed the hotel TVs. It freaked us out. I couldn't put another's life in danger. Barrabás was a key player. But . . . they had me beat.'

When the players arrive for the team meeting before the crunch game against the USA no one speaks. Eventually coach Maturana arrives, his thick, black hair having seemingly gained streaks of grey at the temples overnight, tears in his eyes. He reveals the line-up. Sure enough, Barrabás is dropped. In comes Hernán Gaviria. It adds a whole new dimension to the footballing phrase 'enforced change'. Everyone in that room is under no illusion, their careers, their livelihoods, their very lives and those of their families, hang in the balance. Such is the power of the Cali Cartel now that Pablo is gone. They call their loved ones in Colombia, and find that, as Medellín once more erupts into violence, police have been dispatched to their homes. Football is suddenly the furthest thing from their minds, and yet here they are, about to play one of the most important games of their careers, one of the biggest matches in the history of their nation.

The Colombian team have a strong record against the USA, having bested Los Gringos in a number of friendlies. But in the changing room before the game, as they walk hesitantly out onto the bright green grass of the Pasadena pitch, and as they stand stock still for the national anthem, their haunted eyes betray them. Their actions seem awkward, robotic, automatic and lacking that essential human quality, that joy and hope and energy, with which they had begun the game against Romania. Everything has changed.

If the Romania game was a valiant, heroic and ill-deserved defeat, the game against the USA is a brutal slow-motion car crash. The home commentators bill it as the biggest game in the history of US 'soccer'. The USMNT (United States Men's National Team) have not won a World Cup game since a famous victory over England in 1950. Switzerland, coached by Englishman Roy Hodgson, have already pulled off a comprehensive and somewhat unexpected 4-1 win over Romania, leaving Colombia knowing that failure in their game will put qualification out of their own hands. It's an added pressure they could do without.

Another sell-out crowd of over 90,000 pack the Pasadena Rose

Bowl, swollen with an army of Los Cafeteros fans, brightly bedecked in yellow, red and blue. Again the afternoon sun beats down on the pristine emerald-green pitch. As the camera pans across the Colombia players in the pre-kick-off line-up they stare vacantly from hooded eyes, resigned to a fate of which none of us yet know. Carlos Valderrama, Leonel Álvarez, Andrés Escobar – all stand still as statues, not a smile between them.

Maturana has made two changes – as well as bringing in Gaviria for Barrabás, he has also dropped the bullish Valencia for the quicksilver Antony de Ávila. Back home in Colombia there is confusion and consternation, and many begin to question who is really picking the team and why – for surely the strongest strike pairing is Asprilla and Valencia? At least this time La Selección are wearing their regular kit: perhaps the yellow shirts, blue shorts and red socks will bring them the luck they need. The US team lacks star power or household names, although Alexei Lalas has quickly become a cult hero due to his ginger locks, goatee and penchant for the guitar. On paper, this should be the game for Colombia to get their tilt at the title back on track.

And, after only a few minutes, there's a sliding doors moment that could have changed the course of modern footballing history. The American goalkeeper is beaten to the ball at the by-line, and the cut back looks destined to reach the perfectly placed de Ávila, only for it to cannon into a retreating US defender and ricochet onto the goalpost. Even then, the ball bounces back out to de Ávila who shoots from four yards out but sees his effort strike the same defender as he stumbles on the line. The rebound is finally cleared by a second defender, the chance is gone and the score remains 0-0.

Colombia launch wave after wave of attacks, Rincón and de Ávila in particular stinging the gloves of US goalie and team captain Tony

Meola – a player without a club contract, who immediately after the World Cup will try, and fail, to swap sports and earn a spot as a place kicker for the NFL's New York Jets. But no matter what Valderrama, Asprilla and co can throw at him, the pony-tailed American stands tall. At the other end the USA are limited to pot shots from the edge of the area, but even then the inexperienced Córdoba looks a little jittery, spilling a routine save and hinting at the nerves that are running through the entire squad.

If those nerves were hidden, they are thrown into stark relief before the half is up. First comes the moment that will define Colombian football for a generation. It starts innocuously enough, just after the half hour mark, when Andrés Escobar plays a pass up the line in the inside left channel to Asprilla. Tino cuts inside and lays off a pass with his right foot – straight to a USA player. The Americans recycle the ball and spray it cross-field from right back to the left wing, where Derby County midfielder John Harkes advances deep into Colombia's half. He's still a good ten yards from the left corner of the penalty area when he cuts inside and curls a dipping ball across the box. There's only one grey-blue US shirt in the vicinity but, as Córdoba starts to scramble along his six-yard line to follow the predicted flight of the ball, Andrés Escobar, ever alert to the danger, ever the spare man mopping up and snuffing out the threat, slides in on the penalty spot to cut out the cross before it reaches its intended target. But, for once, he gets it all wrong. From maybe 16 yards out his long, outstretched leg manages only to divert the ball straight at the centre of his own goal. Córdoba is already too far across, too committed, to get back and stop it rolling agonizingly beyond him. Totally wrong-footed, the young keeper collapses in anguish, arching his back and falling to the turf like a stricken Sergeant Elias in the final moments of Oliver Stone's seminal Vietnam war film *Platoon*. The ball rolls into the net. Time stops. In the background the electric advertising hoarding behind the goal proclaims Gillette to the world. When Escobar can finally drag himself up from the turf and walk disconsolately away he breathes out slowly, puffing his cheeks, a haunted look in his eyes as he takes in the reactions of his teammates.

Back home in Colombia, Andrés' nine-year-old nephew turns to his mother, tears in his eyes: 'Mummy, they're going to kill Andrés!' Her words of comfort: 'No, sweetheart, people aren't killed for mistakes. Everyone in Colombia loves Andrés.'

On the pitch, a shell-shocked Colombia stagger towards half time like a punch-drunk boxer clinging on for the end-of-round bell. Córdoba rushes out of his goal and loses the ball, but is bailed out by his defender – it's an error entirely out of character for the conservative shot-stopper, a move much more in keeping with the mad genius of his predecessor in the number one jersey, El Loco. Colombia are all over the place. A US break ends with a shot clipping the outside of the post. Finally the ref blows to end the first half and Maturana can do his best to repair the psychological damage. But his half-time decisions come as a surprise to everyone watching. He makes a double change to his strike force, as he hooks not only de Ávila but also Asprilla. Valencia, unlucky to have been dropped, is finally on the pitch – but will not be playing alongside his regular partner and provider Tino but instead Iván Valenciano. Faustino Asprilla – a key member of the team that beat Argentina in Buenos Aires and had only lost once in nearly 30 games going into this World Cup, one of the side's only truly world class players and their principal goal threat – will be unable to influence the game any further and must instead watch from the bench as his teammates embark on a 45 minutes that will shape their destinies. It's a bold move by Maturana. Some might call it otherwise . . .

Early in the second half the USA have the ball in the net a second time, a shot crashing in off Córdoba's crossbar, yet Colombia get a lucky reprieve as the goal is chalked off for what looks to be an extremely tight offside call. Los Cafeteros fail to heed the warning, and only three minutes later the Americans get that vital second. USMNT striker Ernie Stewart gets in behind Luis Perea and reaches the ball before the onrushing Córdoba. His gentle shot tickles the inside of the post on its way in. Maturana, normally so calm, remonstrates with his players from the dugout. The only positive is that this goal has come early, that Colombia still have time to try to dig themselves out of the hole.

But while Valenciano continues to shoot wildly high and wide at one end, the USA test Córdoba repeatedly at the other. Nothing is coming off for the Colombians. Every header drops right into the grateful gloves of Meola. Every half-chance is snatched at and scuffed embarrassingly wide.

Then, on 89 minutes, when the USA keeper can only palm a fierce close-range strike up into the air, it drops right at the feet of Adolfo Valencia. Finally, a moment of good fortune. And, finally, the line is not fluffed. El Tren knocks the ball into the empty net. But, with just injury time remaining, the Colombians know it is too little too late. And so it proves. As the whistle goes the Americans celebrate like it's the Fourth of July, Tony Meola sprinting off with his arms windmilling as the stars and stripes wave in the crowd. Soon flags are passed to the heroic keeper and his teammates, and they parade them as they perform a lap of honour. Alone in the centre circle, Leonel Álvarez squats down on his haunches, head in his hands, contemplating his team's fate.

Chapter Twenty-Two

The Darkest Day (1994)

Los Cafeteros are shell-shocked, but they cannot afford to wallow in their despair. They still have a chance to qualify for the knockout stages if they can finish third in the four-team group and earn a spot as one of the best third-place finishers. They'll need to beat Switzerland in the final game, and hope that the Americans can do them a favour and find a way to defeat Romania. It means qualification is out of their hands, but all is not quite yet lost. But, as they say, it's the hope that kills you . . .

The final group game for the Colombians is due to take place at the Stanford Stadium, 350 miles north of the Rose Bowl. And Pacho and El Bolillo have just four days to repair the damage done to their talented squad, who are still reeling not just from the seismic defeat at the hands of the USA but also the aftermath of swirling rumours and constant fear engendered by the flurry of death threats from back home. Meanwhile the Swiss know they are already safely qualified. However, with the possibility of finishing top of the group still on the cards, and thus a potential kinder draw for the first knockout game, manager Roy Hodgson names an unchanged, full-strength side. Fresh from thrashing Romania 4-1, and boasting Borussia Dortmund's dangerous striker Stéphane Chapuisat in attack, the Swiss are not to be underestimated.

Knowing only a victory will give his side any hope of escaping the group, Maturana recalls Tino Asprilla to play alongside El Tren Valencia. As a result, the only difference between the team he picked for the opening game, that bitterly hard to swallow defeat to a Hagi-inspired Romania, and this starting XI is the continued absence of Barrabás Gómez in midfield, his spot once again taken by Hernán Gaviria. It's almost his strongest side, and it gives those watching back home a glimmer of hope that Colombia can somehow survive.

At shortly before 1pm on Sunday 26 June 1994, captain Carlos Valderrama leads his team out in front of over 80,000 fans who have packed out the famous Stanford University's college football stadium. At the same time, far to the south along the Californian coastline, the hero of the USMNT's shock victory over Los Cafeteros, Tony Meola, captains the USA once again in the Pasadena Rose Bowl. For Colombians everywhere, but perhaps especially those in Medellín, there is a fervent, desperate hope that football can somehow bring respite from the chaos and carnage that Pablo Escobar has wrought on their city, their country, their families and friends for over a decade – a chaos that has not abated even with his death. This is Colombia's golden generation; Los Cafeteros have become a symbol of hope, a beacon of national pride when there was nothing else but death and destruction. For them to fail, and so spectacularly, is unthinkable.

The shackles seemingly finally off, Colombia start the game like the proverbial house on fire. Valderrama's clever promptings continually release Asprilla to run at, and torment, the Swiss defence, his teammates Rincón and Valencia profiting from the chaos his unpredictable skills create and raining shots down on the goal of

Swiss keeper Marco Pascolo. But they find the 6ft 2in Servette stopper in fine form, and can only watch as a succession of clean strikes are tipped over the bar or around the post, as the keeper dives bravely at the feet of onrushing strikers when they are clean through. Then a goalmouth scramble ends with Valderrama's shot seemingly striking the arm of a desperate, diving defender. The Colombians appeal, but their remonstrations are in vain and the Danish referee waves them away. Even the ice-cool, dark-suited Maturana looks enervated on the touchline. As the end of the first half looms, the score is still 0-0, and it seems the game might be a repeat of that against Romania.

Forty-four minutes are on the clock as the man all Colombians call El Pibe, the kid, stands over a free kick out on the right, some 35 yards from goal. He knocks in a dipping right-footed cross that clears the first Swiss defenders and is met, unchallenged just on the edge of the six-yard box, by the flying head of Hernán Gaviria – the man Maturana has brought in to replace poor Barrabás Gómez. Distracted by the collisions in front of him, Pascolo fumbles the save, and the ball is in the net. It's 1-0 to Colombia. The dream is still alive, they might still be able to awaken from this nightmare. The celebrations are of relief as much as joy, as Gaviria salutes the Colombia fans from the corner flag. Chonto Herrera and Leonel Álvarez are the first to reach him, to jump on his back, to ruffle his hair, as in the Stanford stands the Birdman waves his brightly coloured wings.

But at half time, the news from Pasadena is a gut punch. Romania are 1-0 up on the United States thanks to a goal from their attacking full back Dan Petrescu. No matter what they do on the pitch, if the USA can't get back into the game at the Rose Bowl, Colombia will be out of the World Cup, falling at the first hurdle of a tournament they had been tipped by many, including Pelé, to win.

The second half is a carbon copy of the first, Colombia unable to find that final ball, that last, telling touch, to kill off the game, Switzerland threatening from range but finding it impossible to beat Córdoba. But, with the score further south also stuck resolutely at 1-0, it all feels academic. The clock ticks by, half chances come and go, the fouls tot up. Then Valderrama threads the ball through, linking midfield and attack. Asprilla jinks and turns and drives towards goal. Pascolo saves. It's yet more déjà vu. But, on 89 minutes, it's hearts in mouths time as Chapuisat collects the ball and shoots, unchallenged, from 16 yards. It's the best chance of the game for the Swiss. But the cultured striker's effort is uncharacteristically wayward, ballooning well over the bar. The Colombians are stung into the realization that a late Swiss equalizer would condemn them, that there may still be a chance for a miraculous comeback by the USA in Pasadena. Just over a minute later, as the clock ticks into injury time, Asprilla is set free to scamper down the right flank. His ball inside is taken on into the box by substitute Harold Lozano. The tall América de Cali midfielder feints to cut inside then takes the ball on the outside of the defender and finishes low past the keeper from a tight angle. There's a moment of joy, the natural reaction to scoring a goal, to winning a match – especially in a World Cup, and in front of over 80,000 spectators. But it's short-lived. The USA have lost, beaten 1-0 by Romania at the Rose Bowl. Colombia will finish last in their group; they're going home uncertain, fearful even, of what their reception will be.

*

World Cup USA '94 will be remembered for many things, most of them – despite the crowds, the razzmatazz and the commercial success – negative. Maradona's demonic grimace into the pitch-side camera presaging yet another positive drugs test for cocaine and his expulsion from the Argentina squad and the tournament; one of the World Cup's least memorable final games, won by Brazil but only thanks to a horrific penalty shoot-out miss from the inspirational Italian striker Roberto Baggio. But few would likely remember how Colombia went from one of the favourites for the cup to finishing bottom of their group and failing to even make the knockout stages without the events that would unfold not long after the return of Los Cafeteros to the motherland.

In Colombia, and in particular in Medellín, the death of the world's most infamous criminal, the narcoterrorist Pablo Escobar, has left a dangerous power vacuum. It is into this uncertain new world that Colombia's footballers return. At a press conference, Pacho Maturana announces he is stepping down as manager of the national team with the words 'I've taken all I can take'. Andrés Escobar, brave to a fault, also takes his turn at the microphone and expresses his sadness that the team could not live up to expectations. He still looks somewhat shell-shocked.

While still in America, he had sent a letter to *El Tiempo* newspaper – desperate to bring healing and hope to Colombia in the aftermath of the violent end to the era of his namesake Pablo, and make sense of the crushing failure of Los Cafeteros in the World Cup. Now, back in Medellín, Andrés begins to put his life back together. He never watches his own goal, the only one he had ever scored in his career, but instead surrounds himself with friends and family.

Doing his best to get back to some semblance of normality, his appeal to his people yet to be published by *El Tiempo*, Andrés decides to show his face in public. The World Cup is still continuing in America, without Colombia, when he calls his close friend Chonto

Herrera and asks if he wants to go out with him. Chonto declines the offer, warning Andrés that they should just stay in and lie low for a while. Ignoring the words of Chonto and the entreaties of Pacho Maturana – who had also warned him to just stay at home, that in Medellín the streets were still dangerous and that here arguments were not merely settled with fists – the 27-year-old footballer gets ready to go out on the town. He's had threats and warnings, but it's not the first time, and so, determined to live his life, he heads out into the Medellín night.

He meets up with a small group of friends and they head to a bar in El Poblado. After a while they leave for the El Indio nightclub. Quiet and reserved, some might even say shy, after a few drinks Andrés is feeling relaxed and happy for the first time in days. He chats to anyone and everyone as the sea of people in the club ebbs and flows around him. As the night progresses his group of friends dwindles as they drift away to drink or dance or leave. In the early hours of the morning of what is now 2 July someone begins to taunt Andrés, aggressively and sarcastically thanking him for scoring such a beautiful own goal. Unwilling to get into an argument in a nightclub, Andrés leaves. He walks out of the doors of the long, low warehouse-like building beneath the giant flashing neon 'El Indio' sign, crosses the parking lot and gets into his car. But as he starts to drive through the car park he finds a group, containing the man who had been goading him in the club, has followed him outside. As he pulls alongside to try to placate them the CCTV cameras, mounted high above, capture the group scuttling like insects to surround his car. One of the men approaches Andrés, and fires his gun six times through the driver's side door and window. The men scatter, and a vehicle drives off. Andrés lies slumped in his car. It is shortly after 3am.

It is still dark when the press inevitably arrives, and the crime scene is like something out of a classic Hollywood noir. The TV footage shows a car with its windshield completely shattered, a man shining a torch on the interior as another peers in through the gaping hole. In the background, his laminated ID clipped to his long white coat, a camera hanging around his neck, another man watches on. The footage catches a glimpse, in a long wing mirror, of a body slumped within. A side window has a spider's web of cracked glass where a bullet has struck. The front seats where the blue fabric is stained dark red, still slick and shiny with blood and gore.

Andrés' fiancée Pamela Cascardo, his sister Maria, his friends and family, his teammates, are woken in the middle of the night by the call they had all feared. Andrés is dead. Chonto Herrera, enveloped by the guilt of having neither managed to dissuade his friend from going out nor accompany him and somehow keep him out of trouble – and still scarred by the kidnapping of his son, the death of his brother and the trauma of the failed World Cup campaign – descends into a dark well of despair. Tino Asprilla and Carlos Valderrama can only remember being unable to stop crying.

The funeral of Andrés Escobar takes place on 3 July 1994, the same day that *El Tiempo* prints his now posthumous letter. His words show a man desperate to offer some explanation, some comfort, some contrition – and yet they are, perhaps like him in that moment, confused, labyrinthine even. He refuses to acknowledge or blame any external factors, and surely to do so would have been to sign his own death warrant. Instead, he attempts to end with a sense of calm and optimism – he calls for respect and offers a comforting hug to all. But it is the final sentence of all that lingers: '*Hasta pronto porque la vida no termina aquí*' ('See you soon, because life doesn't end here').

Around 2,000 mourners process through Medellín. It is somehow both just like the funeral of Pablo Escobar and simultaneously nothing like the funeral of Pablo Escobar. The hearse is flanked by young soldiers in soft cloth caps, its roof adorned with a cornucopia of flowers. The vehicle almost disappears amid the thick throng of people. Nacional flags wave disconsolately. At the grave site even the trees are swarming with observers there to pay their respects. On the slopes a group wave and cheer, sporting Nacional colours, wearing their beloved football shirts, waving their green and white flags – a cluster of football fans saying goodbye to their hero, their captain, in the best way they know how. It is everything Pablo's funeral was not – peaceful, respectful and heart-achingly sombre.

President Gaviria walks over to console Andrés' family. From the microphone come the words: 'Andrés Escobar will remain in our hearts as our hero of moral integrity, as a family man and exemplary Colombian.' When it is his turn to speak, President Gaviria chooses his words deliberately, as he vows: 'We must not lose this match against violence. Colombia must not let its best children be expelled from life's playing field. Our country is shaken. We share this profound pain with Andrés' family. Together we all shoulder this burden.' Andrés' family can't control their grief and the tears flow.

It does not take long for the investigation into Andrés' death to progress. Two separate eyewitnesses provide the same licence plate information to the police, and the getaway vehicle is quickly identified as a car registered to one of the infamous Gallón brothers. It transpires that these two drug traffickers, former members of Pablo Escobar's cartel who had jumped ship and joined the Cali-supported Los Pepes, are the men who had taunted Andrés in the club. The gunman is identified as their bodyguard, Humberto Muñoz Castro.

But the wheels of justice turn slowly and, in the eyes of many, their final destination in this case is misguided. The entire investigation focuses solely on the bodyguard, and the Gallóns are cleared of any involvement in the murder. Even the judge on the case admits it's unusual for a bodyguard to act so decisively without the involvement of his employers. Muñoz is sentenced to 43 years for gunning down 27-year-old footballer Andrés Escobar in cold blood in a nightclub parking lot. He will go free after fewer than a dozen years behind bars. The Gallóns will never be prosecuted for any role in the killing.

In the aftermath of the murder, in the uncertainty over what really happened, over whether Andrés was killed for scoring an own goal, for causing powerful narcos to lose a bet, or for talking back to the wrong people, the world turns upside down for Maturana and his team. Fearing it was a premeditated assassination, the police provide security and bodyguards for Pacho and the players. Faustino Asprilla, Carlos Valderrama and Chonto Herrera all consider quitting the game for good.

At the same time the nation is forced to come to terms with the murder of the model Colombian, a footballer not cut from the Higuita mould – a maverick showman plucked from the barrios – but a quiet, modest, clean-living, religious young man from a middle-class family, a beacon of hope for Colombian football who was about to fly the flag in Milan. And on the streets of Medellín, one tragic truth is admitted – that this would never have been allowed to happen if El Patrón was still alive. For some, there remains the lingering suspicion that one man in particular may have been the invisible hand behind the deaths of these two very different Escobars: Carlos Castaño, the leader of Los Pepes.

Whatever the true reason for it, the killing of Andrés Escobar is the death knell for the glory years of Colombian football. With the fall of Pablo, the days of narcoball were numbered, but following the failure at USA '94 and the murder of the poster boy for the nation, the decline is almost immediate. With Pablo dead, and Los Cafeteros lauded as potential world champions following the miracle of Buenos Aires, the country seemed on the cusp of something magical. Instead, Colombia is left to pick up the pieces. Rather than escaping the violence of the narcos, football in Colombia is now indelibly marked by it – and not just at home but in the eyes of the entire world.

Chapter Twenty-Three

The End of Narcoball
(1994–1995)

In 1994 it is not just footballers who fear for their lives, however. With Pablo dead, his family are at the mercy of Los Pepes and the Cali Cartel. The hotel where they have been staying under government protection insists they pay for their rooms and, when they are threatened with the bill for the extensive security detail too, their situation becomes untenable, and the Escobars are forced to go it alone. Shorn of their protection, hounded by Los Pepes, and with much of El Patrón's immense wealth gone, spent on his unwinnable war, the family are forced to negotiate with Pablo's enemies for their lives. Tata convinces the Rodríguez Orejuela brothers and their allies that the family, and in particular Juan Pablo, is not a threat. Instead, the Escobars adopt new assumed identities and attempt once more to leave the country.

On this occasion they do at least locate somewhere that will take them in – but they find war-torn Mozambique to be so inhospitable that they cannot bear to stay. They spend less than 72 hours in Maputo before making their escape. Eventually they find their way to Buenos

Aires, and it is here, under assumed names and on tourist visas, that they settle and begin to build a new life for themselves.

With Pablo dead and his family gone, it is the Cali Cartel who rise to fill the void back in Colombia. However, their approach is very different from that of Pablo and the Medellín Cartel. The Rodríguez Orejuela brothers do not dream of the presidential palace, nor do they want to wage open war on the government. And, with the authorities clamping down hard on the criminal elements within football, they also more or less withdraw from the sport. Their focus is on their cocaine empire, and that alone – on making as much money as they can from manufacturing and exporting the drug. Everything else is an unwanted distraction.

And so the 1994 Campeonato Colombiano is perhaps the swansong of the narcoball era. The four-way final at the end of the season is contested by the country's four leading narcoball sides – Atlético Nacional and Deportivo Independiente of Medellín, Millonarios of Bogotá and América de Cali. On 18 December, at their shared Atanasio Girardot stadium, Medellín's two sides face off in the sixth and final round of matches. The Nacional side, now coached by another Maturana protégé in Juan José Peláez, is yet again made up of nothing but Colombian players. In goal, the fit again René Higuita is desperate to make up for lost time and to banish the disappointment of missing out on the World Cup campaign. Many of his Nacional teammates had been in that ill-fated Los Cafeteros squad, however: Chonto Herrera, Hernán Gaviria, Víctor Aristizábal and Mauricio Serna all line up alongside El Loco still bearing the psychological scars of their trip to America and the subsequent death of their teammate Andrés Escobar. But this final game of the season is a chance for glory – for victory here will make Atlético Nacional champions of Colombia once again.

For well over an hour there's nothing to separate the two Medellín sides. In the end it is a 19-year-old substitute, a teenage striker by the name of Juan Pablo Ángel, who is the difference. On 71 minutes he arrives late at the back post to meet a perfect ball slid across the box. His right-footed, side-foot shot ricochets between the DIM goalkeeper's legs and dribbles over the line to make it 1-0 to Nacional. He runs to the crowd, pulling off his shirt and waving it in front of a sea of green and white. Higuita, Herrera and company are able to keep the DIM forwards at bay for the remaining 20 minutes and Nacional have their first title since the death of their patron, Pablo Escobar. For Higuita it is vindication, coming barely a year since his release from prison. For Juan Pablo Ángel it is the start of a footballing journey that will eventually make him one of the first major Colombian footballing exports in the post-Pablo era. For at least one half of Medellín it is a release of pure joy, a year after the death of Pablo Escobar and only six months on from the murder of his namesake and Nacional star Andrés.

*

1995 sees the final two nails arrive in the coffin of the era of narcoball, as over the course of the summer the Colombian authorities finally arrest the men who most benefitted from the fall of Pablo: Gilberto and Miguel Rodríguez Orejuela.

On 9 June the Colombian National Police, the PNC, with the assistance of the DEA and the CIA, raid a house in Cali. They turn the property upside down and eventually, crouched in a caleta – a secret compartment – hidden behind a giant television, they discover

Gilberto Rodríguez. He is dragged out and arrested on the spot. When they reveal the arrest, and the role that informants played in the operation, Miguel becomes rightly suspicious, and mounts his own internal investigations into those closest to him and his brother. The DEA loses contact with the informant who gave them the vital tip, and he is feared dead. It is days later when contact is finally resumed – their insider has survived the isolation, interrogation and torture meted out by the cartel without cracking, but the clock is surely ticking now.

Then, at 6am on 15 July, the Search Bloc office in Cali receives a phone call. The male caller asks to speak to one of the DEA agents, and his request is granted, for he is none other than the US agency's top informant in Colombia – the Cali Cartel's head of security, and a former Captain of the Colombian National Army Reserve, Jorge Salcedo Cabrera. Salcedo had become a hero of the army's war against the M-19 guerrillas in the Valle del Cauca in the 1980s but, when the paramilitary group downed its weapons in 1990, he was recruited into the Cali Cartel and rose through the ranks to become the most trusted lieutenant of the Rodríguez Orejuela brothers. He had been turned against his bosses by the DEA just weeks after the death of Pablo Escobar – and the Americans had enough evidence against him to ensure his cooperation. With a potential reward of nearly $2 million paid by the Colombian and American authorities on the line, and the promise of a new identity and a new life in the US, Salcedo was about to come through for his handlers – for the second time, as it was his tip that had led to the arrest of Gilberto – in a big way.

In carefully coded language, Salcedo conveys the information the Search Bloc and DEA have been waiting for – the current whereabouts of Miguel Rodríguez. Just a few hours later a joint DEA and Colombian police team swoops on apartment 402 of the Colinas de Santa Rita building, on the western edge of Cali. They clear the apartment room by room, but there is no sign of Miguel. For six hours they search but come up empty handed. They are about to give up when, at 6pm, Salcedo calls his DEA handler to ask if the raid was a success. When he is told the team of nearly 20 men has spent half a day searching and not found him, Salcedo is adamant his intel is correct and Miguel is indeed still hiding somewhere within. He tells the agent they should knock down the luxury apartment if they have to. Impressed by his informant's certainty, the DEA agent convinces the leader of the team – General Rosso José Serrano – to redouble their efforts. They measure the thickness of the internal walls and drill into them, they search for hidden switches that might open secret doors, they dismantle closets and ransack the library – but all to no avail. At 9pm General Serrano cancels the search.

But at 1am the DEA agent receives a call from Salcedo who has confirmed that his information was accurate and that Miguel was definitely in the apartment when they were searching. He returns to Colinas de Santa Rita with General Serrano – and they are shocked to find several new items on the premises that have appeared as if from nowhere: a pair of jeans and a blue checked shirt, an oxygen canister and mask, and a white towel spotted with blood. They must have drilled into Miguel Rodríguez's secret hiding place in the guest bathroom, and in fact drilled right into his skin, without him making a sound. He has slipped through their fingers – but at least they know Salcedo's tip was correct.

The following month, on 6 August, Salcedo calls in yet again, and this time there is no delay. Fifteen men from the Search Bloc smash down the door of a swanky apartment in the Buenos Aires building, in the wealthy Normandia neighbourhood on the slopes of Cali's Cerro de las Tres Cruces. The lightning raid catches Miguel unawares and he is snatched just before he can once again disappear into yet another caleta.

The brothers are sentenced to 15 years each in prison, but crucially the Colombian constitution no longer allows for extradition to the USA and so they will serve their time in their homeland. The law will change in 1997, but will not permit retrospective action, and so it will take a further case against them in 2002, relating to criminal activities undertaken during their incarceration and indeed after the surprise early release of Gilberto that year, for them to finally be extradited to America, Gilberto in December 2004 and Miguel a few months later in March 2005.

*

As 1995 moves on with El Patrón and El Mexicano both dead, and now with the brothers at the head of the Cali Cartel behind bars, all four of the top narcoball sides – Atlético Nacional, DIM, Millonarios and América de Cali – have been shorn of their billionaire backers. But, with or without the cartel millions, football in Colombia doesn't stop, and in 1995 the champions of Colombia, Atlético Nacional, are bidding to follow their league title with victory in the Copa Libertadores. Just three days after the arrest of Miguel Rodríguez the Medellín side face Argentinian giants River Plate in the first leg of the semi-finals.

Nacional are in good form, qualifying from their group with just one defeat, to Bogotá rivals Millonarios, and having already overcome Peñarol of Uruguay 6-2 on aggregate in the round of 16 and then earning their revenge by knocking out Millonarios 3-2 over two legs in the quarter-final. René Higuita, Juan Pablo Ángel and their teammates know they must exploit their home advantage in the first leg. The Estadio Atanasio Girardot is packed, the running track and edges of the pitch littered with white streamers. The Medellín side dominate the first half, boasting 65 per cent possession and with eleven shots to River's five, but when the Chilean referee blows his whistle to bring the first 45 to a close it's still 0-0.

In search of the crucial breakthrough, the Colombians make two changes – but still no goal arrives. Then, as the Argentinian side break, Nacional player Carlos Gutierrez is extremely lucky to avoid a red card for a lunging foul. The resulting free kick from Marcelo Gallardo strikes a head in the Nacional defensive wall, wrong-footing Higuita. The ball slams into the crossbar and ricochets away to safety. The Colombians are riding their luck. From the ensuing corner El Loco jumps high to claim the ball and throws out fast and true to start another Nacional attack. But this one too comes to nothing.

Finally, a lovely fast-flowing Nacional attack is unceremoniously ended by a crude foul on the edge of the River Plate penalty area. As the yellow card is brandished a familiar figure makes his way up the pitch from the distant Nacional penalty area: René Higuita. As the River Plate keeper Germán Burgos screams at his defensive wall and spits on his gloves, El Loco picks up the ball and carefully replaces it on the Medellín turf. The Nacional stopper, his keeper's shirt rolled up to his elbows, his trademark curls glistening, his gloves still securely fastened, runs up and strikes the ball right footed. Curling it over and around the outside of the wall with the instep of his boot, he sees his shot leave Burgos rooted to the spot. The ball clips the underside of the bar and nestles in the net. The Estadio Atanasio Girardot erupts. Higuita sprints away, the finger of one gloved hand pointing skyward. He is chased by his teammates who mob him as the coaching staff and substitutes surround the ecstatic huddle. As he finally jogs back to his goal only one sound can be heard echoing around the stadium: *'¡Higuita! ¡Higuita! ¡Higuita!'*

The game ebbs and flows but is never less than feisty, with 35 fouls and 32 shots shared by the rival sides over the 90 minutes. They can't find a second goal but, with 72 per cent possession, Atlético Nacional are at least able to protect their lead and, with the whistle bringing the game to an end, give themselves a one goal advantage going into the second leg in Buenos Aires.

Seven days later, the return leg in Argentina is a brutally partisan affair. Nacional take to the pitch in their green training jackets to a chorus of whistles, before the River Plate players run out to a deafening roar. The white ticker tape rains down like a snowstorm to the popcorn percussion of firecrackers. Against all expectations, Nacional make the early running and come close with two strikes from around the River Plate box. Then comes a barely believable sequence of events, five seconds of football madness. First a volleyed snapshot from the far right-hand side of the Nacional box beats Higuita only to cannon back off the bar. The rebound is hit first time on the volley from the left corner of the six-yard box – and smashes back off the near post at such speed the Nacional defender six yards out who attempts to control it with his chest almost ends up scoring an own goal. Instead, he is eventually able to desperately hook it clear from practically under his own crossbar. The Argentinians can't believe it. The game opens up, and it's end to end as both keepers are called upon to make crucial saves. Every River Plate tackle is cheered to the heavens, yet somehow the Colombian side hold on to ensure the score remains 1-0 on aggregate at the break.

But in the second half the pressure finally tells. With just three minutes played after the restart, Higuita comes off his line to try to punch away a high, looping corner – but gets under the flight of the ball which is headed into the empty net by River Plate's Gaby Amato. The tie is level, and Nacional have almost a full 45 minutes to survive in the cauldron of the Estadio Monumental with its 60,000 baying fans – and if they are to win they'll have to do so without Ángel, who has been replaced at half time. The most notable moment in a tense, scrappy second half occurs on 75 minutes. Nacional's Colombian attacker Víctor Aristizábal is sent off for a waist-high challenge on Ricardo Altamirano. But the referee ensures neither side gains an advantage by also brandishing a red card at the River Plate defender for his reaction to the tackle. A quarter of an hour of ten versus ten brings no further goals – although an audacious *rabona* attempt from outside the box from goalscorer Amato has Higuita backpedalling to claw it away from under the crossbar. And so the Copa Libertadores semi-final ends, as so many crucial Atlético Nacional matches seem to have done, with a penalty shoot-out. Having scored his side's only goal of the tie, it's yet another chance for René Higuita, the hero of Medellín, to rescue his beloved Nacional.

For the first penalty he dives the right way but cannot get to Marcelo Gallardo's truly struck effort. The pressure is on as El Loco steps up to take his team's first spot kick. The crowd whistles. Burgos beats his chest. And Higuita, the showman with ice in his veins, chips a delicate Panenka-style finish beyond the mistimed dive of his opposite number. It's one apiece. The two teams then trade a series of emphatic finishes although it is Higuita who repeatedly comes closest to making a save, several of the Argentinian strikes coming agonizingly close to his outstretched fingertips. When Gabriel Cedrés scores from the spot to make it 5-4 to River, Mauricio Serna knows he has to score to keep Colombian hopes alive. He does, calmly sending Burgos the wrong way. The shoot-out heads into sudden death. The very next effort, from River's Celso Ayala, looks bound for the bottom corner when Higuita pounces and gets two good hands on the ball. Somehow it squirms beyond his grip and trickles over the line before his despairing hands can claw it back.

It's a perfect seven from seven for both sides, when Matías Almeyda steps up to take River Plate's eighth spot kick. His effort, to Higuita's left side, lacks real venom and is chipped at a saveable height. The Colombian keeper, having guessed right, almost dives beyond the ball but is able to twist his upper body and block the strike with his right hand. It's a vital, trademark penalty save from the Nacional icon – and if Francisco Foronda can score, Nacional will be in the final. The 20-year-old defender stands, black-gloved hands on his hips, as Burgos stares at him from his goal line. He runs up, Burgos goes early to his left, and Foronda places the ball perfectly to the right. Atlético Nacional win 8-7 on penalties in Buenos Aires. René Higuita will have the chance to add a 1995 Copa Libertadores winners medal to his trophy cabinet. The only side standing between Nacional and the Copa? Brazil's Grêmio.

El Loco and his teammates don't have long to wait. It is just a week after the shoot-out in Argentina when they take to the pitch in Porto Alegre, Brazil for the first leg of the final in front of a capacity crowd packed into the Estádio Olímpico Monumental. Right from the kick-off the home side look sharp; roared on by their fans they snap into tackles, pen the Colombians back and draw a series of saves from Higuita within just the first five minutes. As the clock ticks on, and the pattern of the game refuses to change, it seems certain the dam will break, but El Loco is inspired – saving a free header from barely seven yards out with a flying save to tip the ball over the bar.

Gradually Nacional battle their way back into the contest, but a yellow card for Ángel for a lunging tackle after his poor touch let the ball get away from him is testament to the Colombian side's frustrations. They make it to the halfway point in the first half without conceding, then to 30 minutes. But then, with ten minutes to go until half time, catastrophe. A series of robust challenges sees the ball pop out to the Grêmio right flank, where Paolo Nunes takes a touch out of his feet and crosses it in. Backpedalling towards the penalty spot, Nacional defender Víctor Marulanda swings his left boot at the ball to prevent it reaching the predatory Mario Jardel lurking just behind him. But his attempted clearance is horribly sliced, skewing wildly off the top of his boot and looping up over Higuita before it drops just beneath the bar and into the net. Jardel celebrates almost as if he had scored himself. It's harsh on Higuita but no less than the Brazilian side deserve. And worse is to come for Nacional.

With just seconds to go until half time a cross-shot comes in from the left corner of the Nacional box. The ball dips late and Higuita fumbles, and can only manage to palm the ball to the feet of Jardel who needs no further invitation to tuck it away and double his side's advantage. It's a hammer blow.

The second half has only just begun when a Grêmio corner is headed back across goal by Jardel, hits a falling defender and is slammed into the net. But the goal is disallowed for a barely discernible nudge by Jardel. This time it's Grêmio who are unlucky, but the Colombians' reprieve is short-lived. On 55 minutes the Brazilian side's fifth corner is headed at Higuita from point-blank range. His goal line save only succeeds in diverting the ball straight back out to the onrushing Paolo Nunes who pokes it home from a yard out. At 3-0 the Colombians look dead and buried.

But on 72 minutes a sliver of that most dangerous of things: hope. Nacional play some of the best football of the match: a series of tight passes keeps possession inside the Grêmio half before Jaime Arango breaks two tackles to slip through the pass for which Juan Pablo Ángel has been waiting all night. His lunging strike hits the roof of the net. At 3-1, with the home leg in Medellín to come, the Colombians know they still have a chance. And, when the whistle finally goes to bring the first leg to a close, Atlético Nacional know that if they can play as they did in the final 20 minutes of the game in the return fixture back in Colombia they might just be able to reverse the scoreline.

And so, on 30 August 1995, 49,000 take their seats in the Atanasio Girardot hoping for, dreaming of, one more footballing miracle. A breathless, end-to-end opening fuels the crowd and the stadium announcers. On five minutes, the Grêmio keeper seemingly uses every part of his body to keep a series of Nacional strikes out. The Colombians have started just as they left off in Porto Alegre and, although Jardel and Nunes continue to look dangerous on the break, the home crowd can smell blood. With 12 minutes gone, Nacional get a deserved breakthrough. A high ball is met with a speculative volley on the edge of the box, but the block from a jumping Grêmio defender only diverts the ball into the path of the onrushing Víctor Aristizábal who dinks it over keeper Danrlei. 1-0 on the night, 2-3 on aggregate, and with almost 80 minutes left to play with their home crowd roaring them on, it's game on for Atlético Nacional. But that's the thing about dreams, they rarely come true.

For the rest of the half the Colombians are well on top, but for all their dominance they cannot find the equalizing goal. The second half is more of the same – with Nacional dominating possession but unable to create a clearcut chance, and every minute they go without scoring brings Grêmio closer to the trophy. One of the longest serving of the Medellín players, Chonto Herrera, is brought on just shy of the hour mark. With five minutes left in the tie he goes shoulder to shoulder with Nunes on the edge of the Nacional box. Their untidy tussle continues into the area, and both players fall to the turf. The referee blows his whistle and points to the spot. Penalty to Grêmio. Now all the fans can do is pray that Higuita can be their saviour once again, and whistle and shriek as Dinho prepares to take his kick. But when Higuita dives the wrong way, and the Brazilian's effort sails into the opposite corner, the air is sucked out of the stadium. For this year at least, the dream is over.

In the end the 1995 Copa Libertadores is a bridge too far for Nacional who, despite fielding the likes of Higuita and Ángel, seem like a shadow of the team that Pacho Maturana, with the financial muscle of Pablo Escobar, had built in the late 80s and early 90s. In fact, that team's achievement in winning the Copa will not be equalled by a Colombian side until the unexpected 2004 triumph by the unheralded Once Caldas.

Higuita has fallen one agonizing step short of winning the Campeonato Colombiano and the Copa Libertadores within two years of his release from prison. But he does have one more moment of magic to share before the year is out. In 1995, now back in the Colombian squad after missing the World Cup, he is once again one of the footballers, in fact one of the celebrities, most in demand from advertisers. Over the summer he had been shooting a commercial for a popular soft drink when, while larking about for the cameras, he had improvised a new kind of save. With the dedication of a true showman, he spends the next few months practising his secret move in training whenever he can. But, when he's playing in a big game, with the cameras on his every move, the ball is never quite delivered in the way he needs in order to risk attempting to pull off his new party piece.

On 6 September 1995, just days after Nacional's defeat to Grêmio, Higuita and his Colombia teammates are in London, to play England at Wembley. It is seven years since El Loco played at the home of football, when he wowed the crowd with his eccentric skills and Pacho Maturana's side, skippered by Carlos Valderrama, earned a draw, and the respect of their hosts, courtesy of the only ever international goal scored for Colombia by Andrés Escobar. This time round Los Cafeteros are coached by Pacho's understudy and former Nacional player and manager Hernán Darío Gómez – aka El Bolillo – who has been in charge for just a matter of months. In the opposite dugout is not Bobby Robson but, just a year into the job, Terry Venables. It's an England side looking to rebound, having missed out on USA '94 altogether under the stewardship of Graham Taylor and with Euro '96 in England less than a year away. It's a strong 'Three Lions' line-up featuring David Seaman, Tony Adams, Graeme Le Saux, Steve Howey, Gary Neville, Jamie Redknapp, Dennis Wise, Steve McManaman, Nick Barmby, Paul Gascoigne and Alan Shearer. El Bolillo also has some big names at his disposal; Higuita, Valderrama, Asprilla (a key player for Serie A side Parma) and Rincón (now at European royalty Real Madrid) are all there. But one thing is noticeable – there are only two Atlético Nacional players in the starting XI (Higuita, and the right back José Santa), a stark contrast to the Pacho Maturana sides that had earned such plaudits after games at Wembley in 1988 and in Buenos Aires in 1993.

In an open, entertaining first half Shearer hits the bar with a lobbed effort from a perfect Gascoigne through ball, then sees his powerful strike tipped around the post by a flying Higuita. For the

Colombians, a 35-yard Rincón piledriver is destined for the top corner before Seaman fingertips it over. But, despite these brief flashes, in the annals of footballing history this autumn friendly would be largely forgettable – if not for a moment that will come to be replayed on TV screens and in playgrounds and football pitches the world over.

Midway through the first half the ball is knocked back inside to Jamie Redknapp. The Liverpool midfielder, making his England debut, takes a right-footed snapshot from a good 30 yards out. It's an innocuous looking effort that is bound for the dead centre of the goal at an eminently catchable height – and it's finally the perfect trajectory for which René 'El Loco' Higuita has been waiting. At the home of football, the Colombian icon, sporting dark tracksuit bottoms on this dark, damp London evening, makes the ultimate 'one for the cameras' save. Springing forwards, he brings his feet up behind his head, meeting the shot on the full with the studs of both boots and clearing the ball all the way back whence it came. Just like that, the world of football is forever changed, as the 'scorpion kick' is born.

No one watching can quite comprehend what they have just witnessed. The UK television commentary sums it up perfectly:

'Goodness me, have you ever seen something like that in your life from a goalkeeper? That is quite the most remarkable piece of goalkeeping I have ever seen. Extraordinary piece of work by Higuita.'

The rest of the half is entertaining. Gazza hits a post and McManaman stings Higuita's palms from the edge of the box, while at the other end Valenciano, feeding off the feints and flicks from the lively Tino Asprilla, repeatedly shoots from distance for the Colombians. But nothing, in either half, will match that moment of genius from the man from Medellín. In the second half, Dennis Wise hits the bar and Gazza narrowly misses the target with a free kick – but perhaps it's fitting that Higuita's goal continues to lead a charmed life, and his clean sheet ensures the occasion is remembered for one thing only, his moment of magic, the birth of the 'scorpion kick'.

For England the signs are positive, green shoots showing in this Venables performance that hint at the excitement to come at Euro '96. For the Colombians it's a solid performance but indicative of the decline of the side that, heading into the USA '94 World Cup, had been ranked fourth in the world by FIFA. Following their failure in America, the death of Andrés Escobar and the end of the investment in domestic football that characterized the era of narcoball, Los Cafeteros drop like a stone, plummeting to 34th in the rankings by 1997. The golden generation has lost its lustre, their decline mirrored by that of their talismanic captain Carlos Valderrama. He may still have that unmistakable head of blond curls, but as he gets closer to 40 than to 30 he seems a lifetime away from the dynamic, sprightly El Pibe of his youth. His eye for a pass remains but, with his legs starting to go, Colombia lack some of the impetus they had at their peak.

Chapter Twenty-Four

Strange Pilgrims
(1995–2023)

One last link between the cartels and the clubs is severed just eight days after the draw at Wembley. The head of the Colombian Football Federation, and former president of América de Cali, Juan José Bellini, is arrested. He is sentenced to six years in prison after he is unable to explain how he came to receive two cheques for 100 million pesos from the Rodríguez Orejuela brothers. The spectre of El Patrón has even faded sufficiently for Colombia's leading novelist Gabriel García Márquez to publish his non-fiction account of the darkest days in Colombia's recent past: *Noticia de un Secuestro*, 'News of a Kidnapping'. The time of narcoball may be over, but the lives of the key players who rose to prominence in that thrilling – but deadly – era continue, as does the story of Colombian football.

With their patrons and their former president all in jail, América de Cali do nevertheless manage to finish second in the 1995 Campeonato Colombiano, behind Junior of Barranquilla. As a result, they qualify for the 1996 Copa Libertadores. It has been almost a decade since the third of their three consecutive defeats in the final during their narcoball heyday, and in that time they have seen their hated rivals Atlético Nacional become the tournament's first ever Colombian champions in 1989, and come within a whisker of repeating the feat just a few months ago.

The red devils manage to top their group as they finish ahead of Junior, and then an easy win in the round of 16 over Venezuelan side Minervén sets up a juicy quarter-final tie between the two Colombian sides. América manage to narrowly defeat their domestic champions Junior over two legs, the decisive goal scored by the still-lethal Antony de Ávila. In the semi-finals they face Grêmio, the defending champions who had seen off Higuita and Nacional in the final a year earlier. After a 1-0 defeat in Porto Alegre, Mario Jardel stuns the Cali crowd when, on 16 minutes, he scores to make it 2-0 on aggregate. Things are not looking good. But América mount a stunning comeback and romp to a 3-1 victory in the Estadio Olímpico Pascal Guerrero thanks to two goals from their Colombian international centre back Jorge Bermúdez. The 3-2 aggregate win puts them in the final, where they will face River Plate – the team knocked out in the semis of the previous year by Higuita and Nacional.

The two-legged final is a tale of two strikers. América de Cali play at home first, and earn a 1-0 win thanks to Antony de Ávila, his 11th strike in the competition putting him at the top of the goalscorers charts. But a week later, at the Estadio Monumental in Buenos Aires, it is the Argentinian Hernán Crespo who steals the show – and wins his side the trophy. His two goals, his ninth and tenth of the 1996 edition of the Copa, turn the tie on its head, and secure a 2-1 aggregate win for River Plate. And, in a final blow to the fans of América, the 1996 domestic season ends with their city rivals Deportivo Cali crowned as champions of Colombia.

Despite the decline in the domestic game and the breaking up of the golden generation, Los Cafeteros do manage to qualify for the 1998 World Cup – and the tournament in France will be their third in a row, no mean feat for a nation who had only ever been to one World Cup before 1990. Propelled by the goals of Asprilla – most notably a hat trick in a 4-1 home demolition of Chile in Barranquilla – they finish third in the CONMEBOL qualifying behind Argentina and surprise package Paraguay, and just ahead of the Iván Zamorano-inspired Chile. After their win in America, Brazil are the defending champions and so have already secured their place at France '98.

Thanks to their efforts in qualification, Colombia have climbed back into FIFA's top ten – but this side somehow lacks the energy and enthusiasm of the team that drew with Germany at Italia '90, and the strength in depth of quality players at their very peak that carried them so imperiously to USA '94. El Bolillo's side, for he is back in the dugout, might have El Pulpo Asprilla but with Higuita gone, and the captain Valderrama now 36 and plying his trade with MLS expansion team the Miami Fusion, they are very much a squad in transition. More than ever before, with the decline of Atlético Nacional, they lack a nucleus of domestic teammates. Full back José Santa and reserve goalkeeper Miguel Calero are the only Nacional players, and the squad features members playing in eight different countries. The team with the single most players represented in the Colombian national squad isn't even Colombian – it's Boca Juniors of Argentina.

Los Cafeteros are drawn in Group G, alongside old foes Romania, an England side now coached by Glenn Hoddle, and Tunisia. In a repeat of their ill-fated 1994 campaign, Colombia will face Romania in their opening game on 15 June 1998. At the Stade de Gerland in Lyon a stylish strike by Adrian Ilie in first-half stoppage time is enough to give Romania the win and the three points. It's not the start they'd hoped for, but with Tunisia up next El Bolillo and his team know they have a chance to get things back on track.

However, a massive spanner is thrown in the works when Asprilla, a maverick personality in the Higuita mould, publicly criticizes his coach. El Bolillo, deeming El Pulpo to be a divisive influence in the dressing room, casts his star player from the squad.

Just a few days later, and without the cutting edge provided by the absent Parma forward, it takes until the 82nd minute of the tie for Colombia to break the deadlock against Tunisia and score their first goal of the tournament. It's an uninspiring display in Montpellier against the projected whipping boys of the group, the only positive aside from the three points being the goal, scored by one of El Bolillo's three substitutes, the young Santa Fe striker Léider Preciado.

The final game, in Lens, still offers hope, however. With Romania having beaten England 2-1, with a 90th minute Dan Petrescu goal and despite an 81st minute goal for 18-year-old substitute Michael Owen, there is still a chance for Colombia to qualify for the round of 16. In the newly expanded World Cup format only the top two teams in each group will reach the knockout stages. England and Colombia both have three points each, having both lost to Romania and defeated Tunisia, but England have a better goal difference. For England, a draw will be enough. For Colombia, only a win will see them survive.

But, with Asprilla still absent and with the 35-year-old de Ávila joined up front by the youthful but untested Preciado, Los Cafeteros rarely threaten to score the goals they need to overcome Hoddle's side.

In fact, the game is all but over as a contest within half an hour – as goals on 20 and 29 minutes from Darren Anderton and David Beckham, the latter a trademark free kick, give the Three Lions a comfortable 2-0 lead. El Bolillo hooks both de Ávila and Preciado at half time, along with defensive midfield stalwart Mauricio Serna, a sign of his frustration and desperation, but even with three strikers – Adolfo 'El Tren' Valencia, Víctor Aristizábal and Middlesbrough's Hamilton Ricard – replacing them, Colombia can't trouble the scorers. The game ends 2-0. England will progress, and Los Cafeteros – riven by internal issues once more – are going home after the group stages again.

Colombia will fail to qualify for the next three World Cups, missing the tournaments in Japan and South Korea, Germany, and South Africa and only returning to the top table of global football in 2014. The only bright spark in the intervening 16 years comes in 2001.

The 2001 Copa América is a symbol of all that is good, and bad, in Colombian history, politics and football. It is an echo, an aftershock, of the days of narcoball. The tournament is due to be hosted by Colombia – for the first time in their history – in July 2001, but to all intents and purposes the country is still at war. The Cali and Medellín cartels might have crumbled, but the problems of organized crime, civil war and violence still remain as the FARC, the narcos, the death squads and the government forces in their US-backed war on drugs all fight for supremacy. Key host cities Cali, Medellín and Bogotá all suffer bombings in the run-up to the tournament, with a dozen dead and hundreds injured. A car bomb hits several Colombian footballers in Cali. President Pastrana deploys troops across the country. Then, two weeks before the first kick-off is due, the vice-president of the Colombian FA, Hernán Campuzano, is kidnapped by the FARC. On 1 July, just ten days before it is due to start, CONMEBOL announce the cancellation of the tournament. But at the last moment Campuzano is released, and he and Pastrana lobby desperately for the Colombian cause, aware of how much the tournament means to the country and its people. CONMEBOL are convinced by their entreaties, and on 6 July re-confirm Colombia as the hosts. A national ceasefire is announced and five days later the event kicks off with back-to-back games at the Estadio Metropolitano in Barranquilla. After Chile thrash an Ecuador side now managed by El Bolillo 4-1, Colombia take on Venezuela in the second Group A game. It's a comfortable 2-0 win for Los Cafeteros, who are once again under the stewardship of the tactician who masterminded their rise in the late 80s and early 90s – Francisco 'Pacho' Maturana. His youthful squad has a noticeably more domestic bias – its only member to be playing outside of the Americas is captain and Inter Milan defender Iván Córdoba. Pacho's Colombia 2.0 is a breath of fresh air, and a source of hope and joy for the nation once again as arms are downed and TV sets are turned on. A 1-0 win over Pacho's protégé El Bolillo and his Ecuador side and a 2-0 win against Chile put Colombia top of the four-team group – with the rejuvenated Víctor Aristizábal having scored in each of the three games so far – and Los Cafeteros are into the knockout stages. In Armenia's Estadio Centenario three goals in sixteen second-half minutes, two of them from Aristizábal, blow away Peru in the quarters. In the semi-final the striker scores again, taking his tally to six, as Colombia knock out Honduras in Manizales. The Honduran side had been a last-minute addition to the tournament, flown in by the Colombian Air Force the day before their first game, to replace Argentina – who had pulled out due to security concerns.

Colombia's opposition in the final are guest side Mexico; the venue is the Estadio El Campín in Bogotá, scene of Atlético Nacional's dramatic triumph in the 1989 Copa Libertadores. Around 47,000 cram into the stadium to see if their new heroes can win the Copa América for the first time in Colombia's history. The first half is goalless and tournament top scorer Aristizábal is forced off injured but, with Colombia having made it all the way to the final without conceding a single goal, Pacho knows that a single strike might well be enough for his side. He's not wrong, and on 65 minutes it arrives. Fittingly it is the team's captain and defensive rock Iván Córdoba who arrives in the box to glance a header from Iván López's free kick into the corner of the net. The fans in the El Campín send yellow ticker tape raining down onto the pitch in a collective outpouring of joy. Even a scrappy and ill-tempered end to the game, with two Mexican players sent off in the final minutes, cannot spoil the celebrations. Colombia have hosted their first Copa América and won their first ever major international trophy all without conceding a single goal, are awarded the fair play award and even the ceasefire has held throughout the entirety of the tournament. Unfortunately, the success on the pitch, and the peace off it, are both short-lived.

Colombia fail to qualify for the 2002 World Cup and Pacho takes a job coaching Al-Hilal in Saudi Arabia. El Bolillo's fate is quite different, however. First, he is shot in the leg for leaving the son of Ecuador's fugitive president out of the national squad. Then, when he leaves and returns home to his native Colombia, thousands of Ecuadorians take to the streets of Quito begging for his return. He does – and leads the country to their first ever World Cup in 2002.

*

The decade after the 2001 Copa América triumph is a dark period for Colombian football. In 2002 one of the last remaining stars of the golden age, René Higuita, tests positive for cocaine while playing for Ecuadorian side Aucuas. In 2005 he retires, takes part in a reality TV competition format, and undergoes plastic surgery. El Loco returns to football in 2007, but only plays 32 games over three seasons for three different minor clubs before finally hanging up his gloves for good in 2010. But, although he goes out with more of a whimper than a bang, he will go down in history as one of the game's legends. Over his career he scored over 40 goals, invented a completely new 'skill', and revolutionized his position.

Also in 2002, Higuita's former Atlético Nacional and Colombia teammate Hernán Gaviria is playing for Deportivo Cali. The 32-year-old midfielder broke into the Nacional side in 1990, the year after Higuita had helped them lift the Copa Libertadores for the first time – and is perhaps best remembered for scoring for Los Cafeteros against Switzerland at USA '94, in a 2-0 win that was too little, too late to save them from elimination. It is 24 October, and Gaviria is taking part in team training in Cali when the weather worsens. A storm erupts, and Gaviria and his teammate Giovanni Córdoba are struck by a bolt of lightning. Gaviria dies instantly, Córdoba dies three days later in hospital. The 32-year-old Gaviria leaves behind a wife and two children.

On 11 February 2004, one of the heroes of the pivotal year of 1989, Albeiro 'El Palomo' Usuriaga, who scored in Atlético

Nacional's victories over Danubio and Olimpia as they won the Copa Libertadores, and netted the only goal in the play-off against Israel that meant Los Cafeteros qualified for the 1990 World Cup in Italy, is playing in a card game in his hometown of Cali. He is a year retired, having struggled for games and goals in a chequered career that has seen him play in Spain, Argentina, Paraguay, Ecuador, Mexico and Venezuela as well as for half a dozen clubs in his native Colombia. He never regained the heights of 1989 – he was even omitted from the 1990 World Cup squad due to disciplinary problems, and in the mid-90s was banned by the Argentinian Football Association for two years after a positive test for cocaine while playing for Independiente. As the former footballer plays cards in the Doce de Octubre barrio in Cali, the game is interrupted by a gunman who shoots El Palomo to death. It takes several years before authorities uncover the reason why. It eventually transpires that the assassin was Luis Eduardo Suárez Prieto, also known as *El Soltero* – 'The Bachelor' – and that he was hired by the boyfriend of El Palomo's former lover to kill his love rival. It's a messy end for yet another one of the tragic heroes of the narcoball era.

That year there is one major positive though – as Colombian minnows Once Caldas somehow win the Copa Libertadores. Their triumph over Boca Juniors in yet another penalty shoot-out, is the first time since Nacional in 1989, and only the second time ever, that a Colombian side has won the Copa.

The following year Atlético Nacional hire a new manager – their former player Santiago Escobar, brother of Andrés. Under the tutelage of their former defensive midfielder the Medellín side win their eighth Colombian league title as they romp to the 2005 Campeonato Apertura, the first of the two championships contested across the year.

Escobar moves on almost immediately, but will return to Nacional in 2010 and help them to yet another title in 2011.

In 2010 Bogotá's legendary side Millonarios, without a domestic championship since the back-to-back titles of 1987 and 1988 under the patronage of El Mexicano, go bankrupt. It's a mighty fall for the former aristocrats of Colombian football, who are bought up by a collective of 4,000 fans. But Millonarios are not the only Colombian club side to have suffered since the end of the era of narcoball – in the same year the owners of all but four of the eighteen teams in the Colombian top flight warn their sides are at risk of filing for bankruptcy. Strangely, one of the only clubs not seemingly at risk is Independiente Santa Fe, a side who have not won a Colombian league title since 1975. But by the end of the year it becomes clear why – they are rumoured to have been used to launder money for emerald smuggler turned drug lord Julio Alberto Lozano whose El Dorado cartel has emerged from the shadows of Medellín and Cali to claim top spot in Colombia's organized crime underworld.

Yet somehow, 20 years after the tragedy of Colombia's 1994 World Cup campaign in America, in 2014 there is one more chance for glory. After three consecutive missed tournaments, Los Cafeteros qualify for the competition, to be hosted by Brazil, having finished second in the CONMEBOL, qualifying just two points behind winners Argentina. This is a new side, with a new manager – the Argentinian José Pékerman, and soon they are being touted as a second 'golden generation' and potential dark horses for the World Cup itself. The squad is strong and, in Monaco duo Radamel *El Tigre* Falcao and James Rodríguez, has two world class players at the top of their game. Their 30 points in qualifying is Colombia's best ever haul, and they go to Brazil back in the FIFA top ten and full of confidence. Even when

Falcao – whose nine goals had fired them to qualification – is ruled out, having failed to recover from an anterior cruciate ligament (ACL) knee injury sustained while playing for Monaco, Los Cafeteros are determined to do their country proud.

First comes a 3-0 win over Greece, then a tight 2-1 victory over fellow dark horses Ivory Coast. The final game, a 4-1 win over Japan in which James Rodríguez scores for the third consecutive match, ensures Colombia not only qualify but become only the third South American team in history, after Brazil and Argentina, to win all three of their group stage games. In the round of 16 they face a strong Uruguay side – albeit one shorn of their own talismanic striker Luis Suárez, the Liverpool forward suspended after biting Giorgio Chiellini in their crucial group stage match against Italy. It is this game against Uruguay that once more brings Colombian football briefly but beautifully back to the top table of the global game – as James Rodríguez announces himself on the world stage with two more goals, the first of which is one of the most sublime ever to grace the tournament. When, on 28 minutes, defensive midfielder Abel Aguilar's looped header drops towards James, his back to goal some 30 yards out, there looks to be no danger to Fernando Muslera's goal. But a deft touch off his chest sets it up for an unerring left foot volley on the turn that sends the ball arrowing past the Uruguay stopper and in off the bar. His fourth goal in four games will later earn him the Puskás Award for the best goal of the year. His fifth, just five minutes after the restart, is a sublime team effort – James sweeping home right-footed this time from six yards from a cushioned header back across goal by one of the side's other emerging stars, Juan Cuadrado – and has the Colombian players dancing, smiles on their faces, in front of their colourful and ever-loyal travelling fans. It's a far cry from USA '94. When the whistle blows at full time a 2-0 win means Colombia are in the quarter-finals of the World Cup for the first time ever.

The quarter-final match in Fortaleza on 4 July 2014 is against the hosts, Brazil. Billed as a classic shoot-out between the precocious talents of James and Brazil's superstar Neymar, it is anything but. An early goal for Brazil – Thiago Silva bundling home from close range from a corner – forces Colombia to make the running, but they, and James in particular, are kicked out of the game by a robust Brazil who somehow avoid serious sanction from the referee. They will end the match having committed 31 fouls. Then a Colombian goal for defender Mario Yepes is ruled out, and within minutes a stunning long range free kick by David Luiz doubles Brazil's advantage. But this new generation of Colombian players refuse to give up, and on 80 minutes they get a lifeline – a penalty awarded after Carlos Bacca is brought down by Brazil keeper Julio Cesar gives James the chance to score for the fifth consecutive game. Despite the best efforts of the Brazilian players he keeps his cool and sends the goalie the wrong way to halve the deficit and ensure the hosts face a nervy last ten minutes. In the end Colombia come up short, unable to find a second goal to take the game to extra time. They are out, and the hosts progress, but in James Rodríguez Colombia have the tournament's top scorer, with Juan Cuadrado topping the assists table too. FIFA even award Los Cafeteros the fair play award. The side have restored pride to their country, their thrilling run, full of flair, creativity, goals and attacking intent, has once again reminded the world of the joy of football and the talent that still exists in Colombia.

It is a bittersweet form of revenge served cold when Brazil are humiliated 7-1 in the semi-final by a rampant Germany, the home fans shell-shocked by the capitulation of their heroes. Missing talisman Neymar to a fractured vertebra caused by Colombian defender Juan Zuñiga in the ill-tempered quarter-final, the host nation inexplicably find themselves five goals down inside half an hour, and it's 7-0 when they finally get on the scoresheet in the 90th minute. Even a third-place finish is beyond the hosts, as they slump to a 3-0 defeat to The Netherlands, a Robin van Persie penalty starting the rot as early as the third minute.

If the 2014 World Cup in Brazil stands as the high-water mark in the history of the Colombia national team in the 21st century, then it is only two years later when an even more extraordinary series of events sets a new bar for the reputation of Colombian club football.

In 2016 Atlético Nacional's own new golden generation embark on their Copa Libertadores campaign having won the 2015 Torneo de Finalización and in doing so finally overtaking Millonarios with a record 15 domestic titles. They are bidding to become the first Colombian side to win the Copa twice, nearly 30 years after their maiden triumph that will forever be tainted by the bloody hands of Pablo Escobar. *Los Verdolagas* look the team to beat as they waltz through the group stages with five wins and a draw in their six games, scoring a dozen goals without conceding a single one in reply. In the round of 16 they overcome Argentina's Huracán 4-2 on aggregate, and see off their compatriots Rosario Central in the quarters, 3-2. Then they make a mockery of what looks like their sternest test yet, when they beat Brazilian powerhouses São Paolo 2-0 away, and 2-1 at home in Medellín, for a convincing 4-1 aggregate victory. All four Nacional goals are scored by new cult hero Miguel Borja, playing in his first games for the club.

The two-legged final is against the year's surprise package, Independiente del Valle of Ecuador. It is Nacional's first Copa Libertadores final since 1995, and the first in 25 years that has not featured at least one side from either Brazil or Argentina. Things appear to be going to plan for Los Verdolagas in the first leg, away in Quito, when Orlando Berrío gives the Colombians a 35th minute lead. But five minutes from the end at the Estadio Olímpico Atahualpa, Arturo Mina strikes for the home side to set a grandstand finish in Medellín. On 27 July 2016, 46,000 fans pack the Atanasio Girardot to see if their new heroes can once again win the Copa – this time without the influence of the world's biggest narco and their most infamous supporter Pablo Escobar. An eighth-minute goal from Borja settles the nerves in Medellín, and in the end settles the tie in Nacional's favour. They are the champions of South America once again.

Yet this triumph, welcome as it is for the long-suffering fans in Medellín, is not the thing that restores their reputation in the eyes of the world. That comes in the aftermath of a tragedy just a few months later. On 28 November Los Verdolagas are awaiting the arrival of their Brazilian opponents Chapecoense, who are flying to Medellín to take on the Colombian side in the first leg of the Copa Sudamericana, the continent's second tier cup competition. But flight AMI2933, flying from Santa Cruz in Bolivia, runs out of fuel and crashes into the hillside outside Colombia's second city. Of the 77 passengers and crew on board 71 lose their lives, among them 19 members of the Chapecoense squad and coaching team. Nacional immediately request that the two-legged final is cancelled and the victory and the trophy awarded to Chapecoense. Their act of sportsmanship results in the presentation of the FIFA Fair Play Award for 2016, an honour bestowed on the club in the governing body's ceremony in Zurich in January 2017. Twenty-three years after the death of Pablo Escobar, and twenty-eight years after his influence had helped them win their first Copa Libertadores, Atlético Nacional of Medellín have finally earned their redemption in full in the eyes of the world.

*

In 2020 Jhon Jairo Velásquez Vásquez, the man who will forever be remembered as Popeye – Pablo Escobar's baby-faced and deadliest sicario and the man who arranged many of El Patrón's deadliest attacks – dies in prison of oesophageal cancer aged 57.

Two years later, in a prison medical centre in California, Gilberto Rodríguez Orejuela dies of lymphoma. His brother Miguel remains incarcerated at the Loretto Federal Correctional Institution. Inmate number 14022-059 is due for release on 15 July 2028, when he will be 84 years old.

Carlos Lehder, aged 70, was released from prison in the USA in 2020 and escorted to Germany where he is now under the care of the German authorities and undergoing treatment for prostate cancer.

Roberto Escobar lost his eyesight after opening a letter bomb in prison shortly after the death of his brother Pablo. For seven years he lives under guard within the hospital clinic that is attempting to repair his eyes. In 2004 he is freed, and in 2008 he is awarded damages relating to parts of his sentencing. Since his release El Osito has given guided tours of Pablo's Medellín, written his autobiography, tried to sue Netflix for $1 billion over their drama series *Narcos* and attempted to launch his own folding smartphone and cryptocurrency. He turned 77 in January 2024.

Hugo Martínez, the leader of the Search Bloc, retired from active duty in 1999 after 40 years of service in the National Police. In 2003 his son Hugo Martínez Jr, the young man who tracked down Pablo, is killed in a road traffic accident. Martínez Sr dies from a heart attack in 2020.

After many years living in Argentina under the assumed name Sebastián Marroquín, Juan Pablo Escobar has finally been able to safely return to Colombia and has embarked on a new life promoting peace and reconciliation alongside two unlikely allies: the sons of the men his father murdered, former Justice Minister Rodrigo Lara Bonilla and presidential candidate Luis Carlos Galán. After 30 years together he and Ángeles eventually parted ways, but not before welcoming a baby boy, Juan Emilio, into the world. Today Tata, Pablo Escobar's widow Victoria Eugenia Henao, lives in a small apartment in Buenos Aires and is a doting grandmother to the young boy.

After years of lying in ruin, the prison complex known as La Catedral is eventually loaned by the Colombian government to a group of Benedictine monks. It is rumoured that the ghost of the building's infamous former resident occasionally appears to roam the halls at night. The famous hippos, the pride and joy of Don Pablo's menagerie at Hacienda Nápoles, are officially named an 'invasive species' in 2022 after their numbers reach dangerous levels in and around the Magdalena River. The authorities continue to struggle to control the levels of these enormous beasts and are planning a combination of culling, sterilizing and relocating abroad.

El Pibe, Colombia captain Carlos Valderrama, saw out the twilight of his career in Major League Soccer (MLS) in America, playing for Tampa Bay Mutiny and Miami Fusion. A 40ft-high solid bronze statue of him, weighing 7 tons, stands outside the now-derelict stadium of his first club Unión Magdalena.

René 'El Loco' Higuita and Francisco 'Pacho' Maturana are reunited at their beloved Atlético Nacional in Medellín. Pacho is the club's sporting director, René the side's goalkeeping coach.

One of the new generation of Colombian footballing superstars, Luis Díaz, is hoping to bring World Cup glory to his country. But his journey has been an extraordinary one. Of Wayuu origin, he is the first indigenous Colombian to represent his country. In 2021 he helps Colombia finish third in the Copa América, and ends the tournament as joint top goalscorer alongside Lionel Messi of Argentina.

But on 28 October 2023, Díaz's parents are kidnapped – a chilling reminder that, despite the end of the narcoball era and the fall of Pablo and the Medellín cartel, Colombia is still at times a dangerous place. Armed men on motorbikes snatch them from a petrol station in their hometown of Barrancas. The next day, with *Lucho* left out of the squad, Diego Jota nets a first-half goal for Liverpool against Nottingham Forest and runs to the bench to display a Díaz number 7 shirt to the cameras in support of his teammate. The same day his mother, Cilenis, is found alive and well, left behind in a car as Colombian forces closed in on the kidnappers – but there is no sign of his father.

It becomes apparent that Luis Manuel 'Mane' Díaz has been snatched by members of the *Ejército de Liberación Nacional* – the National Liberation Army known as the ELN. But the leadership of the ELN, a left-wing Marxist group and the only significant guerrilla army still operating in Colombia following the end of the FARC in 2016–17, face a huge national backlash over the kidnapping of the father of the country's newest footballing superstar. They swiftly move to distance themselves – claiming the actions were those of a group of their members but were not officially sanctioned.

On 5 November, with his side trailing Premier League newcomers Luton Town 1-0 and fewer than 10 of the 90 minutes remaining, manager Jürgen Klopp looks to his bench and summons Lucho, who is back in the squad after an absence of two games. With 83 minutes on the clock the Colombian replaces Ryan Gravenberch as Klopp gambles in search of an equalizer. Deep into injury time Harvey Elliott sends a cross into the box and the ball is met by the firm head of Lucho – and sails into the net. Liverpool have snatched a vital point at the death. An emotional Díaz is mobbed by his teammates. The Colombian winger lifts his shirt to reveal a poignant message written in black pen on the white undershirt beneath – 'LIBERTAD PARA PAPA', freedom for dad.

Finally, with the ELN admitting their mistake, and after 12 days held in the jungle on the border with Venezuela, Mane Díaz is released unharmed and reunited with his family. And, on 16 November 2023, exactly a week after gaining his freedom, and proudly wearing his bright yellow Colombia football shirt, Mane Díaz is in the stands of the Estadio Metropolitano in Barranquilla to see his son play in a vital World Cup qualifier against Brazil. The five-time former world champions score after just four minutes through Arsenal striker Gabriel Martinelli, but in the second half lightning strikes twice – as an inspired Díaz scores two headed goals in the space of four minutes to win the game for Los Cafeteros. It is the first time Colombia have ever beaten Brazil in a World Cup qualifier. In the stands Mane cannot contain his emotions, writhing uncontrollably with the joy and ecstasy of the moment. On the pitch his son cannot hold back the tears as he dedicates his goals, and the win, to his father.

Thankfully the Colombia of today is nothing like the land of violence and terror of the 1980s and 1990s. And while kids still play football on the pitches built by El Patrón, the name of Pablo Escobar no longer adorns them. The threat of violence still remains as long as the spectre of the cartels, the guerrilla groups and warring factions within Colombia continue to exist, but the future looks bright for Luis Díaz and perhaps this new generation of Los Cafeteros will be the one to finally – and once and for all – exorcise the ghost of USA '94, of Pablo and of narcoball . . .

Acknowledgements

This book only exists thanks to the vision and enthusiasm of my brilliant agent Charlotte Robertson at Robertson Murray who saw the potential in my passion project from the very beginning and has encouraged me every step of the way. Thank you Fiona Kimbell at Arlington Management for the serendipitous, life-changing introduction!

My editor Trevor Davies has been a champion of this book from the get-go, and he and the whole team at Octopus Books and Cassell have been a pleasure to work with.

Throughout this process I have also benefitted hugely from the unwavering support of my wife, Irma. I couldn't have done it without the love she, and our daughter Ivy, show me every single day.

This story is born from my heritage – for which I have my Anglo-Colombian family and my parents John and Carolina to thank.

My cousin Leopoldo Guerra Lleras in Colombia, also offered his time, help and support.

ACKNOWLEDGEMENTS

But most of all, thanks must go to my mother for taking me to Wembley on 24 May 1988, for taking me to Colombia so many times in my childhood, for instilling in me a love of her homeland – and in the written word – from birth, and for her invaluable input into the drafts of this book.

And thanks to you – I hope you have enjoyed reading *Narcoball* as much as I have writing it.

David

Appendix

In the process of researching *Narcoball* I read many fascinating books, watched numerous documentaries and listened to several podcasts in order to get an overview of the life and death of Pablo Escobar, to uncover his true love of Atlético Nacional and the beautiful game itself, and to chart the rise and fall of Colombian domestic and international football. As with any historical story as long, complex and contentious as that of Pablo Escobar there are numerous versions of 'the truth' out there, and we will undoubtedly never know all that really came to pass, but here are just some of the sources I relied upon, and which I offer here in case you wish to further explore the tales laid out in these pages:

BOOKS

Mrs Escobar: My Life with Pablo by Victoria Eugenia Henao (Ebury Digital, 2019)

Escobar: Drugs, Guns, Money, Power by Roberto Escobar and David Fisher (Hodder & Stoughton, 2010)

Manhunters: How We Took Down Pablo Escobar by Steve Murphy and Javier F. Peña (Headline, 2020)

Killing Pablo: The Hunt for the World's Greatest Outlaw by Mark
    Bowden (Atlantic Books, 2012)
The Ball is Round: A Global History of Football by David Goldblatt
    (Penguin Books, 2007)

DOCUMENTARIES

The Two Escobars (Dir: Jeff & Michael Zimbalist, 2010)
Escobar by Escobar (Dir: Thomas Misrachi, David Périssere, 2021)
The Rise & Fall of Pablo Escobar (Dir: Michael Driscoll, 2018)
Diego Maradona (Dir: Asif Kapadia, 2019)
Higuita: The Way of the Scorpion (Dir: Luis Ara, 2023)

PODCASTS

Real Narcos (Noiser, 2020)

ARTICLES

https://blogs.elespectador.com/cultura/el-magazin/el-informe-
    nacional
https://english.elpais.com/usa/2021-12-24/pablo-escobar-unseen-
    portraits-of-a-drug-lord.html
https://www.thedailybeast.com/the-sicarios-tale-part-4-the-
    cuckold-who-brought-down-the-cartels
https://www.theguardian.com/football/2015/jul/30/oscar-pareja-fc-
    dallas-colombia-pablo-escobar
https://www.washingtonpost.com/archive/sports/2002/05/11/
    ecuadors-berth-of-a-nation/2dc1825a-4ce6-4a05-a5db-4b63e
    8f12124/
https://www.theguardian.com/world/2010/dec/28/colombia-
    football-drug-cartels

Picture Credits

Index

About the Author

David Arrowsmith worked in the television industry for over 20 years – originating, developing and producing documentaries and unscripted programming for companies such as October Films, DSP, OSF, Zig Zag, Channel 5, Granada Television and the BBC. He is passionate about sport, history, biography and true crime, and some of his key commissions include *1966: Who Stole the World Cup?*, *Hatton*, *Britain's Bloodiest Dynasty*, *8 Days That Made Rome* and *Adolf & Eva: Love & War*. He was also involved in the development of the award-winning, Nobel Peace Prize-nominated documentary *Sri Lanka's Killing Fields*.

David was born and raised in London but is proudly half-Colombian. In fact, he is the great-grandson of a former president and directly descended from four more. He now lives in Hove, where his paternal great-grandfather worked in a butcher's shop, with his family. He has played football for over 35 years and has no plans to stop just yet.